EVERYDAY
Slow Cooker
& ONE DISH RECIPES

TASTE OF HOME BOOKS • RDA ENTHUSIAST BRANDS, LLC • MILWAUKEE, WI

PEACHY SERRANO
PEPPER WINGS
PAGE 82

Taste*of*Home

© 2018 RDA Enthusiast Brands, LLC.
1610 N. 2nd St., Suite 102, Milwaukee WI
53212-3906

Pictured on front cover and title page:
Slow Cooker Quinoa Chili, p. 61

Pictured on back cover:
Teriyaki Beef Roast, p. 14;
Pork Tenderloin
with Three-Berry Salsa, p. 141;
Shrimp & Crab Pizza, p. 223.

Printed in U.S.A.
1 3 5 7 9 10 8 6 4 2

**International Standard
Book Number:**
978-1-61765-801-3

**International Standard
Serial Number:**
1944-6382

Component Number:
119400047H

Cover Photographer:
Dan Roberts

Set Stylist:
Stacey Genaw

Food Stylist:
Shannon Roum

Contents

Get Social with Us!

 Like Us:
facebook.com/Tasteofhome

 Follow Us:
@tasteofhome

 Pin Us:
pinterest.com/taste_of_home

 Tweet Us:
twitter.com/tasteofhome

To find a recipe: tasteofhome.com

To submit a recipe: tasteofhome.com/submit

To find out about other *Taste of Home* **products:**
shoptasteofhome.com

Simple dishes are so nice to come home to!

Discover how easy dinner can truly be with 357 recipes for the slow cooker, stovetop and oven in this three-in-one cookbook.

Sometimes simplicity is best. Homey, comforting and satisfying, there's something heartwarming about a dish that comes together without much fuss, complicated cooking methods or unique ingredients. Those are the types of mouthwatering specialties you'll find inside this enticing collection. Choose from 110 slow-cooker recipes ready when you are; 105 incredible oven-baked entrees; and 100+ skillet and stovetop dinners that simmer up fast when time is tight. Get back to the flavor simplicity offers, and share that goodness today.

GINGER BEER
PULLED PORK
PAGE 71

HANDY ICONS IN THIS BOOK

EAT SMART Recipes are lower in calories, fat and/or sodium, as determined by a registered dietitian nutritionist. Consider these dishes when you want to eat lighter.

FREEZE IT Freeze It recipes may be stored in the freezer These fix-ahead dishes include directions for freezing and reheating.

76

23

Slow-cook with Confidence

Follow these tips for slow-cooking success every time.

PLAN AHEAD TO PREP AND GO.
In most cases, you can prepare and load ingredients into the slow cooker insert beforehand and store it in the refrigerator overnight. But an insert can crack if exposed to rapid temperature changes. Let the insert sit out just long enough to reach room temperature before placing in the slow cooker.

USE THAWED INGREDIENTS.
Although throwing frozen chicken breasts into the slow cooker may seem easy, it's not a smart shortcut. Thawing foods in a slow cooker can create the ideal environment for bacteria to grow, so thaw frozen meat and veggies ahead of time. The exception is if you're using a prepackaged slow-cooker meal kit and follow the instructions as written.

LINE THE CROCK FOR EASE OF USE.
Some recipes in this book call for a **foil collar** or **sling.** Here's why:

▶ A **foil collar** prevents scorching of rich, saucy dishes, such as Potluck Bacon Mac & Cheese, near the slow cooker's heating element. To make a collar, fold two 18-in.-long pieces of foil into strips 4 in. wide. Line the crock's perimeter with the strips; spray with cooking spray.

▶ A **sling** helps you lift layered foods, such as Slow Cooker Cheesy White Lasagna, out of the crock without much fuss. To make, fold one or more pieces of heavy-duty foil into strips. Place on bottom and up sides of the slow cooker; coat with cooking spray.

TAKE THE TIME TO BROWN.
Give yourself a few extra minutes to brown your meat in a skillet before placing in the slow cooker. Doing so will add rich color and more flavor to the finished dish.

KEEP THE LID CLOSED.
Don't peek! It's tempting to lift the lid and check on your meal's progress, but resist the urge. Every time you open the lid, you'll have to add about 30 minutes to the total cooking time.

ADJUST COOK TIME AS NEEDED.
Live at a high altitude? Slow cooking will take longer. Add about 30 minutes for each hour of cooking the recipe calls for; legumes will take about twice as long.

Want your food done sooner? Cooking one hour on high is roughly equal to two hours on low, so adjust the recipe to suit your schedule.

Stovetop Suppers Are Super Convenient

Stovetop cooking is quick and easy. Many stovetop meals in this book are ready in just one pot, which makes cleanup a breeze. These tips will help you enjoy cooking on the stove.

CHOOSE THE RIGHT PAN FOR THE JOB.

The right cookware can simplify meal preparation when cooking on the stovetop. The basic skillets every kitchen needs include a 10- or 12-in. skillet with lid and an 8- or 9-in. saute/omelet pan.

Good quality cookware conducts heat quickly and cooks food evenly. The type of metal and thickness of the pan affect performance. There are pros and cons to each of the most common cookware metals:

Copper conducts heat the best. However, it is expensive, it tarnishes (and usually requires periodic polishing), and it reacts with acidic ingredients, which is why the interior of a copper pan is usually lined with tin or stainless steel.

Aluminum is a good conductor of heat and is less expensive than copper. However, aluminum reacts with acidic ingredients.

Anodized aluminum has the same positive qualities as aluminum, but the surface is electrochemically treated so it will not react to acidic ingredients. The surface is resistant to scratches and is nonstick.

Cast iron conducts heat very well. It is usually heavy. Cast iron also needs regular seasoning to prevent sticking and rusting.

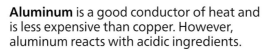

Nonstick is especially preferred for cooking delicate foods, such as eggs, pancakes or thin fish fillets. It won't scorch foods if you're cooking in batches. It can be scratched easily and has maximum temperature limitations.

Stainless steel is durable and retains its new look for years. It isn't a good conductor of heat, which is why it often has an aluminum or copper core or bottom.

MASTER THESE COMMON STOVETOP COOKING TECHNIQUES.

Sauteeing Add a small amount of oil to a hot skillet and heat over medium-high heat. For best results, cut food into uniformly sized pieces before adding. Don't overcrowd in pan. Stir frequently while cooking.

Searing Heat oil in a large skillet over medium-high heat until it almost begins to smoke. Pat food dry. Cook the food until a deeply colored crust has formed, being careful not to crowd the pan. Reduce heat if food browns too quickly.

Braising Season meat; coat with flour if recipe directs. In Dutch oven, brown meat in oil in batches. To ensure nice browning, do not crowd. Set meat aside; cook vegetables, adding flour if recipe directs. Add broth gradually, stirring to deglaze pan and to keep lumps from forming. Return meat to pan and stir until mixture comes to a boil.

Steaming Place a steamer basket or bamboo steamer in a pan with water. Bring water to a boil (boiling water shouldn't touch the steamer) and place food in the basket; cover and steam. Add more boiling water to pan as necessary, making sure pan does not run dry.

206

189

Oven Entrees Bake Hands-Free

And they warm up the kitchen on a chilly day, too! Follow these tips for success every time.

CHOOSE THE RIGHT BAKEWARE.

Metal baking pans These great conductors of heat create nice browning on rolls, coffee cakes and other baked goods. Metal is a safe, smart choice for under the broiler. It may react with acidic foods such as tomato sauce or cranberries and create a metallic taste or discoloration.

Glass baking dishes Glass provides slower, more even baking for egg dishes, custards and casseroles. It takes longer to heat than metal, but once heated, the dish holds the heat longer. This is undesirable for many desserts, as sugary batters may overbrown in glass. If you wish to bake in a glass dish even though the recipe calls for a metal pan, decrease the oven temperature by 25º.

Other baking dishes Ceramic or stoneware baking dishes generally perform like glass, but are more attractive. They may be safe for higher temperatures than glass; refer to the manufacturer's instructions.

CONFIRM THE OVEN'S TEMPERATURE.

Use an oven thermometer to check. Preheat oven to the desired temperature; place an oven thermometer on the center rack. Close the oven door and leave the oven on at the set temperature. Keep thermometer in the oven for 15 minutes before reading. Adjust the oven temperature accordingly to ensure the best baking results.

NEGATE HOT OR COOL SPOTS.

To test your oven for uneven temperatures, try the bread test. Heat the oven to 350° while arranging six to nine slices of white bread on a large cookie sheet. Place in oven for 5-10 minutes; check if slices are starting to brown or burn. If some slices are noticeably darker or lighter than others, the oven may have hot or cool spots. To negate this, rotate your pans while baking.

ELIMINATE SPILLS—THE SMART WAY.

Line a rimmed baking sheet with foil and place it on the bottom oven rack directly below the baking dish. Any drips or spills from the recipe will fall onto the foil-lined pan instead of the oven bottom.

We don't recommend lining the bottom of your oven with aluminum foil or other liners, as there's a chance that they could melt and stick to the oven, causing damage.

Want to clean up a drip while it's still hot? Grab your oven mitt, a pair of tongs and a damp dishcloth. Using the tongs to move the cloth will help prevent burns.

162

TERIYAKI BEEF ROAST
PAGE 14

40

33

66

Slow Cooker

Whether you spend your days at home or away, nothing beats the set-it-and-forget-it convenience of a slow cooker meal. Give yourself the gift of more time—and a hot, homey dinner that's ready when you are—with these 110 favorites from family cooks just like you. Discover breakfasts, appetizers and desserts from the slow cooker, too!

85

Beef & Ground Beef

SLOW COOKER
TATER TOT CASSEROLE

SLOW COOKER TATER TOT CASSEROLE

What's not to love about classic Tater Tot casserole—especially when it's made in the slow cooker? You may want to add this potluck favorite to the regular recipe rotation.
—Nick Iverson, Denver, CO

PREP: 25 min.
COOK: 6 hours + standing
MAKES: 12 servings

- 2 lbs. ground beef
- 1 large onion, chopped
- 1 lb. sliced fresh mushrooms
- 3 garlic cloves, minced
- 2 cans (10¾ oz. each) condensed cream of mushroom soup, undiluted
- ½ tsp. salt
- ½ tsp. pepper
- 1 lb. frozen cut green beans
- 1 bag (32 oz.) frozen Tater Tots
- 1 cup shredded cheddar cheese

1. In a large skillet cook beef over medium-high heat, 5-6 minutes or until no longer pink, breaking into crumbles; drain and transfer to a 5-qt. slow cooker. Add the onions and mushrooms to skillet; cook over medium-high heat until vegetables are tender, 8-10 minutes. Add garlic; cook 1 minute more. Stir in condensed soup, salt and pepper. Place the meat mixture in slow cooker; add green beans and stir to combine. Top with Tater Tots and cheese.
2. Cook, covered, on low 6-8 hours. Let stand, uncovered, for 15 minutes before serving.
1 SERVING: 383 cal., 22g fat (7g sat. fat), 58mg chol., 941mg sod., 27g carb. (3g sugars, 4g fiber), 20g pro.

TEST KITCHEN TIP
For more color, use frozen mixed vegetables in place of green beans in this family-friendly dish.

BEEF DAUBE
PROVENCAL

BEEF DAUBE PROVENCAL

This dish is perfect on cold winter days, after we have been out cutting wood or white-tail hunting. If you are lucky enough to have venison, try it here for melt-in-your-mouth goodness.
—Brenda Ryan, Marshall, MO

PREP: 30 min. • **COOK:** 5 hours
MAKES: 8 servings

- 2 tsp. olive oil
- 1 boneless beef chuck roast or venison roast (about 2 lbs.), cut into 1-in. cubes
- 1½ tsp. salt, divided
- ½ tsp. coarsely ground pepper, divided
- 2 cups chopped carrots
- 1½ cups chopped onions
- 12 garlic cloves, crushed
- 1 Tbsp. tomato paste
- 1 cup dry red wine
- 1 can (14½ oz.) diced tomatoes
- ½ cup beef broth
- 1 tsp. chopped fresh rosemary
- 1 tsp. chopped fresh thyme
- 1 bay leaf

Dash ground cloves
Hot cooked pasta or mashed potatoes
Fresh thyme leaves, optional

1. In a large skillet, heat the oil over medium-high heat. Sprinkle meat with ½ tsp. salt and ¼ tsp. pepper; brown meat in batches. Transfer beef to 4-qt. slow cooker.
2. Add the carrots, onions, garlic and remaining salt and pepper to skillet; cook and stir until golden brown, 4-6 minutes. Add tomato paste; cook and stir 1 minute until fragrant. Add wine, stirring to loosen browned bits from pan; bring to a boil.
3. Transfer meat mixture, tomatoes, broth and seasonings to slow cooker. Cook, covered, on low until tender, 5-7 hours. Discard bay leaf. Serve with hot cooked pasta or mashed potatoes. If desired, sprinkle with fresh thyme.
1 CUP BEEF MIXTURE: 237 cal., 12g fat (4g sat. fat), 74mg chol., 651mg sod., 8g carb. (3g sugars, 2g fiber), 23g pro.
DIABETIC EXCHANGES: 3 lean meat, 1 vegetable.

MOM'S SPAGHETTI SAUCE

Mom made this when we were kids, and it was always my first choice for birthday dinners. Now I do the prep work in the morning and just let it simmer all day. When I get home, all I have to do is boil spaghetti and brown garlic bread. Dinner is on!
—Kristy Hawkes, South Weber, UT

PREP: 20 min. • **COOK:** 4 hours
MAKES: 12 servings

- 1 lb. ground beef
- 1 medium onion, chopped
- 1 medium green pepper, chopped
- 8 to 10 fresh mushrooms, sliced
- 3 celery ribs, chopped
- 1½ tsp. minced garlic
- 2 cans (14½ oz. each) Italian stewed tomatoes
- 1 jar (26 oz.) spaghetti sauce
- ½ cup ketchup
- 2 tsp. brown sugar
- 1 tsp. sugar
- 1 tsp. salt
- 1 tsp. dried oregano
- 1 tsp. chili powder
- 1 tsp. prepared mustard
   Hot cooked spaghetti

1. In a large skillet, cook the beef with the onion, green pepper, mushrooms and celery over medium heat until meat is no longer pink. Add the garlic; cook 1 minute longer. Drain.
2. In a 3-qt. slow cooker, combine the tomatoes, spaghetti sauce, ketchup, sugars, salt, oregano, chili powder and mustard. Stir in the beef mixture. Cover and cook on low for 4-5 hours or until heated through. Serve with hot spaghetti.
FREEZE OPTION: Cool before placing in a freezer container. Cover and freeze for up to 3 months. To use, thaw in the refrigerator overnight. Place in a large saucepan; heat through, stirring occasionally. Serve with spaghetti.
¾ CUP SAUCE: 145 cal., 6g fat (2g sat. fat), 20mg chol., 779mg sod., 15g carb. (9g sugars, 3g fiber), 9g pro.

FRENCH DIP TACOS

I came up with this idea when we had a dab of leftover French dip. So much fun and a nice twist to leftovers. These are also good with a little hot sauce on the side.

—Kelly Williams, Forked River, NJ

PREP: 10 min. • **COOK:** 6 hours
MAKES: 16 servings

- 1 boneless beef chuck roast (about 3 lbs.)
- 1 envelope onion soup mix
- 1 envelope ranch salad dressing mix
- 2 cans (10½ oz. each) condensed beef broth, undiluted
- 2 Tbsp. Worcestershire sauce
- 16 mini flour tortillas, warmed
  Optional toppings: shredded lettuce, chopped tomatoes, provolone cheese strips, sliced pepperoncini and sour cream

1. Place the roast in a 5- or 6-qt. slow cooker; sprinkle evenly with the soup and dressing mixes. Add broth and Worcestershire sauce. Cook, covered, on low until meat is tender, 6-8 hours.
2. Remove roast from slow cooker. Skim fat from cooking juices; keep warm. Shred beef with two forks; serve in tortillas with toppings as desired. Serve with juices for dipping.
1 MINI TACO: 221 cal., 10g fat (4g sat. fat), 55mg chol., 710mg sod., 11g carb. (1g sugars, 1g fiber), 19g pro.

ANCIENT GRAIN BEEF STEW

My version of beef stew is comfort food with a healthy twist. I use lentils and red quinoa rather than potatoes. If leftover stew seems too thick, add more beef stock when reheating.

—Margaret M. Roscoe, Keystone Heights, FL

PREP: 25 min. • **COOK:** 6 hours
MAKES: 10 servings

- 2 Tbsp. olive oil
- 1 lb. beef stew meat, cut into 1-in. cubes
- 4 celery ribs with leaves, chopped
- 2 medium carrots, peeled, chopped
- 1 large onion, chopped
- 1½ cups dried lentils, rinsed
- ½ cup red quinoa, rinsed
- 5 large bay leaves
- 2 tsp. ground cumin
- 1½ tsp. salt
- 1 tsp. dried tarragon
- ½ tsp. pepper
- 2 cartons (32 oz. each) beef stock

Heat oil in a large skillet over medium heat. Add beef; brown on all sides. Transfer meat and drippings to a 5- or 6-qt. slow cooker. Stir in the remaining ingredients. Cook, covered, on low until meat is tender, 6-8 hours. Discard bay leaves.
NOTE: Look for quinoa in the cereal, rice or organic food aisle.
1⅓ CUPS: 261 cal., 7g fat (2g sat. fat), 28mg chol., 797mg sod., 29g carb. (5g sugars, 5g fiber), 21g pro. **DIABETIC EXCHANGES:** 2 starch, 2 lean meat, ½ fat.

ANCIENT GRAIN BEEF STEW

COUNTRY
BACON-
BEEF MAC
& CHEESE

SLOW-COOKED SIRLOIN

My family of five likes to eat beef, so this recipe is a favorite. I usually serve it with homemade bread or rolls to soak up the tasty gravy.
—Vicki Tormaschy, Dickinson, ND

PREP: 20 min. • **COOK:** 3½ hours
MAKES: 6 servings

- 1 beef top sirloin steak (1½ lbs.)
- 1 medium onion, cut into 1-in. chunks
- 1 medium green pepper, cut into 1-in. chunks
- 1 can (14½ oz.) reduced-sodium beef broth
- ¼ cup Worcestershire sauce
- ¼ tsp. dill weed
- ¼ tsp. dried thyme
- ¼ tsp. pepper
  Dash crushed red pepper flakes
- 2 Tbsp. cornstarch
- 2 Tbsp. cold water

1. In a large nonstick skillet coated with cooking spray, brown the beef on both sides. Place onion and green pepper in a 3-qt. slow cooker. Place beef on top. Combine the broth, Worcestershire sauce, dill, thyme, pepper and pepper flakes; pour over beef. Cover and cook on high for 3-4 hours or until the meat reaches desired doneness and the vegetables are crisp-tender.
2. Remove beef and keep warm. Mix cornstarch and water until smooth; gradually stir into cooking juices. Cover and cook on high for about 30 minutes or until slightly thickened. Return beef to the slow cooker; heat through.
3 OZ.: 199 cal., 6g fat (2g sat. fat), 68mg chol., 305mg sod., 8g carb. (2g sugars, 1g fiber), 26g pro. **DIABETIC EXCHANGES:** 3 lean meat, 1 vegetable.

"Have made this many times. The gravy is delicious on mashed potatoes. I did cut the black pepper back a bit the second time I made it."
—SKOOTER941, TASTEOFHOME.COM

COUNTRY BACON-BEEF MAC & CHEESE

Wow. This meaty slow cooker mac and cheese dinner couldn't be much easier to make. Kids always love it!
—Nancy Heishman, Las Vegas, NV

PREP: 35 min. • **COOK:** 1½ hours
MAKES: 12 cups

- 5 bacon strips, chopped
- 1½ lbs. ground beef
- 1 medium onion, chopped
- 3 garlic cloves, minced
- 1 medium sweet red pepper, chopped
- 1 large carrot, coarsely grated
- 1 Tbsp. dried parsley flakes
- ¼ tsp. salt
- 1 tsp. pepper
- 3 cups uncooked protein plus or whole wheat elbow macaroni
- 1 can (14½ oz.) reduced-sodium beef broth
- 1 cup sour cream
- 2 cups shredded sharp cheddar cheese
- 2 cups shredded part-skim mozzarella cheese

1. In a large skillet, cook bacon, stirring occasionally, over medium heat until crisp, 5-6 minutes. Remove with a slotted spoon; drain on paper towels. Discard all but 1 Tbsp. of drippings. Brown ground beef in drippings; remove from pan. Add onion to the skillet; cook and stir until translucent, 2-3 minutes. Stir in the garlic; cook 1 minute more.
2. Combine red pepper, carrot, seasonings and pasta in a 4-qt. slow cooker. Layer with ground beef, bacon and onion mixture (do not stir). Pour in broth.
3. Cook, covered, on low until meat and vegetables are tender, about 1 hour. Thirty minutes before serving, stir in sour cream and cheeses.
1½ CUPS: 591 cal., 36g fat (17g sat. fat), 113mg chol., 719mg sod., 29g carb. (5g sugars, 3g fiber), 38g pro.

MEATBALL CABBAGE ROLLS

My mother would often have these cabbage rolls simmering in her slow cooker when my family and I arrived at her house for weekend visits. The mouthwatering meatballs tucked inside made these stand out from any other cabbage rolls I've tried.

—Betty Buckmaster, Muskogee, OK

PREP: 25 min. • **COOK:** 8 hours
MAKES: 4 servings

- 1   large head cabbage
- 1   can (8 oz.) no-salt-added tomato sauce
- 1   small onion, chopped
- ⅓   cup uncooked long grain rice
- 2   Tbsp. chili powder
- ¼   tsp. garlic powder
- ⅛   tsp. salt
- 1   lb. lean ground beef (90% lean)
- 1   can (15 oz.) tomato sauce

1. In a Dutch oven, cook cabbage in boiling water just until leaves fall off head. Set aside 12 large leaves for rolls. (Refrigerate remaining cabbage for another use.) Cut out the thick vein from the bottom of each reserved leaf, making a V-shaped cut.
2. In a large bowl, combine no-salt tomato sauce, onion, rice, chili powder, garlic powder and salt. Crumble beef over mixture; mix well. Shape into 12 balls. Place one meatball on each cabbage leaf; overlap cut ends of leaf. Fold in sides, beginning from the cut end. Roll up leaf to encase meatball. Secure with toothpicks.
3. Place in a 5-qt. slow cooker. Pour remaining tomato sauce over the cabbage rolls. Cover and cook on low for 8 hours or until the meat is no longer pink and cabbage is tender. Discard toothpicks.
3 ROLLS: 323 cal., 11g fat (4g sat. fat), 71mg chol., 762mg sod., 31g carb. (8g sugars, 7g fiber), 28g pro. **DIABETIC EXCHANGES:** 3 lean meat, 1½ starch, 1 vegetable.

TERIYAKI BEEF ROAST

TERIYAKI BEEF ROAST

My father and I created this pot roast with a hint of Japanese flair. It will make your taste buds dance! Try this for family get-togethers or company.
—Mary Flurkey, Golden, CO

PREP: 30 min. • **COOK:** 7 hours
MAKES: 6 servings

- 4   medium potatoes, peeled and quartered
- 1½ cups fresh baby carrots
- 1   medium green pepper, seeded and cut into ½-in. strips
- 1   medium yellow onion, quartered
- ¼   cup all-purpose flour
- 1   boneless beef chuck roast (about 2 lbs.)
- 2   Tbsp. canola oil
- 8   oz. medium fresh mushrooms, cut into thick slices
- ¼   cup packed brown sugar
- ½   cup teriyaki sauce
- 2   tsp. ground ginger
- 1   tsp. beef base
- 1   tsp. dried oregano
- 1   tsp. pepper
- 2   to 3 green onions (green portion only), thinly sliced

1. Place the potatoes, carrots, green pepper and onion in a 5- or 6-qt. slow cooker. Rub flour over roast. In a large skillet, heat the oil over medium heat; brown roast on all sides. Transfer roast and drippings to slow cooker; arrange mushrooms around roast and sprinkle roast with brown sugar.
2. Combine the teriyaki sauce, ginger, beef base, oregano and pepper in a small bowl. Drizzle sauce slowly over mushrooms and roast.
3. Cook, covered, on low until roast is tender, 7-8 hours. Remove roast and vegetables to a serving platter; top with green onions. If desired, skim fat and thicken cooking juices for gravy; serve with roast.
NOTE: Look for beef base near the broth and bouillon.
1 SERVING: 494 cal., 19g fat (6g sat. fat), 98mg chol., 1024mg sod., 43g carb. (16g sugars, 3g fiber), 35g pro.

SLOW COOKER SPANISH RICE

Here's an economical dish with authentic Tex-Mex taste. Even the little ones will go for this Spanish rice.
—Sharon Tipton, Casselberry, FL

PREP: 30 min. • **COOK:** 4 hours
MAKES: 8 servings

- 1½ lbs. ground beef
- 2 medium onions, chopped
- 1 medium green pepper, chopped
- 1 celery rib, chopped
- 2 garlic cloves, minced
- 1½ cups uncooked converted rice (not instant)
- 1 can (28 oz.) diced tomatoes, drained
- 1 can (6 oz.) tomato paste
- 1 tsp. salt
- 1 tsp. sugar
- 1 tsp. chili powder
  Dash pepper
- 1½ cups water
- 1 can (2¼ oz.) sliced ripe olives, drained
- ½ cup shredded cheddar cheese

1. In a large skillet over medium-high heat, cook beef, onions, pepper and celery 7-8 minutes or until meat is no longer pink, breaking into crumbles. Add the garlic; cook 1 minute longer. Drain and transfer meat mixture to a 4- or 5-qt. slow cooker. Add the next eight ingredients.
2. Cook, covered, on low until rice and vegetables are tender, 4-5 hours, stirring once. Top with olives and cheese before serving.
1¼ CUPS: 378 cal., 13g fat (5g sat. fat), 60mg chol., 632mg sod., 42g carb. (7g sugars, 3g fiber), 22g pro.

SLOW COOKER
SPANISH RICE

EAT SMART
SWEET & SOUR BRISKET

At our home, this is one dish that never seems to get old. It's tender and juicy, with a sweet and sour twist.
—Jolie Albertazzie, Moreno Valley, CA

PREP: 15 min. • **COOK:** 8 hours
MAKES: 10 servings

- 1 can (28 oz.) crushed tomatoes
- 1 medium onion, halved and thinly sliced
- ½ cup raisins
- ¼ cup packed brown sugar
- 2 Tbsp. lemon juice
- 3 garlic cloves, minced
- 1 fresh beef brisket (3 lbs.)
- ½ tsp. salt
- ¼ tsp. pepper

1. In a small bowl, combine the tomatoes, onion, raisins, brown sugar, lemon juice and garlic. Pour half into a 4- or 5-qt. slow cooker coated with cooking spray. Sprinkle meat with salt and pepper. Transfer to slow cooker. Top with remaining tomato mixture. Cook, covered, on low until meat is tender, 8-10 hours.
2. Remove brisket to a serving platter and keep warm. Skim fat from cooking juices. Thinly slice meat across grain. Serve with tomato mixture.
NOTE: This is a fresh beef brisket, not corned beef.
4 OZ. COOKED BEEF WITH ⅓ CUP SAUCE: 248 cal., 6g fat (2g sat. fat), 58mg chol., 272mg sod., 19g carb. (11g sugars, 2g fiber), 30g pro. **DIABETIC EXCHANGES:** 4 lean meat, 1 starch.

ASIAN SLOW-COOKED SHORT RIBS

HORSERADISH POT ROAST

We tasted a dish similiar to this while at a horseradish festival in Illinois. I like to serve it over noodles. This recipe is easily adaptable for the stovetop, too.
—Barbara White, Katy, TX

PREP: 10 min. • **COOK:** 8¼ hours
MAKES: 6 servings

- 1 boneless beef chuck roast (2 to 3 lbs.)
- ½ tsp. salt
- ½ tsp. pepper
- 2 medium onions, thinly sliced into rings
- 1 jar (6 to 6½ oz.) prepared horseradish
- ¼ cup dry white wine or beef broth
- 1 Tbsp. butter, melted
- 1 garlic clove, minced
- 1 Tbsp. sugar
- 2 Tbsp. all-purpose flour
- 2 Tbsp. cold water
  Hot cooked egg noodles
  Minced fresh thyme, optional

1. Place roast in a 6-qt. slow cooker; sprinkle with salt and pepper. Top roast with onions. In a small bowl, combine next five ingredients; pour over roast and onions. Cook, covered, on low until meat is tender, 7-8 hours.
2. Remove roast; cool slightly and shred with two forks. Skim fat from cooking juices. Mix flour and water until smooth; gradually stir into juices. Return beef to the slow cooker. Cook, covered, on high 15-30 minutes or until sauce is thickened. Serve with noodles. If desired, top with minced thyme.
1 SERVING: 320 cal., 17g fat (7g sat. fat), 103mg chol., 395mg sod., 11g carb. (6g sugars, 2g fiber), 31g pro.

ASIAN SLOW-COOKED SHORT RIBS

After a long day of sledding, the aroma of these beautiful short ribs says *welcome home.* Warm and comforting, they make a worthy low-maintenance dinner.
—Amy Chase, Vanderhoof, BC

PREP: 10 min. • **COOK:** 6 hours
MAKES: 4 servings

- 1 can (28 oz.) stewed tomatoes
- 1 medium onion, chopped
- 4 garlic cloves, minced
- 2 Tbsp. honey
- 2 Tbsp. soy sauce
- 1 Tbsp. Worcestershire sauce
- 1 Tbsp. chili garlic sauce
- 2 bay leaves
- 1 tsp. pepper
- ½ tsp. salt
- 8 bone-in beef short ribs (about 4 lbs.)
  Hot cooked rice, optional

In a 4- or 5-qt. slow cooker, combine the first 10 ingredients. Add the short ribs; cook, covered, on low until meat is tender, 6-8 hours. Discard bay leaves. If desired, serve with rice.
1 SERVING: 466 cal., 21g fat (9g sat. fat), 110mg chol., 1338mg sod., 29g carb. (21g sugars, 2g fiber), 39g pro.

DID YOU KNOW?

Worcestershire sauce was originally considered a mistake. In 1835, an English lord commissioned two chemists to duplicate a sauce he had tried in India. The pungent batch was disappointing and wound up in their cellar. When the pair stumbled upon the aged concoction 2 years later, they were pleasantly surprised by its unique taste.

HORSERADISH
POT ROAST

ZIPPY BEEF FAJITAS

Steak fajitas go big on flavor with aromatic ingredients including garlic and gingerroot. There's even a can of cola in the recipe.

—Laurie Sadowski, St. Catharines, ON

PREP: 20 min. • **COOK:** 6 hours
MAKES: 6 servings

- 1 beef flank steak (1½ lbs.)
- 2 tsp. ground ginger
- 2 tsp. crushed red pepper flakes
- ¾ tsp. garlic powder
- ¼ tsp. pepper
- 1 medium sweet red pepper, cut into strips
- 1 medium green pepper, cut into strips
- 1 can (12 oz.) cola
- 5 green onions, chopped
- ⅓ cup soy sauce
- 2 Tbsp. minced fresh gingerroot
- 2 Tbsp. tomato paste
- 1 garlic clove, minced
- 6 flour tortillas (8 in.), warmed

1. Cut steak in half lengthwise. In a small bowl, combine ground ginger, pepper flakes, garlic powder and pepper; rub over steak. Transfer to a 3-qt. slow cooker; add the red and green peppers. Combine cola, green onions, soy sauce, gingerroot, tomato paste and garlic; pour over top.
2. Cook, covered, on low until meat is tender, 6-7 hours. Shred the meat with two forks; return to the slow cooker and heat through. Spoon beef mixture onto tortillas using a slotted spoon.
1 SERVING: 365 cal., 12g fat (4g sat. fat), 48mg chol., 1125mg sod., 37g carb. (9g sugars, 2g fiber), 26g pro.

SPECIAL SLOW-COOKED BEEF

SPECIAL SLOW-COOKED BEEF

This hearty entree is easy to prepare for Sunday dinner, giving the chef time to attend to the other details. With mashed potatoes on the side, it's comfort food for the cool months.
—Juli George, Grandville, MI

PREP: 35 min.
COOK: 6 hours
MAKES: 8 servings

- 1 boneless beef chuck roast (3 lbs.), cubed
- 1 Tbsp. canola oil
- 1 Tbsp. Italian seasoning
- 1 tsp. salt
- 1 garlic clove, minced
- ½ cup sliced ripe olives, drained
- ⅓ cup oil-packed sun-dried tomatoes, drained and chopped
- 1 cup beef broth
- ½ cup fresh pearl onions, peeled
- 1 Tbsp. cornstarch
- 2 Tbsp. cold water

1. In a large skillet, brown meat in oil in batches; drain. Transfer to a 5-qt. slow cooker. Sprinkle with Italian seasoning, salt and garlic; top with the olives and tomatoes. Add the broth and onions. Cook, covered, on low until meat is tender, 6-8 hours.
2. With a slotted spoon, remove beef and onions to a serving platter and keep warm. Pour cooking juices into a small saucepan; skim fat.
3. Combine cornstarch and water until smooth; gradually stir into cooking juices. Bring to a boil; cook and stir for 2 minutes or until thickened. Spoon over beef mixture.
1 SERVING: 332 cal., 20g fat (7g sat. fat), 111mg chol., 551mg sod., 3g carb. (0 sugars, 1g fiber), 34g pro.

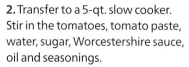

STAMP-OF-APPROVAL SPAGHETTI SAUCE

My father is pretty opinionated, especially about food. He gave this recipe his nearly unattainable stamp of approval—and no one else seems to disagree.
—Melissa Taylor, Higley, AZ

PREP: 30 min.
COOK: 8 hours
MAKES: 12 servings (3 qt.)

- 2 lbs. ground beef
- ¾ lb. bulk Italian sausage
- 4 medium onions, finely chopped
- 8 garlic cloves, minced
- 4 cans (14½ oz. each) diced tomatoes, undrained
- 4 cans (6 oz. each) tomato paste
- ½ cup water
- ¼ cup sugar
- ¼ cup Worcestershire sauce
- 1 Tbsp. canola oil
- ¼ cup minced fresh parsley
- 2 Tbsp. minced fresh basil or 2 tsp. dried basil
- 1 Tbsp. minced fresh oregano or 1 tsp. dried oregano
- 4 bay leaves
- 1 tsp. rubbed sage
- ½ tsp. salt
- ½ tsp. dried marjoram
- ½ tsp. pepper
  Hot cooked spaghetti

1. In a Dutch oven, cook the beef, sausage, onions and garlic over medium heat until meat is no longer pink; drain.

2. Transfer to a 5-qt. slow cooker. Stir in the tomatoes, tomato paste, water, sugar, Worcestershire sauce, oil and seasonings.

3. Cook, covered, on low 8-10 hours. Discard bay leaves. Serve with hot spaghetti or other pasta.

FREEZE OPTION: Cool before placing in a freezer container. Cover and freeze for up to 3 months. Thaw in refrigerator overnight. Place in a large saucepan; heat through, stirring occasionally. Serve with spaghetti.

1 CUP: 335 cal., 16g fat (5g sat. fat), 62mg chol., 622mg sod., 27g carb. (16g sugars, 5g fiber), 22g pro.

MINESTRONE STEW

I add green chilies to spice up my simple slow-cooked stew. You will like that it's made from convenient pantry ingredients.
—Janie Hoskins, Red Bluff, CA

PREP: 10 min. • **COOK:** 4 hours
MAKES: 8 servings (2 qt.)

- 1 lb. ground beef
- 1 small onion, chopped
- 1 can (19 oz.) ready-to-serve minestrone soup
- 1 can (15 oz.) pinto beans, rinsed and drained
- 1 can (14½ oz.) stewed tomatoes
- 1 can (11 oz.) whole kernel corn, drained
- 1 can (4 oz.) chopped green chilies
- 1 tsp. salt
- ½ tsp. garlic powder
- ½ tsp. onion powder

In a large skillet, cook beef and onion over medium heat until meat is no longer pink; drain. Tranfer to a 3-qt. slow cooker. Stir in the remaining ingredients. Cook, covered, on low for 4-6 hours or until heated through.
1 CUP: 221 cal., 6g fat (3g sat. fat), 29mg chol., 901mg sod., 24g carb. (6g sugars, 5g fiber), 15g pro.

STAMP-OF-APPROVAL SPAGHETTI SAUCE

SLOW-COOKED ITALIAN MEATBALLS

Freeze the cooled meatballs and the sauce in freezer containers. To use, partially thaw in refrigerator overnight. Heat through in a covered saucepan, stirring gently and adding a little water or broth if necessary. Serve as directed.
8 MEATBALLS: 432 cal., 24g fat (8g sat. fat), 128mg chol., 1168mg sod., 24g carb. (8g sugars, 1 fiber), 24g pro.

POTATO PIZZA CASSEROLE

I plan on this slow-cooker casserole for those weeknights when everyone comes home hungry at the same time. Meaty and cheesy, it's a dish makes the whole family happy.
—Tyler Sherman, Williamsburg, VA

PREP: 25 min. • **COOK:** 4 hours
MAKES: 8 servings

- 1 lb. ground beef
- ½ lb. sliced fresh mushrooms
- 1 medium green pepper, chopped
- 1 small onion, chopped
- 2 jars (14 oz. each) pizza sauce
- 1 can (10¾ oz.) condensed cheddar cheese soup, undiluted
- ½ cup 2% milk
- 1 tsp. Italian seasoning
- ½ tsp. garlic salt
- ¼ tsp. crushed red pepper flakes
- 1 pkg. (32 oz.) frozen cubed hash brown potatoes, thawed
- 15 slices pepperoni, chopped
- 2 cups shredded Italian cheese blend

1. In a large skillet, cook the beef, mushrooms, green pepper and onion until the meat is no longer pink; drain.
2. Meanwhile, in a large bowl, combine the sauce, soup, milk, Italian seasoning, garlic salt and pepper flakes. Stir in the potatoes, pepperoni and beef mixture.
3. Transfer half of the meat mixture to a 5-qt. slow cooker. Sprinkle with half of the cheese; repeat the layers. Cook, covered, on low until potatoes are tender, 4-5 hours.
1½ CUPS: 402 cal., 18g fat (8g sat. fat), 62mg chol., 1155mg sod., 34g carb. (8g sugars, 4g fiber), 24g pro.

SLOW-COOKED ITALIAN MEATBALLS

FREEZE IT

SLOW-COOKED ITALIAN MEATBALLS

These meatballs are delectable on pasta, in a sandwich or alongside mashed potatoes. They're also wonderful served as an appetizer straight out of the slow cooker.
—Jason Romano, Downingtown, PA

PREP: 50 min.
COOK: 3 hours
MAKES: 8 servings

- 2 Tbsp. olive oil
- 1 small onion, finely chopped
- 3 garlic cloves, minced
- 1 cup Italian-style panko (Japanese) bread crumbs
- 2 large eggs, lightly beaten
- ½ cup grated Parmesan cheese
- ½ cup minced fresh parsley
- ¼ cup water
- ¼ cup minced fresh basil
- 2 Tbsp. Worcestershire sauce
- ½ tsp. salt
- ½ tsp. pepper
- 1 lb. ground beef
- ½ lb. ground pork
- ½ lb. ground veal
- 4 cups spaghetti sauce
   Minced fresh parsley, optional

1. Preheat oven to 400°. In a small skillet, heat oil over medium heat. Add the onion and garlic; cook until onion is tender and golden brown, 5-9 minutes. Cool slightly.
2. In a large bowl, combine the bread crumbs, eggs, cheese, parsley, water and seasonings. Add ground meats; mix lightly but thoroughly. Shape into 1-in. balls. Place on greased racks in shallow baking pans. Bake until browned, 20-25 minutes.
3. Transfer to a 4- or 5-qt. slow cooker. Pour spaghetti sauce over top. Cook, covered, on low until meatballs are cooked through, 3-4 hours. If desired, serve with minced parsley.

SLOW COOKER
SHREDDED BEEF
LETTUCE CUPS

SLOW COOKER SHREDDED BEEF LETTUCE CUPS

The slow cooker is our summertime go-to for cool kitchen cooking. After swim lessons and activities, it's so nice to come back to a tasty, light dinner. If you can't find Bibb or Boston, green leaf lettuce is less sturdy but can work in a pinch.

—Elisabeth Larsen, Pleasant Grove, UT

PREP: 20 min.
COOK: 6 hours
MAKES: 8 servings

1   boneless beef chuck roast (2 lbs.)
3   medium carrots, peeled and chopped
2   medium sweet red peppers, chopped
1   medium onion, chopped
1   can (8 oz.) unsweetened crushed pineapple, undrained
½   cup reduced-sodium soy sauce
2   Tbsp. packed brown sugar
2   Tbsp. white vinegar
1   garlic clove, minced
½   tsp. pepper
3   Tbsp. cornstarch
3   Tbsp. water
24   Bibb or Boston lettuce leaves
     Sliced green onions, optional

1. In a 4- or 5-qt. slow cooker, combine roast, carrots, peppers and onion. Stir together next six ingredients in small bowl; pour over roast. Cook, covered, on low until roast is tender, 6-8 hours.
2. Remove roast from slow cooker. Cool slightly; shred the meat with two forks.
3. Skim fat from the cooking juices; transfer juices and vegetables to a small saucepan. Bring to a boil over high heat. In a small bowl, combine cornstarch and water. Gradually stir cornstarch mixture into juices; cook until sauce is thickened, 3-4 minutes. Return beef, sauce and vegetables to slow cooker; cook until heated through, 10-15 minutes.
4. Serve the beef in lettuce leaves. If desired, sprinkle with green onions.
3 LETTUCE CUPS: 271 cal., 11g fat (4g sat. fat), 74mg chol., 642mg sod., 18g carb. (11g sugars, 2g fiber), 24g pro. **DIABETIC EXCHANGES:** 3 lean meat, 1 starch.

TEST KITCHEN TIP
Water chestnuts would be a pleasing addition to this recipe, and they'll hold up well in the slow cooker. For even more crunch, top lettuce cups with shredded carrots and radishes.

Poultry

**SLOW COOKER
CHICKEN TINGA**

FREEZE IT
SLOW COOKER CHICKEN TINGA

I first fell in love with Chicken Tinga at a taco stand inside a gas station. This is how I now make it at home. Chicken Tinga has a nice zing to it, but it's not overly spicy.
—Ramona Parris, Canton, GA

PREP: 25 min. • **COOK:** 4 hours
MAKES: 8 servings

- 8 oz. fresh chorizo
- 1½ lbs. boneless, skinless chicken thighs
- 1 large onion, cut into wedges
- 1 can (14½ oz.) fire-roasted diced tomatoes
- ½ cup chicken broth
- 3 Tbsp. minced chipotle peppers in adobo sauce
- 3 garlic cloves, minced
- 2 tsp. ground cumin
- 1 tsp. dried oregano
- ½ tsp. salt
- 16 corn tortillas (6 in.)
  Shredded lettuce and pico de gallo, optional

1. In a small skillet, fully cook chorizo over medium heat, breaking meat into crumbles, 6-8 minutes; drain. Transfer to a 3- or 4-qt. slow cooker. Add the next nine ingredients; stir to combine. Cook, covered, on low until chicken is tender, 4-5 hours.
2. Remove chicken; cool slightly. Shred with two forks. Remove and discard onions; strain cooking juices and skim fat. Return cooking juices and chicken to slow cooker; heat through. Serve chicken in tortillas. If desired, top with shredded lettuce and pico de gallo.
FREEZE OPTION: Freeze cooled chicken mixture in freezer containers. To use, partially thaw in refrigerator overnight. Heat through in a saucepan, stirring occasionally and adding a little broth if necessary.
2 TACOS: 363 cal., 16g fat (5g sat. fat), 82mg chol., 800mg sod., 27g carb. (3g sugars, 4g fiber), 25g pro.

**SLOW COOKER
GREEN CHILI CHICKEN
ENCHILADA PIE**

SLOW COOKER GREEN CHILI CHICKEN ENCHILADA PIE

My husband likes some heat in our meals, but our children—not so much. This is the best of both worlds. Serve with additional chopped cilantro and a dollop of sour cream if desired.
—Dana Beery, Ione, WA

PREP: 30 min.
COOK: 4 hours + standing
MAKES: 6 servings

- 3 cups shredded cooked chicken
- 1 can (15 oz.) black beans, rinsed and drained
- 1 can (10½ oz.) condensed cream of chicken soup, undiluted
- 1 can (10 oz.) mild green enchilada sauce
- 1 can (4 to 4½ oz.) chopped green chilies
- ¼ cup minced fresh cilantro
- 1 Tbsp. lime juice
- 9 corn tortillas (6 in.)
- 3 cups shredded Colby-Monterey Jack cheese
  Minced fresh cilantro, lime wedges, salsa and sour cream, optional

1. In a large bowl, combine the first seven ingredients. Cut three 30x6-in. strips of heavy-duty foil; crisscross so they resemble spokes of a wheel. Place strips on bottom and up sides of a 4- or 5-qt. slow cooker. Coat the strips with cooking spray. Spread ¼ cup chicken mixture over bottom of slow cooker. Top with three tortillas, overlapping and tearing them to fit, a third of the chicken mixture and a third of the cheese. Repeat twice.
2. Cook, covered, on low until a thermometer reads 165°, about 4 hours. To avoid scorching, rotate slow cooker insert one-half turn midway through cooking, lifting carefully with oven mitts. Turn off slow cooker; let stand, uncovered, 15 minutes before serving. Using the foil strips as handles, remove pie to a platter. Cut into wedges. If desired, serve with additional cilantro, salsa, sour cream and lime wedges.
1 SERVING: 541 cal., 27g fat (15g sat. fat), 116mg chol., 1202mg sod., 36g carb. (2g sugars, 6g fiber), 39g pro.

TEST KITCHEN TIP
To complete the meal, serve the enchilada pie with Spanish rice or a green salad.

TEX-MEX CHICKEN & RICE

TEX-MEX CHICKEN & RICE

Pantry and freezer basics inspired this deliciously healthy combo.
—Tracy Long, Bellwood, NE

PREP: 10 min. • **COOK:** 4 hours
MAKES: 6 servings

- 4 boneless skinless chicken breast halves (about 6 oz. each)
- 1 can (10½ oz.) reduced-fat condensed cream of chicken soup, undiluted
- 1 can (10 oz.) diced tomatoes and green chilies
- 1 cup salsa verde
- ½ tsp. ground cumin
- 1½ cups (about 7½ oz.) frozen corn
- 1 cup uncooked instant brown rice
  Shredded cheddar cheese, reduced-fat sour cream, cubed avocado, chopped cilantro, and sliced ripe olives, optional

1. In a 3- or 4-qt. slow cooker, combine first five ingredients. Cook, covered, on low until chicken is tender, 3-4 hours. Remove chicken from slow cooker. Cool slightly; shred chicken with two forks. Return meat to slow cooker. Add corn and rice; cook, covered, on low 1 hour longer.
2. If desired, serve with cheese, sour cream, avocado and olives.
1 SERVING: 254 cal., 4g fat (1g sat. fat), 65mg chol., 757mg sod., 28g carb. (2g sugars, 2g fiber), 27g pro. **DIABETIC EXCHANGES:** 3 lean meat, 2 starch.

TEST KITCHEN TIP
Place leftover filling in flour tortillas or lettuce cups. Create a Tex-Mex salad by serving over a bed of lettuce or a crispy shell.

SLOW COOKER
CHICKEN PARMESAN

SLOW COOKER CHICKEN PARMESAN

When the Packers play the Bears, I always plan a party and make sure this is on the menu. Using the slow cooker means I get to watch the game, too! I serve the chicken on submarine rolls with a bit of the sauce and some chopped lettuce. Or cut the chicken breasts in half and make sliders.
—Bonnie Hawkins, Elkhorn, WI

PREP: 25 min. • **COOK:** 4 hours
MAKES: 4 servings

- ½ cup seasoned bread crumbs
- ½ cup grated Parmesan cheese
- ½ tsp. Italian seasoning
- ½ tsp. pepper
- ¼ tsp. salt
- 1 large egg, lightly beaten
- 1 Tbsp. water
- 4 (6 oz. each) boneless skinless chicken breast halves
- 1 jar (24 oz.) marinara sauce
- 4 slices part-skim mozzarella cheese
  Hot cooked pasta, optional

1. In a shallow bowl, combine the bread crumbs, Parmesan cheese, Italian seasoning, pepper and salt. In another bowl, combine egg and water. Dip chicken in egg mixture, then in crumb mixture to coat both sides (patting to help adhere). Repeat.
2. Transfer chicken to the slow cooker. Pour sauce over chicken and top with cheese. Cook, covered, on low until a thermometer inserted in chicken reads 165°, about 4-6 hours. If desired, serve with hot cooked pasta.
1 SERVING: 475 cal., 17g fat (7g sat. fat), 171mg chol., 1689mg sod., 27g carb. (11g sugars, 4g fiber), 50g pro.

LEMON-ROSEMARY CHICKEN & VEGETABLES

SWEET & SPICY PEANUT CHICKEN

Chicken thighs and a slow cooker—that's a marriage made in culinary heaven! Juicy and flavorful, this simple dish will make you swoon when you return home and find it ready. The filling is also excellent in lettuce wraps.
—Janice Elder, Charlotte, NC

PREP: 25 min. • **COOK:** 6 hours
MAKES: 6 servings

- 1½ lbs. boneless skinless chicken thighs
- 1 cup chicken broth
- 1 cup pepper jelly
- ½ cup creamy peanut butter
- ¼ cup reduced-sodium soy sauce
- 2 garlic cloves, minced
- ¼ tsp. salt
- ¼ tsp. pepper
- ½ cup chopped dry roasted peanuts
- ½ cup chopped sweet red pepper
  Hot cooked rice and lime wedges, optional

1. Place chicken in a 3- or 4-qt. slow cooker. Combine broth, jelly, peanut butter, soy sauce and garlic in small bowl; pour over the chicken. Cook, covered, on low until the chicken is tender, 6-8 hours.
2. Remove chicken from slow cooker and cool slightly. Shred with two forks. Skim fat from cooking juices. Return meat to slow cooker. Stir in the salt and pepper.
3. Sprinkle each serving with peanuts and red pepper. If desired, serve with rice and lime wedges.
1 SERVING: 525 cal., 25g fat (5g sat. fat), 76mg chol., 914mg sod., 48g carb. (32g sugars, 3g fiber), 30g pro.

TEST KITCHEN TIP
Serve leftover filling in taco shells, flour tortillas or lettuce cups. Try take-out taste at home by combining filling with prepared rice noodles.

EAT SMART
LEMON-ROSEMARY CHICKEN & VEGETABLES

Even a beginner cook can make this and have it turn out perfectly. Prep time is minimal, and slow cooking brings all the flavors together in a most savory way.
—Anita Bell, Hermitage, TN

PREP: 15 min.
COOK: 6 hours + standing
MAKES: 6 servings

- 2 medium carrots, peeled, halved lengthwise and cut into 3-in. pieces
- 2 celery ribs, halved lengthwise and cut into 3-in. pieces
- 8 small red potatoes, quartered
- ¾ tsp. salt, divided
- ⅛ tsp. pepper
- 1 medium lemon, halved
- 2 garlic cloves, minced
- 1 broiler/fryer chicken (3 to 4 lbs.)
- 1 Tbsp. dried rosemary, crushed
- 1 Tbsp. lemon juice
- 1 Tbsp. olive oil
- 2½ tsp. paprika

1. Place carrots, celery and potatoes in a 6-qt. slow cooker; sprinkle with ¼ tsp. salt and pepper. Place lemon halves and garlic in chicken cavity. Tuck wings under chicken; tie the drumsticks together. Place chicken over vegetables in the slow cooker, breast side up. Mix together rosemary, lemon juice, oil, paprika and remaining salt in small bowl; rub over chicken.
2. Cover and cook on low until a thermometer inserted in thigh reads at least 170° and vegetables ----are tender, about 6-8 hours.
3. Remove chicken from slow cooker; tent with foil. Let stand 15 minutes before carving. Serve with vegetables.
3 OZ. COOKED CHICKEN WITH ⅔ CUP VEGETABLES: 329 cal., 17g fat (4g sat. fat), 88mg chol., 400mg sod., 14g carb. (2g sugars, 3g fiber), 29g pro.

SWEET & SPICY
PEANUT CHICKEN

TANGERINE
CHICKEN TAGINE

TANGERINE CHICKEN TAGINE

My family and friends enjoy foods from around the world, especially Moroccan entrees, so I developed this flavorful dish. Cooking it in the slow cooker keeps every morsel moist.
—Brenda Watts, Gaffney, SC

PREP: 20 min. • **COOK:** 6 hours
MAKES: 8 servings

- 2 Tbsp. brown sugar
- 1 tsp. curry powder
- 1 tsp. ground cinnamon
- 1 tsp. cumin seeds
- ½ tsp. ground ginger
- 1 roasting chicken (5 to 6 lbs.), patted dry
- 1 lb. fresh baby carrots, peeled and thinly sliced
- 1 lb. medium parsnips, peeled and thinly sliced
- 2 large tangerines, peeled and sliced
- 1 cup chopped dried apricots
- ½ cup slivered almonds
- ½ cup chicken broth

Combine first five ingredients; rub spice mixture over chicken until well coated. Arrange carrots, parsnips, tangerines, apricots and almonds in bottom of a 6-qt. slow cooker. Place chicken breast side up on vegetables; pour in broth. Cook, covered, on low until a thermometer inserted in thigh reads 170° and chicken is tender, 6-8 hours. Remove chicken, vegetables and fruits to a serving platter; let stand 5-10 minutes before carving chicken.
1 SERVING: 503 cal., 24g fat (6g sat. fat), 112mg chol., 232mg sod., 35g carb. (20g sugars, 6g fiber), 39g pro.

TEST KITCHEN TIP
Tagine isn't just the name of the delicious stuff inside — it's also the name of the cone-lidded clay pot traditionally used to cook the dish.

SLOW COOKER TURKEY PESTO LASAGNA

SLOW COOKER TURKEY PESTO LASAGNA

My cheesy, noodley lasagna makes any slow-cooker skeptic a believer. It's easy to prep while my kids nap, and dinner's ready when their dad walks in the door at night. We bring more pesto and marinara to the table for our resident sauce lovers.
—Blair Lonergan, Rochelle, VA

PREP: 25 min.
COOK: 3 hours + standing
MAKES: 8 servings

- 1 lb. ground turkey
- 1 small onion, chopped
- 2 tsp. Italian seasoning
- ½ tsp. salt
- 2 cups shredded part-skim mozzarella cheese, divided
- 1 container (15 oz.) whole-milk ricotta cheese
- ¼ cup prepared pesto
- 1 jar (24 oz.) marinara sauce
- 9 no-cook lasagna noodles
  Grated Parmesan cheese

1. Cut three 25x3-in. strips of heavy-duty foil; crisscross so they resemble the spokes of a wheel. Place the strips on bottom and up sides of a greased 5-qt. slow cooker. Coat strips with cooking spray.
2. In a large skillet, cook turkey and onion over medium heat 6-8 minutes or until turkey is no longer pink, breaking up turkey into crumbles; drain. Stir in Italian seasoning and salt.
3. In a small bowl, mix 1 cup mozzarella cheese, ricotta cheese and pesto. In prepared slow cooker, layer a third of each of the following: marinara sauce, noodles (breaking noodles if necessary to fit), turkey mixture and cheese mixture. Repeat layers twice. Sprinkle with remaining mozzarella cheese.
4. Cook, covered, on low until noodles are tender, 3-4 hours. Turn off slow cooker; remove insert. Let stand, uncovered, 30 minutes before serving. Using foil strips, remove lasagna to a platter. Serve with Parmesan cheese.
1 SLICE: 397 cal., 19g fat (8g sat. fat), 79mg chol., 883mg sod., 28g carb. (9g sugars, 3g fiber), 28g pro.

CHICKEN WITH BEANS & POTATOES

This all-in-one entree is another way to do meat and potatoes. Build a pot of slow-cooked goodness.
—*Taste of Home* Test Kitchen

PREP: 20 min. • **COOK:** 4 hours
MAKES: 10 servings

- 2 lbs. boneless skinless chicken breasts, cut into 1-in. cubes
- ½ tsp. lemon-pepper seasoning
- 1 Tbsp. canola oil
- 1 lb. fresh green beans, trimmed
- 1 lb. small red potatoes, quartered
- ½ lb. medium fresh mushrooms, halved
- ½ cup thinly sliced sweet onion
- 2 cans (14½ oz. each) chicken broth
- 2 Tbsp. onion soup mix
- 2 tsp. Worcestershire sauce
- 1 tsp. grated lemon peel
- ½ tsp. salt
- ½ tsp. pepper
- ¼ tsp. garlic powder

1. Sprinkle chicken with lemon-pepper. In a large skillet, cook chicken in oil over medium heat for 4-5 minutes or until lightly browned.
2. In a 5- or 6-qt. slow cooker, layer the green beans, potatoes, mushrooms and onion. In a small bowl, combine the remaining ingredients; pour over vegetables. Top with chicken.
3. Cover and cook on low until the vegetables are tender, 4-5 hours. Serve with a slotted spoon.
1¼ CUPS: 209 cal., 5g fat (1g sat. fat), 63mg chol., 324mg sod., 15g carb. (3g sugars, 3g fiber), 26g pro. **DIABETIC EXCHANGES:** 3 lean meat, 1 vegetable, ½ starch.

TEST KITCHEN TIP
Potatoes and other dense foods can take a long time to cook in the slow cooker. They are often layered in the bottom of the slow cooker, where they can be closer to the heat than other ingredients placed on top.

CHICKEN STEW

Rely on this slow cooker stew on busy weekends when you'd rather not be in the kitchen. Chicken, vegetables and seasonings blend beautifully, and it's lower in fat than most stews.
—Linda Emery, Bearden, AR

PREP: 10 min. • **COOK:** 4½ hours
MAKES: 10 servings

- 2 lbs. boneless skinless chicken breasts, cut into 1-in. cubes
- 2 cans (14½ oz. each) reduced-sodium chicken broth
- 3 cups cubed peeled potatoes
- 1 cup chopped onion
- 1 cup sliced celery
- 1 cup thinly sliced carrots
- 1 tsp. paprika
- ½ tsp. pepper
- ½ tsp. rubbed sage
- ½ tsp. dried thyme
- 1 can (6 oz.) no-salt-added tomato paste
- ¼ cup cold water
- 3 Tbsp. cornstarch
  Shredded Parmesan cheese, optional

1. In a 5-qt. slow cooker, combine the first 11 ingredients; cover and cook on high for 4 hours.
2. Mix the water and cornstarch until smooth; stir into stew. Cook, covered, 30 minutes more or until vegetables are tender. If desired, sprinkle with Parmesan cheese.
1 CUP: 193 cal., 3g fat (0 sat. fat), 59mg chol., 236mg sod., 16g carb. (0 sugars, 0 fiber), 24g pro. **DIABETIC EXCHANGES:** 3 lean meat, 2 vegetable, ½ starch.

CHICKEN STEW

KING-SIZE DRUMSTICKS

Let your slow cooker do the work when these tender turkey legs are on the menu. Enchilada sauce, chilies and cumin give these king-sized drummies a zesty treatment.
—*Taste of Home* Test Kitchen

PREP: 15 min. • **COOK:** 8 hours
MAKES: 6 servings

- 1 can (10 oz.) enchilada sauce
- 1 can (4 oz.) chopped green chilies, drained
- 1 tsp. dried oregano
- ½ tsp. garlic salt
- ½ tsp. ground cumin
- 6 turkey drumsticks (12 oz. each), skin removed
- 3 Tbsp. cornstarch
- 3 Tbsp. cold water

1. In a large bowl, combine enchilada sauce, chilies, oregano, garlic salt and cumin. Place the drumsticks in a 5-qt. slow cooker; top with sauce. Cook, covered on low, until a thermometer in turkey reads 180°, 8-10 hours.
2. Remove turkey to a serving platter; keep warm. Skim fat from cooking juices; transfer to a small saucepan. Bring liquid to a boil. Combine the cornstarch and water until smooth. Gradually stir into the pan. Bring to a boil; cook and stir for 2 minutes or until juices are thickened. Serve with turkey drumsticks.
1 DRUMSTICK: 306 cal., 7g fat (2g sat. fat), 202mg chol., 640mg sod., 7g carb. (1g sugars, 0 fiber), 51g pro.

BBQ CHICKEN & SMOKED SAUSAGE

My party-ready barbecue recipe works for weeknights, too. With just a few minutes of prep time, you still get that low-and-slow flavor everybody craves (thanks, slow cooker!). Throw in some minced jalapenos for extra *oomph*.
—Kimberly Young, Mesquite, TX

PREP: 30 min. • **COOK:** 4 hours
MAKES: 8 servings

- 1 medium onion, chopped
- 1 large sweet red pepper, cut into 1-in. pieces
- 4 bone-in chicken thighs, skin removed
- 4 chicken drumsticks, skin removed
- 1 pkg. (12 oz.) smoked sausage links, cut into 1-in. pieces
- 1 cup barbecue sauce
  Sliced seeded jalapeno pepper, optional

1. Place first five ingredients in a 4- or 5-qt. slow cooker; top with barbecue sauce. Cook, covered, on low until chicken is tender and a thermometer inserted in chicken reads at least 170°-175°, 4-5 hours.
2. Remove the chicken, sausage and vegetables from slow cooker; keep warm. Transfer cooking juices to a saucepan; bring to a boil. Reduce heat; simmer, uncovered, until thickened, 15-20 minutes, stirring occasionally.
3. Serve the chicken, sausage and vegetables with sauce. If desired, top with jalapeno.
1 SERVING: 331 cal., 18g fat (6g sat. fat), 91mg chol., 840mg sod., 17g carb. (13g sugars, 1g fiber), 24g pro.

SLOW COOKER
PAD THAI

ITALIAN CHICKEN
CHARDONNAY

SLOW COOKER PAD THAI

I love pad Thai, but I hate standing over a hot stir-fry—especially in the summer. This slow cooker version lets me keep my cool and enjoy pad Thai, too.
—Shawn Barto, Winter Garden, FL

PREP: 20 min. • **COOK:** 4 hours
MAKES: 4 servings

3 boneless skinless chicken breast halves (5 to 6 oz. each)
¼ cup packed brown sugar
¼ cup lime juice
2 Tbsp. soy sauce
2 garlic cloves, minced
1 tsp. fish sauce or additional soy sauce
¼ tsp. crushed red pepper flakes
8 oz. uncooked Asian lo mein noodles
2 tsp. butter
2 large eggs, beaten
3 green onions, thinly sliced
¼ cup chopped salted peanuts
¼ cup chopped fresh cilantro

1. Place chicken in a 1½- or 3-qt. slow cooker. In a small bowl, combine the next six ingredients; pour over the chicken. Cook, covered, on low until a thermometer inserted in chicken reads 165°, about 4 hours. Remove chicken; cool slightly. Shred chicken with two forks; return to slow cooker.
2. In a large saucepan, cook noodles according to package directions. In a small nonstick skillet, heat butter over medium heat. Pour in eggs; cook and stir until eggs are thickened and no liquid egg remains.
3. Drain noodles. Stir eggs and noodles into slow cooker. Top with green onions, peanuts and cilantro.
FREEZE OPTION: Double the chicken mixture. Freeze half of cooled chicken mixture in freezer containers. To use, partially thaw in refrigerator overnight. Heat through in a saucepan, stirring occasionally and adding a little water if necessary. Prepare noodles and eggs as directed; stir into chicken mixture. Garnish as desired.
1 SERVING: 482 cal., 12g fat (3g sat. fat), 157mg chol., 891mg sod., 59g carb. (14g sugars, 2g fiber), 34g pro.

ITALIAN CHICKEN CHARDONNAY

Knowing that we needed dinner ready one night when we walked in the door, I gave a favorite skillet dish a slow cooker make-over. It's perfect for an everyday meal but nice enough for company.
—Judy Armstrong, Prairieville, LA

PREP: 20 min.
COOK: 5 hours
MAKES: 6 servings

2 tsp. paprika
1 tsp. salt
1 tsp. pepper
¼ tsp. cayenne pepper
3 lbs. bone-in chicken breast halves, skin removed
½ lb. baby portobello mushrooms, quartered
1 medium sweet red pepper, chopped
1 medium onion, chopped
1 can (14 oz.) water-packed artichoke hearts, rinsed and drained
1½ cups chardonnay
1 can (6 oz.) tomato paste
3 garlic cloves, minced
2 Tbsp. minced fresh thyme or 2 tsp. dried thyme
¼ cup minced fresh parsley
   Hot cooked pasta
   Shredded Romano cheese

1. Combine the paprika, salt, pepper and cayenne; sprinkle over chicken. Place the chicken, mushrooms, red pepper, onion and artichokes in a 5-qt. slow cooker. In a small bowl, combine the chardonnay, tomato paste, garlic and thyme; pour over vegetables.
2. Cook, covered, on low until chicken is tender, 5-6 hours. Stir in parsley. Serve with pasta; sprinkle with cheese.
1 SERVING: 282 cal., 5g fat (2g sat. fat), 103mg chol., 550mg sod., 16g carb. (6g sugars, 5g fiber), 43g pro. **DIABETIC EXCHANGES:** 5 lean meat, 1 starch.

SLOW-COOKED
MOROCCAN
CHICKEN

TURKEY & PORK MEATBALLS

Treat yourself to homemade meatballs, already simmering in sauce, at the end of a busy day.
—Suzanne Wagg, Madison, ME

PREP: 20 min. • **COOK:** 4 hours
MAKES: 6 servings

- 3 slices whole wheat bread
- ½ cup grated Romano or Parmesan cheese
- 1 large egg, beaten
- 1 Tbsp. ketchup
- 1 Tbsp. minced fresh parsley
- 1 tsp. minced fresh oregano
- 1 tsp. minced fresh basil
- 1 tsp. seafood seasoning
- 1 lb. ground turkey
- ¼ lb. ground pork
- 1 can (29 oz.) tomato sauce
  Hot cooked pasta, Parmesan cheese, and chopped fresh parsley, optional

1. Pulse bread in a food processor until fine crumbs form. Transfer to a large bowl. Combine bread crumbs with the next seven ingredients. Add turkey and pork; mix lightly but thoroughly. With wet hands, shape into twenty-four 1½-in. balls.
2. Transfer to a 3- or 4-qt. slow cooker. Pour sauce over top; stir gently. Cook, covered, on low until meatballs are cooked through, 4-5 hours. If desired, serve with hot cooked pasta and sprinkle with parsley.
4 MEATBALLS WITH ⅓ CUP SAUCE: 273 cal., 14g fat (5g sat. fat), 96mg chol., 1049mg sod., 14g carb. (4g sugars, 3g fiber), 27g pro.

TEST KITCHEN TIP
Browning meatballs before placing them in the slow cooker helps develop an intense meaty flavor.

EAT SMART

SLOW-COOKED MOROCCAN CHICKEN

Herbs and spices really work magic on plain chicken in this dish, and the dried fruit adds an exotic touch.
—Kathy Morgan, Ridgefield, WA

PREP: 20 min. • **COOK:** 6 hours
MAKES: 4 servings

- 4 medium carrots, sliced
- 2 large onions, halved and sliced
- 1 broiler/fryer chicken (3 to 4 lbs.), cut up, skin removed
- ½ tsp. salt
- ½ cup chopped dried apricots
- ½ cup raisins
- 1 can (14½ oz.) reduced-sodium chicken broth
- ¼ cup tomato paste
- 2 Tbsp. all-purpose flour
- 2 Tbsp. lemon juice
- 2 garlic cloves, minced
- 1½ tsp. ground ginger
- 1½ tsp. ground cumin
- 1 tsp. ground cinnamon
- ¾ tsp. pepper
  Hot cooked couscous

1. Place carrots and onions in a greased 5-qt. slow cooker. Sprinkle the chicken with salt; add to slow cooker. Top with apricots and raisins. In a small bowl, whisk the broth, tomato paste, flour, lemon juice, garlic and seasonings until blended; add to slow cooker.
2. Cook, covered, on low until chicken is tender, 6-7 hours. Serve with hot cooked couscous.
1 SERVING: 435 cal., 9g fat (3g sat. fat), 110mg chol., 755mg sod., 47g carb. (27g sugars, 6g fiber), 42g pro.

TURKEY & PORK
MEATBALLS

SLOW-SIMMERED CHICKEN WITH RAISINS, CAPERS & BASIL

SLOW-SIMMERED CHICKEN WITH RAISINS, CAPERS & BASIL

Capers, golden raisins and fresh basil give this dish a sweetly savory blend of flavors. And what is even better than that? The kids LOVE it.
—Nadine Mesch, Mount Healthy, OH

PREP: 25 min.
COOK: 4 hours
MAKES: 8 servings

- 2 Tbsp. olive oil, divided
- 8 boneless skinless chicken thighs (4 oz. each)
- 1 tsp. salt
- 1 tsp. pepper
- ½ cup Marsala wine
- 8 oz. sliced fresh mushrooms
- 1 medium sweet red pepper, thinly sliced
- 1 medium onion, thinly sliced
- 1 can (14½ oz.) diced tomatoes, undrained
- ½ cup golden raisins
- 2 Tbsp. capers, drained
- ¼ cup chopped fresh basil
  Hot cooked couscous

1. In a large skillet, heat 1 Tbsp. oil over medium-high heat. Sprinkle chicken with salt and pepper; brown chicken on both sides in batches, adding oil as needed. Transfer chicken to a 5- or 6-qt. slow cooker.
2. Add wine to the skillet, stirring to loosen browned bits; pour into slow cooker. Stir mushrooms, red pepper, onion, and tomatoes, raisins and capers into slow cooker.
3. Cook, covered, until chicken and vegetables are tender, 4-5 hours. Sprinkle with basil before serving. Serve with hot cooked couscous.
1 SERVING: 250 cal., 12g fat (3g sat. fat), 76mg chol., 494mg sod., 13g carb. (9g sugars, 2g fiber), 23g pro. **DIABETIC EXCHANGES:** 3 lean meat, 1 vegetable, 1 fat, ½ starch.

CHICKEN VEGETABLE CURRY

CHICKEN VEGETABLE CURRY

This comfort dish gets fabulous flavor when I add chicken, sweet red peppers, coconut milk and the all-important seasoning, curry powder.
—Roxana Lambeth, Moreno Valley, CA

PREP: 20 min. • **COOK:** 4 hours
MAKES: 6 servings

- 1½ lbs. boneless skinless chicken thighs, cut into 1½-in. pieces
- 2 medium red potatoes, chopped (about 1½ cups)
- 1 small sweet red pepper, coarsely chopped
- 1 medium onion, coarsely chopped
- 1 medium carrot, chopped
- 3 garlic cloves, minced
- 1 can (13.66 oz.) coconut milk
- ½ cup chicken broth
- 3 tsp. curry powder
- 1½ tsp. salt
- 1 tsp. ground cumin
- 1 Tbsp. minced fresh cilantro
  Hot cooked couscous

1. Place first six ingredients in a 3- or 4-qt. slow cooker. In a small bowl, whisk together coconut milk, broth and dry seasonings; stir into chicken mixture.
2. Cook, covered, on low until chicken and vegetables are tender, 4-5 hours. Stir in cilantro. Serve with couscous.
1 CUP CURRY: 339 cal., 22g fat (14g sat. fat), 76mg chol., 755mg sod., 12g carb. (2g sugars, 2g fiber), 24g pro.

TEST KITCHEN TIP
Chicken thighs tend to do better in the slow cooker than chicken breast. They aren't as lean as chicken breast, so the longer cook time won't dry them out. This dish makes plenty of rich sauce, ideal for serving with couscous or rice.

CURRIED CHICKEN WITH PEACHES

I'm always looking for dinners I can prepare ahead of time. The chicken in this recipe cooks for hours in fragrant seasonings, and sweet peaches and raisins round out the amazing flavors.
—Heidi Martinez, CO Springs, CO

PREP: 15 min. **COOK:** 3¼ hours
MAKES: 4 servings

- 1 broiler/fryer chicken (3 lbs.), cut up
- ⅛ tsp. salt
- ⅛ tsp. pepper
- 1 can (29 oz.) sliced peaches
- ½ cup chicken broth
- 2 Tbsp. butter, melted
- 1 Tbsp. dried minced onion
- 2 tsp. curry powder
- 2 garlic cloves, minced
- ¼ tsp. ground ginger
- 3 Tbsp. cornstarch
- 3 Tbsp. cold water
- ¼ cup raisins
  Toasted sweetened shredded coconut, optional

1. Place chicken in a 5-qt. slow cooker; sprinkle with salt and pepper. Drain peaches, reserving ½ cup juice; set peaches aside. In a small bowl, combine broth, butter, onion, curry, garlic, ginger and reserved juice; pour over chicken. Cook, covered, on low 3-4 hours or until chicken is tender.
2. Remove chicken to a serving platter; keep warm. Mix cornstarch and water until smooth; stir into cooking juices. Add raisins. Cook, covered, on high for 15 minutes or until thickened. Stir in peaches and heat through. Serve with chicken. If desired, sprinkle with coconut.
1 SERVING: 423 cal., 15g fat (6g sat. fat), 125mg chol., 360mg sod., 34g carb. (24g sugars, 3g fiber), 39g pro.

EAT SMART
SOUTHWESTERN CHICKEN & LIMA BEAN STEW

I love to have my daughter, son-in-law and grandchildren over for this easy supper. When they fill their bowls again, that's the best compliment.
—Pam Corder, Monroe, LA

PREP: 20 min.
COOK: 6 hours
MAKES: 6 servings

- 4 bone-in chicken thighs (1½ lbs.), skin removed
- 2 cups frozen lima beans
- 2 cups frozen corn
- 1 large green pepper, chopped
- 1 large onion, chopped
- 2 cans (14 oz. each) fire-roasted diced tomatoes, undrained
- ¼ cup tomato paste
- 3 Tbsp. Worcestershire sauce
- 3 garlic cloves, minced
- 1½ tsp. ground cumin
- 1½ tsp. dried oregano
- ¼ tsp. salt
- ¼ tsp. pepper
  Chopped fresh cilantro or parsley

1. Place the first five ingredients in a 5-qt. slow cooker. In a large bowl, combine tomatoes, tomato paste, Worcestershire sauce, garlic and dry seasonings; pour over top.
2. Cook, covered, on low until chicken is tender, 6-8 hours. Remove chicken from slow cooker. When cool enough to handle, remove meat from bones; discard bones. Shred meat with two forks; return to slow cooker and heat through. If desired, sprinkle each serving with cilantro.
1½ CUPS: 312 cal., 7g fat (2g sat. fat), 58mg chol., 614mg sod., 39g carb. (9g sugars, 8g fiber), 24g pro. **DIABETIC EXCHANGES:** 3 lean meat, 2 starch, 1 vegetable.

SOUTHWESTERN CHICKEN & LIMA BEAN STEW

SLOW COOKER
ROAST CHICKEN

SLOW COOKER ROAST CHICKEN

Roast chicken is so easy to make in a slow cooker. We save the shredded chicken to use for other meals throughout the week.
—Courtney Stultz, Weir, KS

PREP: 20 min.
COOK: 4 hours + standing
MAKES: 6 servings

- 2 medium carrots, cut into 1-in. pieces
- 1 medium onion, cut into 1-in. pieces
- 2 garlic cloves, minced
- 2 tsp. olive oil
- 1 tsp. dried parsley flakes
- 1 tsp. pepper
- ¾ tsp. salt
- ½ tsp. dried oregano
- ½ tsp. rubbed sage
- ½ tsp. chili powder
- 1 broiler/fryer chicken (4 to 5 lbs.)

1. Place carrots and onion in a 6-qt. slow cooker. In a small bowl, mix garlic and oil. In another bowl, combine the dry seasonings.
2. Tuck wings under chicken; tie drumsticks together. With fingers, carefully loosen skin from chicken breast; rub garlic mixture under the skin. Secure skin to underside of breast with toothpicks.
3. Place chicken in slow cooker over carrots and onions, breast side up; sprinkle with seasoning mixture. Cook, covered, on low until a thermometer inserted in thigh reads at least 170°, 4-5 hours. Remove chicken from slow cooker; tent with foil. Discard vegetables. Let chicken stand for 15 minutes before carving.
FREEZE OPTION: Cool the chicken and any juices. Freeze in freezer containers. To use, partially thaw in refrigerator overnight. Heat through slowly in a covered skillet until a thermometer inserted in chicken reads 165°, stirring occasionally and adding a little broth or water if necessary.
5 OZ. COOKED CHICKEN: 408 cal., 24g fat (6g sat. fat), 139mg chol., 422mg sod., 1g carb. (0 sugars, 0 fiber), 44g pro.

Other Entrees

SAUSAGE & BLUE
CHEESE STUFFED
PEPPERS

SAUSAGE & BLUE CHEESE STUFFED PEPPERS

This family favorite combines some of our most-enjoyed ingredients: sausage, blue cheese and sweet peppers. The ease of preparation and slow-cooker convenience make this a go-to meal for busy weeknights.
—Peggy Mehalick, Mountain Top, PA

PREP: 15 min. • **COOK:** 3½ hours
MAKES: 4 servings

- 2 medium sweet red peppers
- 2 medium sweet yellow peppers
- 1 jar (14 oz.) pizza sauce or pasta sauce, divided
- 1 lb. uncooked bulk pork sausage
- ¾ cup uncooked instant rice
- 1 small onion, chopped
- 1 small tomato, seeded and chopped
- ½ cup crumbled blue cheese
- 1 large egg, lightly beaten
- 2 Tbsp. chopped ripe olives
- 1½ tsp. dried parsley flakes
- ½ tsp. garlic powder
- ½ tsp. Italian seasoning
- ¼ to ½ tsp. crushed red pepper flakes, optional
  Crumbled blue cheese, optional

1. Cut and discard tops from peppers; remove seeds. Pour sauce into bottom of a 4- or 5-qt. slow cooker, reserving ¾ cup. In small bowl, combine remaining ingredients; add reserved sauce. Spoon mixture into peppers; place in slow cooker. Cook, covered, on low until the peppers are tender, 3½-4½ hours.
2. Spoon cooking juices over peppers. If desired, top with more blue cheese.
1 STUFFED PEPPER: 593 cal., 39g fat (13g sat. fat), 136mg chol., 1510mg sod., 35g carb. (11g sugars, 5g fiber), 25g pro.

TEST KITCHEN TIP
Instant rice works well in the slow cooker, as does converted rice (which has been partially cooked and then dried).

SPICY PORK & BUTTERNUT SQUASH RAGU

FREEZE OPTION: Freeze cooled sauce in freezer containers. To use, partially thaw in the refrigerator overnight. Place in a saucepan and heat through, stirring occasionally.

1 CUP RAGU: 195 cal., 8g fat (3g sat. fat), 52mg chol., 426mg sod., 13g carb. (6g sugars, 2g fiber), 17g pro. **DIABETIC EXCHANGES:** 2 lean meat, 1 starch.

POTATO SAUSAGE SUPPER

I fix this comforting dish at least once a month. At family reunions, the lovely layered casserole always disappears, and it's home again with an empty slow cooker.

—Patricia Ginn, Delphi, IN

PREP: 15 min. • **COOK:** 5½ hours
MAKES: 8 servings

- 4 medium potatoes, peeled and sliced
- 1 lb. smoked kielbasa or Polish sausage, cut into ½-in. slices
- 2 medium onions, sliced and separated into rings
- 1 can (10¾ oz.) condensed cheddar cheese soup, undiluted
- 1 can (10¾ oz.) condensed cream of celery soup, undiluted
- 1 pkg. (10 oz.) frozen peas, thawed

1. In a greased 5-qt. slow cooker, layer a third of each of potatoes, sausage, onions and cheese soup. Repeat the layers twice.
2. Pour celery soup over the top. Cook, covered on low until potatoes are tender, 5-6 hours. Add peas and cook 30 minutes longer.

1½ CUPS: 357 cal., 20g fat (7g sat. fat), 44mg chol., 1226mg sod., 35g carb. (8g sugars, 5g fiber), 14g pro.

SPICY PORK & BUTTERNUT SQUASH RAGU

Perfect for cooler fall weather, this recipe is a marvelously spicy combo that proves satisfying after a day spent outdoors.

—Monica Osterhaus, Paducah, KY

PREP: 20 min. • **COOK:** 5 hours
MAKES: 10 servings

- 2 cans (14½ oz. each) stewed tomatoes, undrained
- 1 pkg. (12 oz.) frozen cooked winter squash, thawed
- 1 large sweet onion, cut into ½-in. pieces
- 1 medium sweet red pepper, cut into ½-in. pieces
- 1½ tsp. crushed red pepper flakes
- 2 lbs. boneless country-style pork ribs
- 1 tsp. salt
- ¼ tsp. pepper
- ¼ tsp. garlic powder
  Hot cooked pasta
  Shaved Parmesan cheese, optional

1. Combine first five ingredients in bottom of 6- or 7-qt. slow cooker. Sprinkle ribs with salt, garlic powder and pepper; place in slow cooker. Cook, covered, on low until pork is tender, 5-6 hours.
2. Remove cover; stir to break pork into smaller pieces. Serve with pasta. If desired, top with Parmesan cheese.

CHOPS WITH FRUIT STUFFING

The aroma that fills the house as this dish slow-cooks is amazing. Serve a green vegetable for an easy complete meal—and consider this one for when company comes to dinner.

—Suzanne Reyes, Tustin, CA

PREP: 10 min. • **COOK:** 3 hours
MAKES: 6 servings

- 6   boneless pork loin chops (4 oz. each)
- 1   Tbsp. canola oil
- 1   pkg. (6 oz.) herb stuffing mix
- 2   celery ribs, chopped
- 1   medium tart apple, peeled and chopped
- 1   cup dried cherries or cranberries
- ½   cup chopped onion
- ⅔   cup chicken broth
- ¼   cup butter, melted

1. In a large skillet, brown pork chops in oil on both sides. In a large bowl, combine the remaining ingredients.
2. Place half of the stuffing mixture in a 3-qt. slow cooker. Top with pork and remaining stuffing mixture. Cook, covered on low until pork is tender, about 3 hours.
1 SERVING: 435 cal., 18g fat (7g sat. fat), 74mg chol., 741mg sod., 41g carb. (20g sugars, 2g fiber), 27g pro.

"This is my all-time favorite slow cooker recipe. The stuffing is fabulous and the pork so tender. Makes my mouth water just thinking about it! Five stars and two thumbs up!"
—LATELYLISA, TASTEOFHOME.COM

WESTERN OMELET CASSEROLE

This is a western-style omelet with ham and hash browns using the slow cooker. From youngest to oldest at brunch, everyone devours it.

—Kathleen Murphy, Littleton, CO

PREP: 15 min.
COOK: 6 hours + standing
MAKES: 8 servings

- 1   pkg. (30 oz.) frozen shredded hash brown potatoes, thawed
- 1   lb. cubed fully cooked ham or 1 lb. bulk pork sausage, cooked and drained
- 1   medium onion, chopped
- 1   medium green pepper, chopped
- 1½ cups shredded cheddar cheese
- 12 large eggs
- 1   cup 2% milk
- 1   tsp. salt
- 1   tsp. pepper

1. In a greased 5- or 6-qt. slow cooker, layer half of each of the following: potatoes, ham, onion, green pepper and cheese. Repeat layers.
2. Whisk together the remaining ingredients; pour over top. Cook, covered, on low until set, 6-7 hours. Turn off slow cooker. Remove insert; let stand, uncovered, 15-30 minutes before serving.
1⅓ CUPS: 363 cal., 17g fat (8g sat. fat), 332mg chol., 1166mg sod., 24g carb. (4g sugars, 2g fiber), 29g pro.

WESTERN OMELET CASSEROLE

SWEET & SOUR
PORK WRAPS

KAPUZTA

Here is a truly authentic Old World recipe—family friends from Poland gave it to my mother years ago—popular for Sunday dinners and at potlucks. After my husband and I moved to our dairy farm, I realized that it's a perfect any-night supper and even better the next day.
—Liz Krocak, Montogomery, MN

PREP: 20 min. • **COOK:** 6 hours
MAKES: 8 servings

- 1 Tbsp. olive oil
- 1½ lbs. pork stew meat
- 1 medium onion, chopped
- 1½ lbs. smoked Polish sausage, cut into ½-in. slices
- 1 qt. sauerkraut, rinsed and well drained
- 2 cups coarsely chopped cabbage
- 1 Tbsp. caraway seeds
- 1 can (10¾ oz.) condensed cream of mushroom soup, undiluted
  Pepper to taste

In a large skillet, heat oil over medium-high heat. Add pork and onion; brown meat. Transfer to a 5-qt. slow cooker. Stir in remaining ingredients. Cook, covered, on low until pork is tender, 6-8 hours.
1 CUP: 519 cal., 39g fat (15g sat. fat), 121mg chol., 1509mg sod., 12g carb. (3g sugars, 3g fiber), 28g pro.

SWEET & SOUR PORK WRAPS

We always make these wraps at our family's annual party. The cabbage and cilantro give them a fresh texture.
—Andrew DeVito, Hartford, CT

PREP: 15 min.
COOK: 6 hours
MAKES: 8 servings

- 1 boneless pork shoulder butt roast (3 to 4 lbs.)
- 1 medium onion, chopped
- 1 cup water
- 1 cup sweet-and-sour sauce
- ¼ cup sherry or chicken broth
- ¼ cup reduced-sodium soy sauce
- 1 envelope onion soup mix
- 1 Tbsp. minced fresh gingerroot
- 3 garlic cloves, minced
- 16 flour tortillas (6 in.), warmed
- 4 cups shredded cabbage
- ¼ cup minced fresh cilantro

1. Place roast and onion in a 6-qt. slow cooker. In a small bowl, whisk water, sweet-and-sour sauce, sherry, soy sauce, soup mix, ginger and garlic until blended; pour over pork. Cook, covered, on low until meat is tender, 6-8 hours.
2. When cool enough to handle, shred pork with two forks. To serve, spoon about ⅓ cup pork mixture onto the center of each tortilla. Top with ¼ cup cabbage; sprinkle with cilantro. Fold bottom of tortilla over filling; fold both sides to close.
2 WRAPS: 523 cal., 23g fat (6g sat. fat), 101mg chol., 1357mg sod., 42g carb. (8g sugars, 1g fiber), 36g pro.

SAUSAGE WITH JALAPENO POTATOES

SAUSAGE WITH JALAPENO POTATOES

While we were in Texas, my husband and I came up with this dish for our weekend cookouts. This one is for meat and potato lovers everywhere.
—Rose Smith, Royalton, IL

PREP: 25 min. • **COOK:** 5 hours
MAKES: 6 servings

- 3 lbs. potatoes (about 6 medium), peeled and cut into 1-in. cubes
- 3 jalapeno peppers, sliced and seeded
- ¼ cup butter, cubed
- 2 Tbsp. water
- 3 garlic cloves, minced
- ¾ tsp. salt
- ¼ tsp. pepper
- 2 medium sweet red peppers, halved and cut into 1-in. strips
- 2 medium sweet yellow or orange peppers, halved and cut into 1-in. strips
- 1 large onion, halved and thinly sliced
- 1 tsp. olive oil
- 5 Italian sausage links (4 oz. each)
  Chopped fresh basil, optional

1. Place the first seven ingredients in a 6-qt. slow cooker; toss to combine. Top with sweet peppers and onion.

2. In a large skillet, heat oil over medium-high heat. Brown sausages on all sides; place over vegetables. Cook, covered, on low until potatoes are tender, 5-6 hours.

3. Remove sausages; cut diagonally into 2- to 3-in. pieces. Remove the vegetables with a slotted spoon; serve with sausage. If desired, sprinkle with fresh basil.

NOTE: Wear disposable gloves when cutting hot peppers; the oils can burn skin. Avoid touching your face.

1 SERVING: 518 cal., 29g fat (11g sat. fat), 71mg chol., 948mg sod., 50g carb. (5g sugars, 7g fiber), 16g pro.

CAROLINA SHRIMP & CHEDDAR GRITS

My family loves shrimp and grits, but we couldn't agree on a recipe. This one with cheddar and Cajun seasoning seems to make everyone happy.
—Charlotte Price, Raleigh, NC

PREP: 15 min. • **COOK:** 2¾ hours
MAKES: 6 servings

- 1 cup uncooked stone-ground grits
- 1 large garlic clove, minced
- ½ tsp. salt
- ¼ tsp. pepper
- 4 cups water
- 2 cups shredded cheddar cheese
- ¼ cup butter, cubed
- 1 lb. peeled and deveined cooked shrimp (31-40 per lb.)
- 2 medium tomatoes, seeded and finely chopped
- 4 green onions, finely chopped
- 2 Tbsp. chopped fresh parsley
- 4 tsp. lemon juice
- 2 to 3 tsp. Cajun seasoning

1. Place the first five ingredients in a 3-qt. slow cooker; stir to combine. Cook, covered, on high 2½-3 hours or until water is absorbed and grits are tender, stirring every 45 minutes.
2. Stir in cheese and butter until melted. Stir in remaining ingredients; cook, covered, on high 15-30 minutes or until heated through.
1⅓ CUPS: 417 cal., 22g fat (13g sat. fat), 175mg chol., 788mg sod., 27g carb. (2g sugars, 2g fiber), 27g pro.

CAROLINA
SHRIMP &
CHEDDAR
GRITS

EAT SMART

SLOW-COOKED FRUITED OATMEAL WITH NUTS

The beauty of this breakfast is that you can set the slow cooker overnight and, with nothing more than a ladle, spoons and bowls, feed a crowd in the morning.
—Trisha Kruse, Eagle, ID

PREP: 15 min. • **COOK:** 6 hours
MAKES: 6 servings

- 3 cups water
- 2 cups old-fashioned oats
- 2 cups chopped apples
- 1 cup dried cranberries
- 1 cup fat-free milk
- 2 tsp. butter, melted
- 1 tsp. pumpkin pie spice
- 1 tsp. ground cinnamon
- 6 Tbsp. chopped almonds, toasted
- 6 Tbsp. chopped pecans, toasted
    Additional fat-free milk

1. In a 3-qt. slow cooker coated with cooking spray, combine the first eight ingredients. Cook, covered, on low until liquid is absorbed, 6-8 hours.
2. Spoon oatmeal into bowls. Sprinkle with almonds and pecans. If desired, drizzle with additional milk.
1 CUP: 306 cal., 13g fat (2g sat. fat), 4mg chol., 28mg sod., 45g carb. (20g sugars, 6g fiber), 8g pro. **DIABETIC EXCHANGES:** 3 starch, 2 fat.

LAMB & WHITE BEAN CHILI

SLOWER COOKER MILK-CAN SUPPER

Here's a slow-cooked version of an old campfire classic. Pioneers and cowboys would cook this kind of meal over a milk can on an open fire, letting the flavors and textures blend together beautifully.
—Nick Iverson, Denver, CO

PREP: 20 min. • **COOK:** 6 hours
MAKES: 8 servings

- 1 Tbsp. canola oil
- 8 uncooked bratwurst links
- 2 lbs. small Yukon Gold potatoes, quartered
- 1 small head cabbage, coarsely chopped
- 2 medium onion, quartered
- 3 medium carrots, peeled and cut into 2-in. lengths
- 3 medium parsnips, peeled and cut into 2-in. lengths
- 6 fresh thyme sprigs
- 2 each garlic cloves, crushed
- 2 each bay leaf
- ½ tsp. salt
- ½ tsp. pepper
- 1 cup light beer
- 1 cup reduced-sodium chicken broth

1. Heat oil in large skillet over medium-heat; add sausages and cook until browned, 3-4 minutes. Remove from heat; set aside.
2. Place potatoes in single layer on the bottom of a 6-qt. slow cooker. Top with the cabbage, onion, carrot and parsnips. Add thyme, garlic, bay leaves, salt and pepper. Add sausages; pour beer and chicken broth over top. Cook, covered, until vegetables are tender, 6-8 hours.

1 SERVING: 457 cal., 27g fat (9g sat. fat), 63mg chol., 967mg sod., 37g carb. (6g sugars, 4g fiber), 15g pro.

LAMB & WHITE BEAN CHILI

I created a fresh take on chili using lamb and Moroccan seasoning with a feta and almond garnish—and made a second batch almost right away for my husband and son. For a spicier chili, add harissa paste or use medium salsa instead of mild.
—Arlene Erlbach, Morton Grove, IL

PREP: 25 min.
COOK: 6 hours
MAKES: 4 servings

- 1 lb. ground lamb
- 1 cup coarsely chopped red onion
- 1 can (15 oz.) cannellini beans, undrained
- 1 jar (16 oz.) mild chunky salsa
- 3 Tbsp. Moroccan seasoning (ras el hanout), divided
- 4½ tsp. finely chopped lemon zest, divided
- 3 Tbsp. orange marmalade
- ¼ cup minced fresh parsley
- ¼ cup crumbled goat cheese
- 2 Tbsp. sliced almonds

Additional chopped red onion and toasted naan flatbread or pita bread, optional

1. In a large nonstick skillet cook lamb and onion over medium-high heat for 6-8 minutes or until meat is no longer pink, breaking into crumbles; drain. Transfer lamb mixture to a 3- or 4-qt. slow cooker. Add beans.
2. In a small bowl, combine the salsa, 1½ Tbsp. Moroccan seasoning and 1 Tbsp. lemon zest. Pour over beans and lamb; stir until well combined. Cook, covered, on low until onions are tender, about 6 hours.
3. In a small bowl, combine marmalade with remaining Moroccan seasoning and lemon zest; stir into slow cooker. Cook, covered, 15 minutes longer. Sprinkle each serving with parsley, cheese and almonds. If desired, serve with additional red onion and naan or pita bread.

1 CUP: 438 cal., 18g fat (8g sat. fat), 84mg chol., 840mg sod., 39g carb. (16g sugars, 7g fiber), 28g pro.

SLOWER COOKER MILK-CAN SUPPER

**SLOW COOKER
CASSOULET WITH
CRUMB CRUST**

SLOW COOKER CASSOULET WITH CRUMB CRUST

Classically inspired, this dish is loaded with chicken thighs, pork and smoked sausage. Tomatoes, beans and wine round out this hearty French stew, and bread crumbs thicken it slightly.
—Marie Rizzio, Interlochen, MI

PREP: 20 min • **COOK:** 7 hours
MAKES: 8 servings

- 1 cup soft bread crumbs
- 2 lbs. boneless skinless chicken thighs
- 1 lb. boneless pork shoulder, trimmed and cut into 1 pieces
- 8 oz. kielbasa, halved lengthwise and cut into ½-in. thick slices
- 2 cans (15 oz. each) cannellini beans, rinsed and drained
- 1 can (14½ oz.) petite diced tomatoes, drained
- 1 cup chopped onion
- 1 cup chicken broth
- ¾ cup white wine
- 1 Tbsp. tomato paste
- ½ tsp. salt
- ½ tsp. pepper
- 2 garlic cloves, crushed
- 2 fresh thyme sprigs
- 1 bay leaf
  Minced fresh parsley, optional

1. Preheat oven to 350°. Place bread crumbs in a 15x10x1-in. baking pan. Bake, uncovered until the crumbs are lightly browned, stirring occasionally, about 8-12 minutes. Set aside.
2. Combine the remaining ingredients in a 5- or 6-qt. slow cooker. Cover and cook on low until meat is tender, 7 hours. Remove and discard thyme sprigs and bay leaf. Stir in ¾ cup bread crumbs. Top individual servings with remaining bread crumbs. If desired, sprinkle with chopped parsley.
1¼ CUPS: 482 cal., 22g fat (7g sat. fat), 129mg chol., 802mg sod., 24g carb. (4g sugars, 6g fiber), 40g pro.

SLOW COOKER HAM & EGGS

SLOW COOKER HAM & EGGS

This dish is appreciated any time of the year, but I most love serving it on holiday mornings. Once started, it requires little attention and is a fun meal for the family.
—Andrea Schaak, Jordan, MN

PREP: 15 min. • **COOK:** 3 hours
MAKES: 6 servings

- 6 large eggs
- 1 cup biscuit/baking mix
- ⅔ cup 2% milk
- ⅓ cup sour cream
- 2 Tbsp. minced fresh parsley
- 2 garlic cloves, minced
- ½ tsp. salt
- ½ tsp. pepper
- 1 cup cubed fully cooked ham
- 1 cup shredded Swiss cheese
- 1 small onion, finely chopped
- ⅓ cup shredded Parmesan cheese

1. In a large bowl, whisk the first eight ingredients until blended; stir in remaining ingredients. Pour into a greased 3- or 4-qt. slow cooker.
2. Cook, covered, on low until eggs are set, 3-4 hours. Cut into wedges.
1 SERVING: 315 cal., 18g fat (9g sat. fat), 256mg chol., 942mg sod., 17g carb. (4g sugars, 1g fiber), 21g pro.

"Easy and good. I made half the recipe and cooked it about 2 hours, and my husband and I enjoyed it. Next time I will use a little less garlic as my personal preference."
—SD20, TASTEOFHOME.COM

CINNAMON BLUEBERRY FRENCH TOAST

I like to do the prep work for this breakfast in the afternoon, let it chill, then put into the slow cooker before I go to bed. It holds wonderfully on the keep warm setting while we sleep. When we wake up, it's ready to go.

—Angela Lively, Conroe, TX

PREP: 15 min. + chilling
COOK: 3 hours
MAKES: 6 servings

- 3 large eggs
- 2 cups 2% milk
- ¼ cup sugar
- 1 tsp. ground cinnamon
- 1 tsp. vanilla extract
- ¼ tsp. salt
- 9 cups cubed French bread (about 9 oz.)
- 1 cup fresh or frozen blueberries, thawed
   Maple syrup

1. Whisk together first six ingredients. Layer half of the bread in a greased 5-qt. slow cooker; top with ½ cup blueberries and half of the milk mixture. Repeat layers. Refrigerate, covered, 4 hours or overnight.
2. Cook, covered, on low until a knife inserted in the center comes out clean, 3-4 hours. Serve warm with syrup.
1 CUP: 265 cal., 6g fat (2g sat. fat), 100mg chol., 430mg sod., 42g carb. (18g sugars, 2g fiber), 11g pro.

"SECRET'S IN THE SAUCE" BBQ RIBS

A sweet, rich sauce makes these ribs so tender that the meat literally falls off the bones. And the aroma is wonderful. Yum!

—Tanya Reid, Winston Salem, NC

PREP: 10 min. • **COOK:** 6 hours
MAKES: 5 servings

- 4½ lbs. pork baby back ribs
- 1½ tsp. pepper
- 2½ cups barbecue sauce
- ¾ cup cherry preserves
- 1 Tbsp. Dijon mustard
- 1 garlic clove, minced

Cut the ribs into serving-size pieces; sprinkle with pepper. Place in a 5- or 6-qt. slow cooker. Combine remaining ingredients; pour over ribs. Cover and cook on low until meat is tender, for 6-8 hours. Serve with sauce.
1 SERVING: 921 cal., 58g fat (21g sat. fat), 220mg chol., 1402mg sod., 50g carb. (45g sugars, 2g fiber), 48g pro.

CINNAMON BLUEBERRY FRENCH TOAST

SLOW COOKER
STUFFED SHELLS

SLOW COOKER STUFFED SHELLS

There's no need to precook the shells in this simple pasta dish. It's almost like magic to lift the lid and find such deliciousness ready to serve. Add garlic bread, and you're golden!
—Sherry Day, Pinckney, MI

PREP: 30 min. • **COOK:** 4 hours
MAKES: 10 servings

1 carton (15 oz.) part-skim ricotta cheese
1 pkg. (10 oz.) frozen chopped spinach, thawed and squeezed dry
2½ cups shredded Italian cheese blend
½ cup diced red onion
½ tsp. garlic powder
2 tsp. dried basil
½ tsp. dried oregano
½ tsp. dried thyme
2 jars (24 oz. each) roasted garlic Parmesan pasta sauce
2 cups water
1 pkg. (12 oz.) jumbo pasta shells
   Additional shredded Italian cheese blend and sliced fresh basil, optional

1. Mix the first eight ingredients (mixture will be stiff). In a greased 6-qt. slow cooker, mix one jar pasta sauce with water. Fill the shells with ricotta mixture; layer in slow cooker. Top with remaining jar of pasta sauce.

2. Cook, covered, on low until pasta is tender, 4-5 hours. If desired, serve with additional cheese and fresh basil.

4 STUFFED SHELLS: 303 cal., 10g fat (6g sat. fat), 34mg chol., 377mg sod., 34g carb. (4g sugars, 3g fiber), 17g pro.
DIABETIC EXCHANGES: 2 starch, 2 medium-fat meat.

DID YOU KNOW?
Relative to other cheeses, ricotta is especially high in calcium. Just ¼ cup of ricotta provides almost 20% of the recommended daily value.

SLOW COOKER CLAM SAUCE

SLOW COOKER CLAM SAUCE

Serve this delectable clam sauce as a hot dip with toasted baguette for holiday get-togethers. The sauce is bright and fresh with pasta, too.
—Frances Pietsch, Flower Mound, TX

PREP: 10 min • **COOK:** 3 hours
MAKES: 4 cups

- 4 Tbsp. butter
- 2 Tbsp. olive oil
- ½ cup finely chopped onion
- 8 oz. fresh mushrooms, chopped
- 2 garlic cloves, minced
- 2 cans (10 oz. each) whole baby clams
- ¾ tsp. dried oregano
- ½ tsp. garlic salt
- ¼ tsp. white pepper
- ¼ tsp. black pepper
- ¼ tsp. Italian seasoning
- 1 bay leaf
- ¼ cup sherry
- 2 tsp. lemon juice
- ½ cup water
- 2 Tbsp. chopped fresh parsley
  Hot cooked pasta
  Grated Parmesan cheese, lemon juice and minced fresh parsley, optional

1. Heat butter and oil in a skillet over medium-high heat. Add onion; cook and stir 5 minutes. Add mushrooms and garlic; cook until vegetables are tender, 5 minutes more.
2. Drain the clams, reserving liquid; coarsely chop. Add clams, reserved clam juice, mushroom mixture and the next nine ingredients in a 5- qt. slow cooker. Cook, covered, on low for 3 hours. Remove and discard bay leaf; stir in parsley. Serve with hot pasta. If desired, serve with cheese, lemon juice or parsley.
½ CUP: 138 cal., 10g fat (4g sat. fat), 40mg chol., 580mg sod., 5g carb. (1g sugars, 0 fiber), 7g pro.

LOW & SLOW HUEVOS RANCHEROS

LOW & SLOW HUEVOS RANCHEROS

We love Mexican food, especially for breakfast, and huevos rancheros are a particular favorite. This is my slow cooker version. Try it rolled into warm flour tortillas for a breakfast crowd.
—Joan Hallford, North Richland Hills, TX

PREP: 25 min.
COOK: 3½ hours + standing
MAKES: 10 servings

- ½ lb. fresh chorizo
- ½ cup chopped onion
- ½ cup chopped sweet red pepper
- 2 jalapeno pepper, seeded and chopped
- 1 garlic clove, minced
- 3 cups frozen cubed hash brown potatoes, thawed
- 8 large eggs, beaten
- 2 cups shredded Colby-Monterey Jack cheese
- 1 cup salsa
- 4 bacon strips, cooked and crumbled
- 20 flour tortillas (6 in.)
  Fresh chopped cilantro and additional salsa, optional

1. In a large skillet, cook the chorizo, onion, pepper, jalapeno and garlic, over medium-high heat 6-8 minutes or until cooked through, breaking into crumbles; drain. Transfer mixture to a 3- or 4-qt. slow cooker. Stir in the next five ingredients.
2. Cook, covered, until potatoes are tender and eggs are set, 3½-4 hours. Turn off slow cooker; remove insert. Let stand 10 minutes before serving. Serve with tortillas. If desired, top with cilantro and additional salsa.
2 TACOS: 488 cal., 25g fat (11g sat. fat), 192mg chol., 1028mg sod., 41g carb. (3g sugars, 4g fiber), 21g pro.

TEST KITCHEN TIP
This is a versatile recipe that can be served with the toppings of your choice. Try it with avocado, sour cream, Mexican crema or lime wedges. For party-sized brunch appetizers, serve the mixture in smaller tortillas —street tacos—or in tortilla chip scoops.

Soups, Sides & Sandwiches

RAVE REVIEW
CHICKEN SOUP

RAVE REVIEW CHICKEN SOUP

Cozy and warm on a cold winter's day, this hearty chicken soup gets rave reviews from my family and friends. It goes nicely with fresh-baked biscuits.
—Caroline Simpson, Fredericton, NB

PREP: 30 min. • **COOK:** 4½ hours
MAKES: 8 servings (3 qt.)

- ¼ cup butter, divided
- 1½ lbs. boneless skinless chicken breasts, cut into 1-in. chunks
- 1 large onion, chopped
- 2 large carrots, peeled and chopped
- 3 celery ribs, chopped
- 1 garlic clove, minced
- 1 can (14½ oz.) diced tomatoes, undrained
- 1 green onion, thinly sliced
- 1 tsp. chicken bouillon granules
- 1 tsp. curry powder
- 1 tsp. dried oregano
- ½ tsp. salt
- ½ tsp. pepper
- 1 carton (32 oz.) chicken broth
- ½ cup heavy whipping cream
- ¼ cup cornstarch
  Minced fresh parsley, optional

1. In a large skillet, heat 2 Tbsp. butter over medium heat. Brown chicken; transfer to a 5-qt. slow cooker. Add remaining butter to skillet; saute onion, carrots and celery until slightly softened. Add garlic; cook 1 minute longer. Transfer onion mixture to slow cooker; add next eight ingredients. Cook, covered, on low 4 hours or until carrots are tender.
2. In a small bowl, mix the cream and cornstarch until smooth; gradually stir into soup. Cook, covered, on high for 15-20 minutes or until the soup is thickened. If desired, sprinkle with minced parsley.
1½ CUPS: 247 cal., 14g fat (8g sat. fat), 82mg chol., 941mg sod., 12g carb. (5g sugars, 2g fiber), 19g pro.

SAUSAGE &
KRAUT BUNS

CHIPOTLE SHREDDED SWEET POTATOES WITH BACON

I crave a little bit of heat with my sweet spuds, so I mix in chipotle peppers. The smoky flavor blends perfectly with this creamy, cheesy side dish.
—Kathi Jones-DelMonte, Rochester, NY

PREP: 30 min. • **COOK:** 4 hours
MAKES: 10 servings

- 2 Tbsp. olive oil
- 1 large sweet onion, finely chopped
- 2 shallots, finely chopped
- ¼ cup minced fresh parsley
- 2 tsp. ground chipotle pepper
- 1 tsp. coarsely ground pepper
- ½ tsp. kosher salt
- 3 lbs. sweet potatoes (about 4 large), peeled and shredded
- 1 pkg. (8 oz.) cream cheese, softened
- 2 cups shredded Manchego or Monterey Jack cheese
- 2 cups shredded Muenster cheese
- 1 pkg. (16 oz.) applewood smoked bacon, cooked and chopped
- ½ tsp. paprika

TOPPING

- 1 cup sour cream
- 2 Tbsp. maple syrup
- ¼ tsp. ground chipotle pepper

1. In a large skillet, heat the oil over medium heat. Add the onion and shallots; cook and stir 4-6 minutes or until softened.
2. Transfer onion mixture to a large bowl; stir in parsley and seasonings. Add sweet potatoes and cheeses, mixing well. Fold in chopped bacon.
3. Transfer mixture to a greased 5- or 6-qt. slow cooker. Sprinkle with paprika. Cook, covered, on low for 4-5 hours or until potatoes are tender.
4. Mix the topping ingredients; serve with sweet potatoes.
¾ CUP WITH ABOUT 4½ TSP. TOPPING: 491 cal., 28g fat (14g sat. fat), 64mg chol., 708mg sod., 42g carb. (19g sugars, 5g fiber), 20g pro.

SAUSAGE & KRAUT BUNS

This recipe has become a regular at our church potlucks. Let's just say I'm in trouble if I show up at a get-together and they don't appear! For a homey dinner spin, try the sausages and kraut over mashed potatoes.
—Patsy Unruh, Perryton, TX

PREP: 20 min. • **COOK:** 4 hours
MAKES: 12 servings

- 2 cans (14½ oz. each) no-salt-added diced tomatoes, drained
- 2 cans (14 oz. each) sauerkraut, rinsed and drained
- ½ lb. sliced fresh mushrooms
- 1 large sweet pepper, thinly sliced
- 1 large onion, halved and thinly sliced
- 2 Tbsp. brown sugar
- ½ tsp. pepper
- 2 pkg. (14 oz. each) smoked sausage, sliced
- 12 pretzel sausage buns, warmed and split partway

1. In a 5- or 6-qt. slow cooker, combine the first seven ingredients. In a large skillet, saute sausage over medium-high heat until lightly browned. Stir into tomato mixture.
2. Cook mixture, covered, on low until vegetables are tender, 4-5 hours. Serve in buns.
1 SANDWICH: 468 cal., 23g fat (8g sat. fat), 44mg chol., 1491mg sod., 51g carb. (12g sugars, 4g fiber), 17g pro.

SMOKY PEANUT BUTTER CHILI

I eliminated beans from my standard chili recipe and added peanut butter and peanuts just for fun. Wow, it was amazing! Tried it on my family, who loved it too.
—Nancy Heishman, Las Vegas, NV

PREP: 25 min. • **COOK:** 4 hours
MAKES: 12 servings (3 qt.)

- 1 Tbsp. peanut oil or canola oil
- 2½ lbs. lean ground beef (90% lean)
- 1 large green pepper, chopped
- 1 large red onion, chopped
- 1 large carrot, peeled and chopped
- 2 garlic cloves, minced
- 2 cans (15 oz. each) tomato sauce
- 2 cans (14½ oz. each) diced tomatoes with basil, oregano and garlic, undrained
- 2 cans (4 oz. each) chopped green chilies
- ½ cup creamy peanut butter
- 1 to 2 Tbsp. ground ancho chili pepper
- 1 tsp. kosher salt
- 1 tsp. smoked paprika
  Shredded smoked cheddar cheese and chopped peanuts, optional

1. In a large skillet, heat the oil over medium-high heat; add beef and cook in batches 7-10 minutes, or until no longer pink, breaking into crumbles. Remove with a slotted spoon; drain. Add green pepper, onion and carrot; cook and stir until slightly browned, about 2 minutes. Add garlic; cook 1 minute longer. Transfer the meat, vegetables and drippings to a 5- or 6-qt. slow cooker.
2. Stir in the next seven ingredients until combined. Cook, covered, on low until the vegetables are tender, about 4 hours. If desired, sprinkle chili with shredded cheese and peanuts.
1 CUP: 279 cal., 15g fat (4g sat. fat), 59mg chol., 878mg sod., 13g carb. (6g sugars, 4g fiber), 23g pro.

SLOW-COOKED GREEN BEANS

I spent hours in search of side dishes for a cooking demo to present to women from my church. These easy green beans became the show's star attraction. They add a lovely splash of color to a traditional holiday meal.
—Alice White, Willow Spring, NC

PREP: 10 min. • **COOK:** 2 hours
MAKES: 12 servings (⅔ cup each)

- 16 cups frozen french-style green beans (about 48 oz.), thawed
- ½ cup butter, melted
- ½ cup packed brown sugar
- 1½ tsp. garlic salt
- ¾ tsp. reduced-sodium soy sauce

Place beans in a 5-qt. slow cooker. Mix the remaining ingredients; pour over beans and toss to coat. Cook, covered, on low until heated through, about 2-3 hours. Serve with a slotted spoon.
⅔ CUP: 143 cal., 8g fat (5g sat. fat), 20mg chol., 320mg sod., 17g carb. (12g sugars, 3g fiber), 1g pro.

SMOKY PEANUT BUTTER CHILI

SHREDDED BUFFALO CHICKEN SANDWICHES

SHREDDED BUFFALO CHICKEN SANDWICHES

My family loves Buffalo chicken wings, but the frying makes them unhealthy. This takes some of the fat out but lets us enjoy that Buffalo chicken taste.
—Terri McKenzie, Wilmington, OH

PREP: 10 min. • **COOK:** 3 hours
MAKES: 6 servings

- 4 boneless skinless chicken breast halves (6 oz. each)
- 3 celery ribs, chopped
- 2 cups Buffalo wing sauce
- ½ cup chicken stock
- 2 Tbsp. butter
- 4 tsp. ranch salad dressing mix
- 6 hoagie buns, toasted
  Blue cheese or ranch salad dressing and celery ribs, optional

In a 3- or 4-qt. slow cooker, combine first six ingredients. Cook, covered, on low until chicken is tender, 3-4 hours. Remove from slow cooker. Cool the mixture slightly; shred meat with two forks and return to slow cooker. Using tongs, serve on hoagie buns. If desired, top with salad dressing and serve with celery ribs.

1 SANDWICH: 398 cal., 12g fat (4g sat. fat), 73mg chol., 2212mg sod., 42g carb. (6g sugars, 2g fiber), 32g pro.

TEST KITCHEN TIP
If you prefer dark meat, substitute chicken thighs for breasts. Top sandwiches with coleslaw for added crunch.

LAMB PITAS WITH YOGURT SAUCE

The spiced lamb in these stuffed pita pockets goes perfectly with the cool cucumber and yogurt. It's like having your own Greek gyro stand right there in the kitchen!

—Angela Leinenbach, Mechanicsville, VA

PREP: 35 min. • **COOK:** 6 hours
MAKES: 8 servings

- 2 Tbsp. olive oil
- 2 lbs. lamb stew meat (¾-in. pieces)
- 1 large onion, chopped
- 1 garlic clove, minced
- ⅓ cup tomato paste
- ½ cup dry red wine
- 1¼ tsp. salt, divided
- 1 tsp. dried oregano
- ½ tsp. dried basil
- 1 medium cucumber
- 1 cup (8 oz.) plain yogurt
- 16 pita pocket halves, warmed
- 4 plum tomatoes, sliced

1. In a large skillet, heat oil over medium-high heat; brown lamb in batches. Transfer lamb to a 3- or 4-qt. slow cooker, reserving drippings in the skillet.

2. In the drippings, saute the onion over medium heat until tender, for 4-6 minutes. Add garlic and tomato paste; cook and stir 2 minutes. Stir in wine, 1 tsp. salt, oregano and basil. Add to lamb. Cook, covered, on low until lamb is tender, 6-8 hours.

3. To serve, dice enough cucumber to measure 1 cup; thinly slice remaining cucumber. Combine diced cucumber with yogurt and remaining salt. Fill pitas with lamb mixture, tomatoes, sliced cucumbers and yogurt mixture.

FREEZE OPTION: Freeze cooled lamb mixture in freezer containers. To use, partially thaw in refrigerator overnight. Heat through in a saucepan, stirring occasionally and adding a little broth or water if necessary.

2 FILLED PITA HALVES: 383 cal., 11g fat (3g sat. fat), 78mg chol., 766mg sod., 39g carb. (5g sugars, 3g fiber), 31g pro.
DIABETIC EXCHANGES: 3 lean meat, 2½ starch, 1 fat.

BUTTERNUT SQUASH & BARLEY SOUP

BUTTERNUT SQUASH & BARLEY SOUP

I love to use my garden produce in this veggie-packed soup. Serve it with hot oatmeal dinner rolls and you've got a delicious, healthy dinner.

—Julie Sloan, Osceola, IN

PREP: 25 min. • **COOK:** 5 ¼ hours
MAKES: 12 servings (3 qt.)

- 1 small butternut squash (2½ to 3 lbs.), peeled and cut into 1-in. cubes (about 6 cups)
- 4 cups water
- 1 carton (32 oz.) reduced-sodium chicken broth
- ¾ cup medium pearl barley
- 2 medium carrots, chopped
- 2 celery ribs, chopped
- 1 small onion, chopped
- 2 Tbsp. minced fresh parsley or 2 tsp. dried parsley flakes
- 2 garlic cloves, minced
- 1 tsp. rubbed sage
- 1¼ tsp. salt
- ½ tsp. curry powder
- ¼ tsp. pepper
- 1 cup cubed cooked turkey

1. Place all ingredients, except turkey, in a 5- or 6-qt. slow cooker. Cook, covered, on low until the squash and barley are tender, 5-7 hours.

2. Stir in turkey; cook, covered until heated through, about 15 minutes.

FREEZE OPTION: Transfer to three 1-qt. freezer containers; cool. Cover; freeze for up to 3 months. To use frozen soup, thaw in the refrigerator. Place in a saucepan and heat through.

1 CUP: 120 cal., 1g fat (0 sat. fat), 12mg chol., 493mg sod., 23g carb. (4g sugars, 6g fiber), 7g pro.
DIABETIC EXCHANGES: 1½ starch.

BUFFALO WING POTATOES

I was getting tired of mashed and baked potatoes, so I decided to create something new. This potluck-ready recipe is an easy and delicious twist on the usual potato dish.
—Summer Feaker, Ankeny, IA

PREP: 15 min. • **COOK:** 6 ¼ hours
MAKES: 12 servings

- 4 lbs. large Yukon Gold potatoes, cut into 1-in. cubes
- 1 medium sweet yellow pepper, chopped
- 1 small red onion, chopped
- ½ cup Buffalo wing sauce
- 1 cup shredded cheddar cheese

Optional toppings: crumbled cooked bacon, sliced green onions and sour cream, optional

1. Place potatoes, yellow pepper and red onion in a 6-qt. slow cooker. Add Buffalo wing sauce; stir to coat. Cook, covered, on low for 6 hours or until potatoes are tender, stirring halfway through. Stir potato mixture; sprinkle with cheese. Cover and cook until the cheese is melted, about 15 minutes.
2. Transfer to a serving bowl. If desired, top potatoes with bacon, green onions and sour cream.
¾ CUP: 182 cal., 4g fat (2g sat. fat), 9mg chol., 382mg sod., 32g carb. (3g sugars, 3g fiber), 6g pro. **DIABETIC EXCHANGES:** 2 starch, ½ fat.

BUFFALO WING POTATOES

TANGY BARBECUE SANDWICHES

Since I prepare the beef for these yummy sandwiches in the slow cooker, it's easy to fix a meal for a hungry bunch. The savory, slightly sweet homemade sauce assures that I never come home with leftovers.
—Debbi Smith, Crossett, AR

PREP: 10 min. • **COOK:** 8 hours
MAKES: 18 servings

- 3 cups chopped celery
- 1 cup chopped onion
- 1 cup ketchup
- 1 cup barbecue sauce
- 1 cup water
- 2 Tbsp. white vinegar
- 2 Tbsp. Worcestershire sauce
- 2 Tbsp. brown sugar
- 1 tsp. chili powder
- 1 tsp. salt
- ½ tsp. pepper
- ½ tsp. garlic powder
- 1 boneless beef chuck roast (3 to 4 lbs.), trimmed and cut in half
- 18 hamburger buns, split

1. In a 5-qt. slow cooker, combine the first 12 ingredients. Add roast. Cover and cook on high for 1 hour. Reduce heat to low and cook 6-8 hours longer or until meat is tender.
2. Remove roast; cool. Shred meat and return to sauce; heat through. Using a slotted spoon, fill each bun with about ½ cup of meat mixture.
1 SERVING: 262 cal., 9g fat (3g sat. fat), 49mg chol., 659mg sod., 26g carb. (8g sugars, 2g fiber), 18g pro.

PINEAPPLE MANGO
PULLED PORK

PINEAPPLE MANGO PULLED PORK

I love mangoes and pineapple. They go so well with pork. Serve these little sandwiches with a spring salad.

—Thomas Faglon, Somerset, NJ

PREP: 20 min. • **COOK:** 8 hours
MAKES: 12 servings

1 tsp. kosher salt
1 tsp. coarsely ground pepper
1 boneless pork shoulder butt roast (about 3 lbs.)
2 cans (11.30 oz. each) mango nectar
1 can (8 oz.) pineapple tidbits, drained
¼ cup mango chutney
2 Tbsp. lemon juice
2 tsp. grated lemon zest
6 green onions, thinly sliced
12 Hawaiian sweet hamburger buns
   Chopped jalapeno peppers, optional

1. Rub salt and pepper over the roast. Transfer to a 5- or 6-qt. slow cooker. In a small bowl, mix the mango nectar, pineapple, chutney, lemon juice and zest. Add to slow cooker. Cook roast, covered, on low until meat is tender, 6-8 hours. Cool slightly.
2. Remove roast from slow cooker. When cool enough to handle, shred meat with two forks. Strain cooking juices, discarding fruit; skim fat. Return the cooking juices and meat to slow cooker. Stir in green onion. Serve on buns. If desired, top with jalapenos.

½ CUP MEAT MIXTURE ON 1 BUN: 249 cal., 11g fat (4g sat. fat), 67mg chol., 291mg sod., 16g carb. (12g sugars, 1g fiber), 19g pro.

TEST KITCHEN TIP
Pair leftover meat with crispy bread, pickles and mustard for an easy Cuban sandwich.

SLOW COOKER QUINOA CHILI

EAT SMART
SLOW COOKER QUINOA CHILI

This is the recipe that finally turned my husband into a quinoa lover. Plus, I made it the day my husband got good news about a new job, and we'll always remember how excited we were as we ate this tasty chili.

—Claire Gallam, Alexandria, VA

PREP: 25 min. • **COOK:** 4 hours
MAKES: 10 servings (about 3½ qt.)

1 lb. lean ground beef (90% lean)
1 medium onion, chopped
2 garlic cloves, minced
1 can (28 oz.) diced tomatoes with mild green chilies, undrained
1 can (14 oz.) fire-roasted diced tomatoes, undrained
1 can (15 oz.) chickpeas or garbanzo beans, rinsed and drained
1 can (15 oz.) black beans, rinsed and drained
2 cups reduced-sodium beef broth
1 cup quinoa, rinsed
2 tsp. onion soup mix
1 to 2 tsp. crushed red pepper flakes
1 tsp. garlic powder
¼ to ½ tsp. cayenne pepper
¼ tsp. salt
   Shredded cheddar cheese, chopped avocado, chopped red onion, sliced jalapeno, sour cream and cilantro, optional

1. In a large skillet, cook beef, onion and garlic over medium-high heat for 6-8 minutes or until no longer pink, breaking into crumbles; drain.
2. Transfer mixture to a 5- or 6-qt. slow cooker. Add next 11 ingredients; stir to combine. Cook, covered, on low for 4-5 hours or until quinoa is tender.
3. Serve chili with optional toppings as desired.

1½ CUPS: 318 cal., 7g fat (2g sat. fat), 37mg chol., 805mg sod., 41g carb. (7g sugars, 8g fiber), 21g pro. **DIABETIC EXCHANGES:** 2½ starch, 2 lean meat.

GREEN CHILI CREAMED CORN

When hosting big meals, I sometimes ran out of burners. Then I realized my slow cooker could help by simmering my signature corn and green chilies with pickled jalapenos.

—Pat Dazis, Charlotte, NC

PREP: 10 min. • **COOK:** 2½ hours
MAKES: 8 servings

- 6   cups fresh or frozen corn (about 30 oz.), thawed
- 1   pkg. (8 oz.) cream cheese, cubed
- 1   jar (4 oz.) diced pimientos, drained
- 1   can (4 oz.) chopped green chilies
- ½   cup vegetable broth
- ¼   cup butter, cubed
- ¼   cup pickled jalapeno slices, coarsely chopped
- 1   Tbsp. sugar
- ⅛   tsp. crushed red pepper flakes

In a 3- or 4-qt. slow cooker, combine all ingredients. Cook, covered, on low for 2½ to 3 hours or until heated through. Stir just before serving.
¾ CUP: 258 cal., 17g fat (10g sat. fat), 44mg chol., 296mg sod., 25g carb. (10g sugars, 3g fiber), 6g pro.

ITALIAN SAUSAGE SLOPPY JOES

My grandma absolutely loves Italian food, so I decided to make a twist on classic sloppy joe sandwiches just for her. The mozzarella and tomato sauce are classic, and pickled hot peppers make it fun.

—Kristen Heigl, Staten Island, NY

PREP: 20 min. • **COOK:** 4 hours
MAKES: 8 servings

- 1   lb. bulk Italian sausage
- 1   medium sweet red pepper, chopped
- 1   medium onion, chopped
- 1½ lbs. lean ground beef (90% lean)
- 2   cans (8 oz. each) no-salt-added tomato sauce
- 1   can (6 oz.) tomato paste
- 1   tsp. garlic powder
- 1   tsp. liquid smoke, optional
- 16 slices smoked mozzarella cheese (about ¾ lb.)
- 8   hoagie buns, split and toasted Pickled hot cherry peppers, optional

1. In a large skillet, cook and crumble sausage with red pepper and onion over medium-high heat until no longer pink, 5-7 minutes. Transfer to a 3- or 4-qt. slow cooker.
2. In the same pan, cook and crumble beef over medium-high heat until no longer pink, 5-7 minutes. Using a slotted spoon, add beef to the slow cooker. Stir in tomato sauce, tomato paste, garlic powder and, if desired, liquid smoke. Cook, covered, on low until flavors are blended, 4-5 hours.
3. To serve, place the cheese on bun bottoms; top with meat mixture and, if desired, peppers. Close sandwiches.
FREEZE OPTION: Freeze cooled meat mixture in freezer containers. To use, partially thaw in refrigerator overnight. Heat through in a saucepan, stirring occasionally and adding a little water if necessary.
1 SANDWICH: 661 cal., 35g fat (14g sat. fat), 121mg chol., 1231mg sod., 46g carb. (9g sugars, 3g fiber), 42g pro.

ITALIAN SAUSAGE SLOPPY JOES

PESTO
BEAN SOUP

SLOW-COOKED CHEESY CAULIFLOWER

When my main course took up the entire oven, I needed a vegetable that I could make in the slow cooker. After searching for a recipe, I ended up writing my own, and the dish turned out better than I could have hoped!
—Heather Corson, Casper, WY

PREP: 15 min. • **COOK:** 5 hours
MAKES: 16 servings (¾ cup each)

- 2 medium heads cauliflower, cut into florets (about 18 cups)
- 1 can (10¾ oz.) condensed cream of chicken soup, undiluted
- 2 cups shredded cheddar cheese
- 1 cup (8 oz.) sour cream
- ½ tsp. salt
- ½ tsp. pepper
- ¼ cup butter, cubed
- 1 cup dry bread crumbs

1. In a 6-qt. slow cooker, combine cauliflower, soup and cheese. Cook, covered, on low until cauliflower is tender, 5-6 hours. Stir in sour cream, salt and pepper.
2. In a small skillet, melt butter over medium heat. Add bread crumbs; cook and stir until golden brown, for about 2-3 minutes. Sprinkle over cauliflower.
¾ CUP: 178 cal., 12g fat (7g sat. fat), 27mg chol., 411mg sod., 11g carb. (3g sugars, 2g fiber), 6g pro.

EAT SMART
PESTO BEAN SOUP

This is one of my favorite vegetarian recipes, especially on those cold winter evenings. I make large batches and freeze it. Homemade pesto is tasty , but you can use store-bought to make the recipe really simple. Serve the soup with garlic toast and a green salad.
—Liz Bellville, Jacksonville, NC

PREP: 10 min. • **COOK:** 4 hours
MAKES: 8 servings

- 1 carton (32 oz.) reduced-sodium vegetable broth
- 1 large white onion, chopped
- 4 garlic cloves, minced
- 2½ cups sliced baby portobello mushrooms
- 3 cans (15 to 15½ oz. each) white kidney or cannellini beans, rinsed and drained
- ¾ cup prepared pesto, divided
- ¼ cup grated Parmigiano-Reggiano cheese
   Grated Parmigiano-Reggiano cheese and prepared pesto, optional

In a 4-qt. slow cooker, combine the first five ingredients. Stir in ½ cup pesto. Cook, covered, on low until vegetables are tender, 4-6 hours. Before serving, stir in reserved pesto and cheese. If desired, serve with additional cheese and pesto.
1¼ CUPS: 244 cal., 9g fat (2g sat. fat), 2mg chol., 586mg sod., 30g carb. (3g sugars, 8g fiber), 9g pro. **DIABETIC EXCHANGES:** 2 starch, 1½ fat, 1 lean meat.

TEST KITCHEN TIP
For a thicker, more velvety texture, mash half of the beans before adding them to the soup mixture.

TANDOORI
CHICKEN PANINI

TANDOORI CHICKEN PANINI

Tandoori-style spices in this chicken give it a bold flavor that's so hard to resist. It tastes incredible when tucked between pieces of naan and grilled for an Indian-inspired panini.

—Yasmin Arif, Manassas, VA

PREP: 25 min. • **COOK:** 3 hours
MAKES: 6 servings

- 1½ lbs. boneless skinless chicken breasts
- ¼ cup reduced-sodium chicken broth
- 2 garlic cloves, minced
- 2 tsp. minced fresh gingerroot
- 1 tsp. paprika
- ¼ tsp. salt
- ¼ to ½ tsp. cayenne pepper
- ¼ tsp. ground turmeric
- 6 green onions, chopped
- 6 Tbsp. chutney
- 6 naan flatbreads

1. Place first eight ingredients in a 3-qt. slow cooker. Cook, covered, on low until chicken is tender, 3-4 hours.
2. Shred chicken with two forks. Stir in green onions.
3. Spread chutney over one side of each naan. Top chutney side of three naan with chicken mixture; top with remaining naan, chutney side down.
4. Cook sandwiches on a panini maker or indoor grill until golden brown, 6-8 minutes. To serve, cut each sandwich in half.

½ **PANINI:** 351 cal., 6g fat (2g sat. fat), 68mg chol., 830mg sod., 44g carb. (12g sugars, 2g fiber), 27g pro. **DIABETIC EXCHANGES:** 3 starch, 3 lean meat.

EAT SMART
SLOW COOKER SPICY SWEET POTATO CHILI

While this recipe contains no meat, it still has plenty of protein—plus vitamins and minerals. I love sweet potatoes, and they're even better mixed with black beans. The chili is great with crackers or even spooned into tortilla shells (yes, I make sweet potato tacos out of this).

—Jennifer Butz, Atlanta, GA

PREP: 20 min. • **COOK:** 4 hours
MAKES: 4 servings

- 2 large sweet potatoes, peeled and cubed
- 1 can (14½ oz.) black beans, rinsed and drained
- 1 can (14½ oz.) diced tomatoes with green peppers and onions, undrained
- 1 cup water
- 1 Tbsp. chili powder
- 1 tsp. ground ginger
- 1 tsp. ground cumin
- ½ tsp. salt
- ½ tsp. pepper
- ¼ cup minced fresh cilantro

In a 3- or 4-qt. slow cooker, combine first nine ingredients. Cook, covered, on low until sweet potatoes are tender, 4-5 hours. Just before serving, stir in cilantro.

1½ CUPS: 300 cal., 1g fat (0 sat. fat), 0 chol., 811mg sod., 64g carb. (21g sugars, 12g fiber), 9g pro.

PINEAPPLE-DIJON HAM SANDWICHES

My kids like ham; the challenge is finding new ways to prepare it. When I slow-cook it with pineapple and Dijon, the juices make an amazing dipping sauce.

—Camille Beckstrand, Layton, UT

PREP: 20 min. • **COOK:** 3 hours
MAKES: 10 servings

- 2 lbs. fully cooked ham, cut into ½-in. cubes
- 1 can (20 oz.) crushed pineapple, undrained
- 1 medium green pepper, finely chopped
- ¾ cup packed brown sugar
- ¼ cup finely chopped onion
- ¼ cup Dijon mustard
- 1 Tbsp. dried minced onion
- 10 hamburger buns, split
- 10 slices Swiss cheese
  Additional Dijon mustard, optional

1. In a greased 4-qt. slow cooker, combine the first seven ingredients. Cook, covered, on low 3-4 hours or until heated through.
2. Preheat broiler. Place bun bottoms and tops on baking sheets, cut side up. Using a slotted spoon, place ham mixture on bottoms; top with cheese. Broil 3-4 in. from heat for 1-2 minutes or until cheese is melted and tops are toasted. Replace tops. If desired, serve with additional mustard.

1 SANDWICH: 396 cal., 8g fat (3g sat. fat), 67mg chol., 1283mg sod., 52g carb. (30g sugars, 2g fiber), 28g pro.

SLOW COOKER SPICY SWEET POTATO CHILI

SLOW COOKER
PARSNIP & APPLE SOUP

SWEET & SPICY SLOPPY JOES

These sandwiches have been the go-to meal for my son's basketball team. Turkey is a wonderful change from ground beef and really absorbs all the flavors. I have also used this for a Friday the 13th celebration at work, calling it 13-Ingredient Sloppy Joes (count salt and pepper separately to get to 13).

—Karen Hildebrand, Labelle, FL

PREP: 30 min. • **COOK:** 4 hours
MAKES: 12 servings

- 2 tsp. canola oil
- 3 lbs. ground turkey
- 1 large onion, chopped
- ½ medium green pepper, chopped
- 3 garlic cloves, minced
- 2 Tbsp. Worcestershire sauce
- 1 tsp. crushed red pepper flakes
- 3 cups ketchup
- ⅔ cup water
- ⅓ cup packed brown sugar
- 3 Tbsp. spicy brown mustard
- ½ tsp. salt
- ¼ tsp. pepper
- 12 hamburger buns, split
  Coleslaw, dill pickle slices, optional

1. Heat oil in a large non-stick skillet over medium-high heat. Cook the turkey in batches until no longer pink, breaking into crumbles, 8-10 minutes per batch. Transfer meat to a 5- or 6-qt. slow cooker. In the same skillet, cook onion and green pepper until tender, 2-3 minutes. Add garlic, Worcestershire and red pepper flakes; cook 1 minute longer. Transfer to slow cooker.
2. In a bowl, combine ketchup, water, brown sugar, mustard, salt and pepper; pour over meat. Cover and cook on low until flavors are blended, 4-5 hours. Serve on buns.

1 SANDWICH: 390 cal., 11g fat (3g sat. fat), 75mg chol., 1206mg sod., 46g carb. (26g sugars, 1g fiber), 27g pro.

SLOW COOKER PARSNIP & APPLE SOUP

Here's a light, lovely soup ideal for a first course at your next special dinner. You'll taste the harmony of fall flavors.
—Shelly L. Bevington, Hermiston, OR

PREP: 15 minutes • **COOK:** 3 hours
MAKES: 8 servings (2 qt.)

- 2 medium tart apples, chopped
- 2 cups chopped parsnips
- 1 cup thinly sliced fresh carrots
- ½ cup chopped onion
- 2 cans (14½ oz. each) vegetable broth
- 2 cups water
- 2 tsp. cider vinegar
- 1½ tsp. minced fresh rosemary, plus more for topping
- ½ tsp. salt
- ¼ tsp. pepper
  Fresh cracked pepper, optional

Combine all ingredients in a 4- or 5-qt. slow cooker. Cook, covered, until the parsnips are tender, 3 hours. If desired, top with additional minced rosemary and cracked pepper.

1 CUP: 61 cal., 0 fat (0 sat. fat), 0 chol., 454mg sod., 15g carb. (7g sugars, 3g fiber), 1g pro. **DIABETIC EXCHANGES:** 1 starch.

**SWEET & SPICY
SLOPPY JOES**

MUSHROOMS MARSALA WITH BARLEY

This satisfying vegetarian recipe is a tasty mashup of chicken Marsala and mushroom barley soup. It's a delicious side dish, with or without the barley.
—Arlene Erlbach, Morton Grove, IL

PREP: 20 min. • **COOK:** 4 hours
MAKES: 6 servings

- 1½ lbs. baby portobello mushrooms, cut into ¾-in. chunks
- 1 cup thinly sliced shallots
- 3 Tbsp. olive oil
- ½ tsp. minced fresh thyme
- ¾ cup Marsala wine, divided
- 3 Tbsp. reduced-fat sour cream
- 2 Tbsp. all-purpose flour
- 1½ tsp. grated lemon zest
- ¼ tsp. salt
- ¼ cup crumbled goat cheese
- ¼ cup minced fresh parsley
- 2½ cups cooked barley

1. In a 4- or 5-qt. slow cooker, combine mushrooms, shallots, olive oil and thyme. Add ¼ cup Marsala wine. Cook, covered, on low until vegetables are tender, 4 hours.
2. Stir in sour cream, flour, lemon zest, salt and remaining Marsala. Cook, covered, on low 15 minutes longer. Sprinkle with goat cheese and parsley. Serve with hot cooked barley.

¾ CUP MUSHROOMS WITH ABOUT ⅓ CUP BARLEY: 235 cal., 9g fat (2g sat. fat), 7mg chol., 139mg sod., 31g carb. (6g sugars, 5g fiber), 7g pro. **DIABETIC EXCHANGES:** 2 starch, 2 fat, 1 vegetable.

MOM'S ITALIAN BEEF SANDWICHES

MOM'S ITALIAN BEEF SANDWICHES

My mom made the best Italian beef. I've added to the recipe over the years, but it's still hers. She made sandwiches like these for all our family reunions, and we couldn't get enough.
—Mary McVey, Colfax, NC

PREP: 20 min. • **COOK:** 8 hours
MAKES: 16 servings

- 1 boneless beef rump roast or bottom round roast (2 lbs.), halved
- 1 boneless beef chuck roast (2 lbs.), halved
- 1 beef sirloin tip roast (1 lb.)
- 2 Tbsp. canola oil
- 2 cups water
- 1 medium onion, chopped
- 4 garlic cloves, minced
- 2 envelopes Italian salad dressing mix
- 1 envelope zesty Italian salad dressing mix
- 1 envelope (0.87 oz.) brown gravy mix
- 1 to 2 Tbsp. crushed red pepper flakes
- 1 Tbsp. Italian seasoning
- 2 tsp. Worcestershire sauce
- 16 hoagie buns, split
  Sliced provolone cheese and giardiniera, optional

1. In a large skillet, brown each roast in oil on all sides. Drain. Transfer meat to a 7-qt. slow cooker. Combine the water, onion, garlic, salad dressing and gravy mixes, pepper flakes, Italian seasoning and Worcestershire sauce; pour over beef. Cover and cook on low for 8-10 hours or until meat is tender.
2. Remove beef; cool slightly. Skim fat from cooking juices. Pour juices into a large bowl. Shred beef with two forks; add to bowl. Using a slotted spoon, place ½ cup on each bun. Top with cheese and giardiniera if desired.
FREEZE OPTION: Cool meat and juices; transfer to freezer containers. Freeze for up to 3 months. To use, thaw in the refrigerator overnight. Place in a Dutch oven; heat through. Using a slotted spoon, place ½ cup on each bun. Top with cheese and giardiniera if desired.
1 SANDWICH: 450 cal., 16g fat (5g sat. fat), 89mg chol., 969mg sod., 39g carb. (8g sugars, 1g fiber), 37g pro.

HAM & WHITE BEAN SOUP

I came up with this recipe when I wanted to make dinner in the slow cooker but didn't have time to go to the grocery store. I went through my freezer and cupboards and threw in whatever I thought would go well together. At the last minute, I decided to add Old Bay. This flavorful soup was a make-again!

—Stacey Cornell, Saratoga Springs, NY

PREP: 20 min. • **COOK:** 6 hours
MAKES: 12 servings (3 qt.)

- 1 carton (32 oz.) chicken broth
- 1 can (28 oz.) diced tomatoes, undrained
- 1 can (15 to 15½ oz.) white kidney or cannellini beans, rinsed and drained
- 1 pkg. (10 to 12 oz.) frozen cooked winter squash, thawed
- 1 pkg. (10 oz.) frozen leaf spinach, thawed and squeezed dry
- 1¾ cups cubed fully cooked ham
- 3 medium carrots, peeled, chopped
- 1 large onion, chopped
- 3 garlic cloves, minced
- 1 tsp. reduced-sodium seafood seasoning
- ¼ tsp. pepper
  Grated Parmesan cheese, optional

In a 5- or 6-qt. slow cooker, combine first 11 ingredients. Cook, covered, on low for 6-8 hours. If desired, sprinkle with Parmesan cheese.

1 CUP: 102 cal., 1g fat (0 sat. fat), 14mg chol., 808mg sod., 15g carb. (4g sugars, 4g fiber), 8g pro.

TEST KITCHEN TIP

To make Pasta e Fagioli, add ditalini or elbow pasta to this soup. For a spicy twist, sprinkle with hot sauce.

CREAMY RANCHIFIED POTATOES

My daughter-in-law gave me this recipe and, over the years, I have adjusted it to our tastes. It's so nice to come home from work to a hot, tasty potato dish that's ready to serve! You can use any cheese you like and also add any leftover meats you may have on hand—chicken, for one.

—Jane Whittaker, Pensacola, FL

PREP: 15 min. • **COOK:** 6 hours
MAKES: 8 servings

- 2 lbs. small red potatoes, quartered
- 1 cup cubed fully cooked ham
- 1 can (10¾ oz.) condensed cream of potato soup, undiluted
- 1 carton (8 oz.) spreadable chive and onion cream cheese
- 3 Tbsp. minced chives
- 1 envelope ranch salad dressing mix
- 1 tsp. pepper
- 6 oz. pepper jack cheese, grated

In a 4-qt. slow cooker, combine first seven ingredients. Cook, covered, on low until potatoes are tender, 6-8 hours. Top the mixture with cheese; stir to combine.

¾ CUP: 297 cal., 15g fat (8g sat. fat), 53mg chol., 933mg sod., 28g carb. (2g sugars, 3g fiber), 14g pro.

HAM & WHITE BEAN SOUP

VEGETABLE LENTIL SOUP

Here's a healthy soup that's ideal for vegetarians and those watching their weight. Butternut squash and lentils make it filling, while herbs and other veggies round out the flavor.
—Mark Morgan, Waterford, WI

PREP: 15 min.
COOK: 4½ hours
MAKES: 6 servings (about 2 qt.)

- 3 cups cubed peeled butternut squash
- 1 cup chopped carrot
- 1 cup chopped onion
- 1 cup dried lentils, rinsed
- 2 garlic cloves, minced
- 1 tsp. dried oregano
- 1 tsp. dried basil
- 4 cups vegetable broth
- 1 can (14½ oz.) Italian diced tomatoes, undrained
- 2 cups frozen cut green beans (about 8 oz.)

1. Place first eight ingredients in a 5-qt. slow cooker. Cook, covered, on low until lentils are tender, about 4 hours.
2. Stir in tomatoes and beans. Cook, covered, on high until heated through, about 30 minutes.
1⅓ CUPS: 217 cal., 1g fat (0 sat. fat), 0 chol., 685mg sod., 45g carb. (11g sugars, 8g fiber), 11g pro.

SLOW-COOKED SUMMER SQUASH

We love squash, but I got tired of fixing it plain or with cheese, so I decided to jazz it up a bit. This was a huge hit with the family.
—Joan Hallford, North Richland Hills, TX

PREP: 15 min. • **COOK:** 2 hours
MAKES: 8 servings

- 1 lb. medium yellow summer squash
- 1 lb. medium zucchini
- 2 medium tomatoes, chopped
- ¼ cup thinly sliced green onions
- ½ tsp. salt
- ¼ tsp. pepper
- 1 cup vegetable broth
- 1½ cups Caesar salad croutons, coarsely crushed
- ½ cup shredded cheddar cheese
- 4 bacon strips, cooked and crumbled

1. Cut squash into ¼-in.-thick slices. In a 3- or 4-qt. slow cooker, combine squash, tomatoes and green onions. Add salt, pepper and broth. Cook, covered, on low until tender, about 2½—3½ hours. Remove the squash with a slotted spoon.
2. To serve, top with croutons, cheese and bacon.
¾ CUP: 111 cal., 6g fat (2g sat. fat), 12mg chol., 442mg sod., 10g carb. (4g sugars, 2g fiber), 6g pro. **DIABETIC EXCHANGES:** 1 vegetable, 1 fat.

SLOW-COOKED
SUMMER SQUASH

GINGER BEER PULLED PORK

GINGER BEER PULLED PORK
This is just one of the many ways I like
to cook pork. My family likes the ginger
flavor, and we also enjoy drinking
ginger beer. Different, but delicious!
—Nancy Heishman, Las Vegas, NV

PREP: 25 min. • **COOK:** 6 hours
MAKES: 10 servings

2 tsp. garlic salt
1 tsp. ground ginger
1 boneless pork shoulder butt
   roast (2½ lbs.)
1 Tbsp. canola oil
1 large onion, diced
1 can (15 oz.) tomato sauce
1 medium green pepper, diced
3 Tbsp. brown sugar

1 Tbsp. tomato paste
1 Tbsp. Worcestershire sauce
½ tsp. salt
1 cup ginger beer
8 sandwich buns, split and toasted
2 cups shredded Monterey Jack
   cheese

1. Combine garlic salt and ginger; rub
onto all sides of roast. In a large skillet,
heat the oil over medium-high heat.
Brown roast on all sides, 5-8 minutes.
Add onion; cook until softened.
2. Transfer pork, onion and drippings
to a 4-qt. slow cooker. Stir in the next
seven ingredients.
3. Cook, covered, on low until meat is
tender, 6-8 hours. Remove roast; cool
slightly. Skim fat from cooking juices.

Shred roast with two forks. Stir
1½ cups cooking juices into the
shredded meat; mix well. Serve on
buns with cheese.
1 SANDWICH: 495 cal., 24g fat (9g sat.
fat), 88mg chol., 1244mg sod., 39g carb.
(12g sugars, 2g fiber), 32g pro.

TEST KITCHEN TIP
Pair this recipe with crunchy
cabbage slaw. Serve it on
slider buns, pretzel or sweet
Hawaiian rolls.

ENGLISH PUB
SPLIT PEA SOUP

ENGLISH PUB SPLIT PEA SOUP

This family favorite is the same recipe my grandmother used. Now with the magic of the slow cooker, I can spend 15 minutes putting it together, walk away for 5 hours, and come back to "soup's on." Finish it with more milk if you like your soup a bit thinner.

—Judy Batson, Tampa, FL

PREP: 15 min. • **COOK:** 5 hours
MAKES: 8 servings (2 qt.)

- 1 meaty ham bone
- 1⅓ cups dried green split peas, rinsed
- 2 celery ribs, chopped
- 1 large carrot, chopped
- 1 sweet onion, chopped
- 4 cups water
- 1 bottle (12 oz.) light beer
- 1 Tbsp. prepared English mustard
- ½ cup 2% milk
- ¼ cup minced fresh parsley
- ½ tsp. salt
- ¼ tsp. pepper
- ¼ tsp. ground nutmeg
  Minced fresh parsley, optional

1. Place ham bone in a 4-qt. slow cooker. Add peas and vegetables. Combine water, beer and mustard; pour over top. Cook, covered, on high 5-6 hours or until peas are tender.
2. Remove ham bone from soup. Cool slightly, trim away fat and remove meat from bone; discard fat and bone. Cut meat into bite-size pieces; return to slow cooker. Stir in the remaining ingredients. If desired, top soup with minced parsley.
1 CUP: 141 cal., 1g fat (0 sat. fat), 1mg chol., 193mg sod., 25g carb. (6g sugars, 9g fiber), 9g pro. **DIABETIC EXCHANGES:** 1½ starch, 1 lean meat.

TEST KITCHEN TIP
Nutmeg is the secret spice in many savory dishes. It's commonly used in white sauces, soups and potatoes. Be careful not to overdo it. A small amount of nutmeg goes a long way.

ROOT BEER BRATS

ROOT BEER BRATS

Here's an easy recipe that's versatile, too. Serve the saucy brats over rice for one meal and have them on buns the next. For extra punch, add a splash of root beer concentrate to the sauce.
— Pamela Thompson, Girard, IL

PREP: 15 min. • **COOK:** 6 hours
MAKES: 10 servings

- 1 can (12 oz.) root beer
- 3 Tbsp. cornstarch
- 3 tsp. ground mustard
- 3 tsp. caraway seeds
- 10 uncooked bratwurst links
- 1 large onion, coarsely chopped
- 1 bottle (12 oz.) chili sauce
- 10 hoagie buns, toasted
  Thinly sliced red onion, optional
  Prepared mustard, optional

1. Whisk first four ingredients until blended. In a large nonstick skillet, brown bratwursts over medium-high heat. Transfer to a 4- or 5-qt. slow cooker. Add onion, chili sauce and root beer mixture.
2. Cook, covered, on low for 6-8 hours (a thermometer inserted in sausage should read at least 160°). Serve in buns. If desired, top brats with onion and mustard.
1 SERVING: 563 cal., 30g fat (10g sat. fat), 63mg chol., 1575mg sod., 54g carb. (16g sugars, 2g fiber), 20g pro.

SWEET & HOT BAKED BEANS

Baked beans belong at a barbecue. They're sweet with heat when you add pineapple and jalapenos.
—Robin Haas, Cranston, RI

PREP: 20 min. • **COOK:** 5 hours
MAKES: 14 servings (½ cup each)

- 4   cans (15 oz. each) white kidney or cannellini beans, rinsed and drained
- 2   cans (8 oz. each) crushed pineapple, undrained
- 2   large onions, finely chopped
- 1   cup packed brown sugar
- 1   cup ketchup
- 10 bacon strips, cooked and crumbled
- ½   cup molasses
- ¼   cup canned diced jalapeno peppers
- 2   Tbsp. white vinegar
- 4   garlic cloves, minced
- 4   tsp. ground mustard
- ¼   tsp. ground cloves

In a 3- or 4-qt. slow cooker, combine all ingredients. Cook, covered, on low for 5-6 hours or until heated through.
½ CUP: 273 cal., 3g fat (1g sat. fat), 6mg chol., 494mg sod., 54g carb. (33g sugars, 5g fiber), 8g pro.

SPICED CARROTS & BUTTERNUT SQUASH

When I've got a lot going on, my slow cooker is my go-to tool for cooking veggies. I toss in cumin and chili powder to bring out the natural sweetness of carrots and squash.
—Courtney Stultz, Weir, KS

PREP: 15 min. • **COOK:** 4 hours
MAKES: 6 servings

- 5   large carrots, cut into ½-in. pieces (about 3 cups)
- 2   cups cubed peeled butternut squash (1-in. pieces)
- 1   Tbsp. balsamic vinegar
- 1   Tbsp. olive oil
- 1   Tbsp. honey
- 1   tsp. ground cinnamon
- ½   tsp. salt
- ½   tsp. ground cumin
- ¼   tsp. chili powder

Place carrots and squash in a 3-qt. slow cooker. In a small bowl, mix remaining ingredients; drizzle over vegetables and toss to coat. Cook, covered, on low for 4-5 hours or until vegetables are tender. Gently stir before serving.
⅔ CUP: 85 cal., 3g fat (0 sat. fat), 0 chol., 245mg sod., 16g carb. (8g sugars, 3g fiber), 1g pro. **DIABETIC EXCHANGES:** 1 vegetable, ½ starch, ½ fat.

SPICED CARROTS & BUTTERNUT SQUASH

**CHICKEN &
LENTIL CHILI**

FREEZE OPTION: Freeze cooled chili mixture in freezer containers. To use, partially thaw in refrigerator overnight. Heat through in a saucepan, stirring chili occasionally and adding a little water if necessary.

1¼ CUPS: 249 cal., 2g fat (0 sat. fat), 23mg chol., 844mg sod., 38g carb. (5g sugars, 9g fiber), 21g pro.

SLOW-COOKED WILD RICE

This recipe has become such a family heirloom that I asked my mother's permission before passing it along. It has traveled to weddings, baptisms, landmark birthdays and wedding anniversaries—and it always makes people happy.
—Janet Mahowald, Rice Lake, WI

PREP: 15 min. • **COOK:** 4 hours
MAKES: 8 cups

- 1 lb. bulk pork sausage
- 4 celery ribs, chopped
- 1 small onion, chopped
- 1 can (10¾ oz.) condensed cream of mushroom soup, undiluted
- 1 can (10¾ oz.) condensed cream of chicken soup, undiluted
- 1 cup uncooked wild rice
- 1 can (4 oz.) mushroom stems and pieces, drained
- 3 cups chicken broth

1. In a large skillet, cook and crumble sausage with celery and onion over medium heat until the sausage is no longer pink and vegetables are tender, 6-8 minutes; drain. Transfer to a 3-qt. slow cooker. Add the soups, rice and mushrooms. Stir in broth.
2. Cook, covered, on low until rice is tender, 4-5 hours.

¾ CUP: 236 cal., 14g fat (4g sat. fat), 30mg chol., 1059mg sod., 19g carb. (2g sugars, 2g fiber), 9g pro.

CHICKEN & LENTIL CHILI

I like to make a simple, hearty slow-cooked recipe at least once a week. You can mix this up the night before and throw it into the crock on your way out the door. Use hotter tomatoes and chilies or salsa if you like more zing.
—Laurie Stout-Letz, Bountiful, UT

PREP: 20 min. • **COOK:** 5 hours
MAKES: 8 servings (2½ qt.)

- 2 boneless skinless chicken breast halves (6 oz. each)
- 1 large onion, chopped
- 1 can (16 oz.) kidney beans, rinsed and drained
- 1 can (15 oz.) black beans, rinsed and drained
- 1 can (14½ oz.) reduced-sodium chicken broth
- 1 can (10 oz.) diced tomatoes and green chilies
- 1 can (8 oz.) tomato sauce
- 1 cup (about 5 oz.) frozen corn
- 1 cup mild salsa
- 1 can (4 to 4½ oz.) chopped green chilies
- ⅔ cup dried lentils, rinsed
- 3 garlic cloves, minced
- 1½ tsp. chili powder
- 1 tsp. ground cumin
- ⅛ tsp. celery salt
- ⅛ tsp. cayenne pepper
   Tortilla chips, shredded Mexican cheese blend and sliced ripe olives, optional

In a 5- or 6-qt. slow cooker combine the first 16 ingredients. Cook, covered, on low until chicken and lentils are tender, about 5-6 hours. Remove chicken; cool slightly and chop. Return chicken to slow cooker; heat through. Serve over tortilla chips and top with cheese and olives, if desired.

Snacks & Sweets

SLOW COOKER CHOCOLATE POTS DE CREME

SLOW COOKER CHOCOLATE POTS DE CREME

Lunch on the go just got a whole lot sweeter. Tuck jars of rich chocolate custard into lunch bags for a midday treat. These desserts in a jar are fun for picnics, too.
—Nick Iverson, Denver, CO

PREP: 20 min. • **COOK:** 4 hours + chilling
MAKES: 8 servings

- 2 cups heavy whipping cream
- 8 oz. bittersweet chocolate, finely chopped
- 1 Tbsp. instant espresso powder
- 4 large egg yolks
- ¼ cup sugar
- ¼ tsp. salt
- 1 Tbsp. vanilla extract
- 8 canning jars (4 oz. each) with lids and bands
- 3 cups hot water
  Whipped cream, grated chocolate and fresh raspberries, optional

1. Place cream, chocolate and espresso in a microwave-safe bowl; microwave on high until the chocolate is melted and cream is hot, about 4 minutes. Whisk to combine.
2. In a large bowl, whisk egg yolks, sugar and salt until blended but not foamy. Slowly whisk in cream mixture; stir in extract.
3. Pour egg mixture into jars. Center lids on jars and screw on bands until fingertip tight. Add hot water to a 7-qt. slow cooker; place jars in slow cooker. Cook, covered, on low until set, 4 hours. Remove jars from slow cooker; cool on counter 30 minutes. Refrigerate until cold, 2 hours.
4. If desired, top with whipped cream, grated chocolate and raspberries.
1 SERVING: 424 cal., 34g fat (21g sat. fat), 160mg chol., 94mg sod., 13g carb. (11g sugars, 1g fiber), 5g pro.

VEGETARIAN BUFFALO DIP

DELUXE WALKING NACHOS

This slow-cooked potluck chili makes an awesome filling for a little bag of walk-around nachos. Cut the bag lengthwise to make it easier to load up your fork.

—Mallory Lynch, Madison, WI

PREP: 20 min. • **COOK:** 6 hours
MAKES: 18 servings

- 1 lb. lean ground beef (90% lean)
- 1 large sweet onion, chopped
- 3 garlic cloves, minced
- 2 cans (14½ oz. each) diced tomatoes with mild green chilies
- 2 cans (15 oz. each) pinto beans, rinsed and drained
- 2 cans (15 oz. each) black beans, rinsed and drained
- 2 to 3 Tbsp. chili powder
- 2 tsp. ground cumin
- ½ tsp. salt
- 18 pkg. (1 oz. each) nacho-flavored tortilla chips
  Optional toppings: shredded cheddar cheese, sour cream, chopped tomatoes and pickled jalapeno slices

1. In a large skillet, cook beef, onion and garlic over medium heat for 6-8 minutes or until the meat is no longer pink. Break the beef into crumbles; drain.
2. Transfer beef mixture to a 5-qt. slow cooker. Drain one can tomatoes, discarding liquid; add to slow cooker. Stir in the beans, chili powder, cumin, salt and remaining tomatoes. Cook, covered, on low 6-8 hours to allow flavors to blend. Mash the beans to desired consistency.
3. Just before serving, cut open tortilla chip bags. Divide chili among bags; add toppings as desired.
FREEZE OPTION: Freeze cooled chili in a freezer container. To use, partially thaw in refrigerator overnight. Heat through in a saucepan, stirring occasionally and adding a little water if necessary.
1 SERVING: 282 cal., 10g fat (2g sat. fat), 16mg chol., 482mg sod., 36g carb. (5g sugars, 6g fiber), 12g pro.

VEGETARIAN BUFFALO DIP

A friend made Buffalo chicken dip and that got me thinking about creating a vegetarian dip with the same flavors. This addictive dip is so amazing, no one will miss the meat.

—Amanda Silvers, Old Fort, TN

PREP: 10 min.
COOK: 1½ hours
MAKES: 6 cups

- 1 container (8 oz.) sour cream
- 8 oz. cream cheese, softened
- 1 envelope ranch salad dressing mix
- 2 cups shredded sharp cheddar cheese
- 1 can (15 oz.) black beans, rinsed and drained
- 8 oz. fresh mushrooms, chopped
- 1 cup Buffalo wing sauce

Sliced green onions and tortilla chips, optional

Combine the sour cream, cream cheese and ranch dressing mix in a bowl until smooth. Stir in the next four ingredients. Transfer to a 3- or 4-qt. slow cooker. Cook, covered on high for 1½ hours. If desired, sprinkle with green onion and serve with tortilla chips.
¼ CUP: 113 cal., 8g fat (5g sat. fat), 21mg chol., 526mg sod., 5g carb. (1g sugars, 1g fiber), 4g pro.

TEST KITCHEN TIP
Serve the dip with celery sticks, carrots or tri-colored tortilla chips.

SWEET & SALTY PARTY MIX

My husband doesn't like traditional party mixes, saying that they are too salty or too sweet. He calls this one his favorite—it's just right.

—Jackie Burns, Kettle Falls, WA

PREP: 20 min. • **COOK:** 1 hour + cooling
MAKES: 16 servings (¾ cup each)

- 3 cups each Corn Chex, Rice Chex and Wheat Chex
- 3 cups miniature pretzels
- 1 cup dried cranberries
- 1 cup sliced almonds
- ½ cup butter, cubed
- 1 cup packed brown sugar
- ¼ cup corn syrup
- ¼ tsp. baking soda

1. Place cereal, pretzels, cranberries and almonds in a greased 6-qt. slow cooker; toss to combine. In a small saucepan, melt butter over medium heat; stir in the brown sugar and corn syrup. Bring to a boil; cook and stir 5 minutes. Remove from heat; stir in baking soda. Drizzle over cereal mixture and toss to coat.
2. Cook, covered, on low 1 hour, stirring halfway through cooking. Spread onto waxed paper; cool completely. Store in airtight containers.
¾ CUP: 288 cal., 9g fat (4g sat. fat), 15mg chol., 363mg sod., 51g carb. (25g sugars, 3g fiber), 4g pro.

HONEY BUFFALO MEATBALL SLIDERS

These little sliders deliver big Buffalo chicken flavor without the usual messiness of wings. The spicy-sweet meatballs are a hit on game day with kids and adults alike.

—Julie Peterson, Crofton, MD

PREP: 10 min. • **COOK:** 2 hours
MAKES: 6 servings

- ¼ cup packed brown sugar
- ¼ cup Louisiana-style hot sauce
- ¼ cup honey
- ¼ cup apricot preserves
- 2 Tbsp. cornstarch
- 2 Tbsp. reduced-sodium soy sauce
- 1 pkg. (24 oz.) frozen fully cooked Italian turkey meatballs, thawed
  Additional hot sauce, optional
  Bibb lettuce leaves
- 12 mini buns
  Crumbled blue cheese
  Ranch salad dressing, optional

1. In a 3- or 4-qt. slow cooker, mix the first six ingredients until smooth. Stir in the meatballs until coated. Cook, covered, on low until meatballs are heated through, 2-3 hours.
2. If desired, stir in additional hot sauce. Serve meatballs on buns lined with lettuce; top with cheese and, if desired, dressing.
2 SLIDERS: 524 cal., 21g fat (6g sat. fat), 110mg chol., 1364mg sod., 61g carb. (29g sugars, 1g fiber), 28g pro.

HONEY BUFFALO MEATBALL SLIDERS

**SLOW COOKER
RICE PORRIDGE**

WARM ROCKY ROAD CAKE

When served warm, this reminds me of super moist lava cake. Until I made this, I didn't think a slow cooker cake could be so attractive. It's a real winner.
—Scarlett Elrod, Newnan, GA

PREP: 20 min. • **COOK:** 3 hours
MAKES: 16 servings

- 1 pkg. German chocolate cake mix (regular size)
- 1 pkg. (3.9 oz.) instant chocolate pudding mix
- 1 cup sour cream
- ⅓ cup butter, melted
- 3 large eggs
- 1 tsp. vanilla extract
- 3¼ cups 2% milk, divided
- 1 pkg. (3.4 oz.) cook-and-serve chocolate pudding mix
- 1½ cups miniature marshmallows
- 1 cup (6 oz.) semisweet chocolate chips
- ½ cup chopped pecans, toasted
  Vanilla ice cream, optional

1. In a large bowl, combine the first six ingredients; add 1¼ cups milk. Beat on low speed for 30 seconds. Beat on medium speed for 2 minutes. Transfer to a greased 4- or 5-qt. slow cooker. Sprinkle cook-and-serve pudding mix over batter.
2. In a small saucepan, heat remaining milk until bubbles form around sides of pan; gradually pour over contents of slow cooker.
3. Cook, covered, on high for 3-4 hours or until a toothpick inserted in the cake portion comes out with moist crumbs.
4. Turn off slow cooker. Sprinkle the marshmallows, chocolate chips and pecans over cake; let stand, covered, 5 minutes or until marshmallows begin to melt. Serve warm. If desired, serve with ice cream.
NOTE: To toast nuts, bake in a shallow pan in a 350° oven for 5-10 minutes or cook in a skillet over low heat until lightly browned, stirring occasionally.
¾ CUP: 386 cal., 17g fat (8g sat. fat), 59mg chol., 431mg sod., 55g carb. (34g sugars, 2g fiber), 6g pro.

SLOW COOKER
RICE PORRIDGE

We Italians have a soft spot for our rice dishes. Whether it's risotto or rice pudding, it's all good. This not-too-sweet treat is a terrific way to finish a meal. Top it off with blueberry or cherry pie filling right before serving ...or stir in a little Amaretto.
—Lorraine Caland, Shuniah, ON

PREP: 15 min • **COOK:** 2½ hours
MAKES: 12 servings (½ cup each)

- 2 Tbsp. melted butter
- 1 cup uncooked long grain rice
- ¼ cup sugar
- 1 pinch salt
- 3 cups whole milk
- 2 cups half-and-half cream
  Additional milk and cherry pie filling, optional
  Toasted sliced almonds, optional

1. Brush the inside of a 5-qt. slow cooker with melted butter. Add rice, sugar, salt, milk and half and half; stir to combine. Cook, covered on high for 2 hours; stir. Cover and cook until liquid is almost absorbed and rice is tender, 30 minutes.
2. If desired, stir in additional milk and top with pie filling and almonds.
½ CUP: 186 cal., 8g fat (5g sat. fat), 31mg chol., 184mg sod., 22g carb. (8g sugars, 0 fiber), 5g pro.

TEST KITCHEN TIP
Replace some of the milk with a can of coconut milk for porridge with coconut flavor. Top servings with toasted coconut.

SLOW-COOKED
POT ROAST SLIDERS

SLOW-COOKED
POT ROAST SLIDERS

This recipe reminds me of my mom's famous pot roast. Best of all, these sandwiches are simple to make, with only five ingredients. I love that I can enjoy the flavors of Mom's roast with the delicious portability of a slider.
—Lauren Drafke, Cape Coral, FL

PREP: 20 min.
COOK: 5 hours
MAKES: 2 dozen

 1 boneless beef chuck roast (3 lbs.)
1½ cups water
 1 envelope (1 oz.) onion soup mix
 1 envelope (1 oz.) au jus gravy mix

 2 pkg. (12 oz. each) Hawaiian sweet rolls, halved
12 slices Swiss cheese (¾ oz. each), cut in half
     Baby arugula, sliced tomato and horseradish sauce, optional

1. Place roast in a 4-qt. slow cooker. In a small bowl, whisk together water, soup and gravy mixes. Pour seasoning mixture over roast. Cook, covered, on low until tender, 5-6 hours. Remove from cooker. Cool slightly; shred meat with two forks.
2. Preheat broiler. Place halved rolls on a baking sheet. On each bottom half, place cheese piece. Broil buns 4-6 in. from heat until cheese is melted and rolls start to brown, 1-2 minutes.

Remove from broiler. Using tongs, place meat mixture on roll bottoms. If desired, top with arugula, tomato and horseradish sauce. Replace roll tops.
2 SLIDERS: 487 cal., 22g fat (11g sat. fat), 124mg chol., 721mg sod., 36g carb. (12g sugars, 2g fiber), 36g pro.

TEST KITCHEN TIP
Try the sandwiches with more flavorful cheeses such as aged Swiss or white cheddar.

SLOW COOKER PIZZA DIP

FREEZE IT

I created this dip for my daughter's pizza-themed birthday party, and it was an instant hit. Pizza dip has proved equally popular at all kinds of parties and gatherings.
—Stephanie Gates, Waterloo, IA

PREP: 15 min. • **COOK:** 2 hours
MAKES: 20 servings (¼ cup each)

- ½ lb. ground beef
- ½ lb. bulk pork sausage
- 1 can (28 oz.) crushed tomatoes
- ½ cup diced green pepper
- ¼ cup grated Parmesan cheese
- 2 Tbsp. tomato paste
- 2 tsp. Italian seasoning
- 1 garlic clove, minced
- ¾ tsp. crushed red pepper flakes
- ¼ tsp. salt
- ¼ tsp. pepper
  Hot garlic bread

1. In a large skillet, cook and crumble beef and sausage over medium heat until no longer pink, 5-7 minutes. Using a slotted spoon, transfer the meat to a 3-qt. slow cooker. Stir in all remaining ingredients except garlic bread.
2. Cook, covered, on low until heated through, for 2-3 hours. Serve with hot garlic bread.
FREEZE OPTION: Freeze cooled dip in freezer containers. To use, partially thaw in refrigerator overnight. Warm dip in a saucepan until heated through, stirring occasionally.
¼ CUP: 68 cal., 4g fat (1g sat. fat), 14mg chol., 198mg sod., 4g carb. (2g sugars, 1g fiber), 4g pro.

STRAWBERRY-BANANA PUDDING CAKE

This luscious pink pudding cake is so easy to put together. Top it with ice cream and fresh fruit for one very happy family.
—Nadine Mesch, Mount Healthy, OH

PREP: 15 min.
COOK: 3½ hours + standing
MAKES: 10 servings

- 1 pkg. strawberry cake mix (regular size)
- 1 pkg. (3.4 oz.) instant banana cream pudding mix
- 2 cups plain Greek yogurt
- 4 large eggs
- 1 cup water
- ¾ cup canola oil
- 2 Tbsp. minced fresh basil
- 1 cup white baking chips
  Optional toppings: vanilla ice cream, sliced bananas, sliced strawberries and fresh basil

1. In a large bowl, combine first six ingredients; beat on low speed for 30 seconds. Beat on medium speed for 2 minutes; stir in basil. Transfer to a greased 5-qt. slow cooker. Cook, covered, on low until edges of the cake are golden brown (center will be moist), 3½ to 4 hours.
2. Remove slow cooker insert; sprinkle cake with baking chips. Let cake stand, uncovered, 10 minutes before serving. Serve with toppings as desired.
1 SERVING: 373 cal., 29g fat (8g sat. fat), 90mg chol., 239mg sod., 23g carb. (21g sugars, 0 fiber), 5g pro.

SLOW COOKER
PIZZA DIP

CRANBERRY-ALMOND
CORNMEAL CAKE

PEACHY SERRANO PEPPER WINGS

Bring the heat and a kiss of sweet peach jam to the table with these irresistible sriracha chicken wings.
—Crystal Holsinger, Waddell, AZ

PREP: 20 min. • **COOK:** 4 hours
MAKES: about 2 dozen

- 3 lbs. chicken wings
- 1 cup all-purpose flour
- 2 cups peach preserves
- ¼ cup chicken broth
- ¼ cup white vinegar
- 1 Tbsp. soy sauce
- 2 to 3 serrano peppers, finely chopped
- 2 shallots, finely chopped
- 1 garlic clove, minced
- ½ tsp. salt
  Minced chives, ranch dip, optional

1. Using a sharp knife, cut through the two chicken wing joints; remove and discard wing tips. Place the remaining wing pieces in a large resealable plastic bag. Add flour; seal and shake to coat. Transfer chicken to a 4- or 5-qt. slow cooker coated with cooking spray.
2. In medium bowl, combine the remaining ingredients; pour over chicken. Cook, covered, on low until chicken juices run clear, 4-5 hours. If desired, top with chives and serve with ranch dip.
1 PIECE: 141 cal., 4g fat (1g sat. fat), 18mg chol., 116mg sod., 20g carb. (16g sugars, 0 fiber), 6g pro.

CRANBERRY-ALMOND CORNMEAL CAKE

This warm, comforting slow cooker dessert is guaranteed to ward off the wintertime blues. Top with vanilla ice cream for an extra layer of flavor.
—Shannon Kohn, Simpsonville, SC

PREP: 15 min. • **COOK:** 2 hours
MAKES: 10 servings

- 1 pkg. (8½ oz.) cornbread/muffin mix
- 1 cup all-purpose flour
- ⅔ cup sugar
- 1 tsp. baking powder
- 3 large eggs, lightly beaten
- 1 cup buttermilk
- ½ cup butter, melted
- 1½ cups dried cranberries
- 1 can (12½ oz.) almond cake and pastry filling
  Vanilla ice cream or whipped cream, optional

1. In large bowl, whisk together the cornbread mix, flour, sugar and baking powder. Stir in eggs, buttermilk and melted butter until combined. Pour batter into a 5-qt. slow cooker coated with cooking spray. Sprinkle batter with cranberries; drop almond filling by heaping tablespoons evenly over cranberries and batter.
2. Cook, covered, on high until a toothpick inserted in center comes out clean, about 2 hours. If desired, serve warm with vanilla ice cream or whipped cream.
1 SERVING: 506 cal., 17g fat (8g sat. fat), 82mg chol., 433mg sod., 84g carb. (50g sugars, 3g fiber), 7g pro.

TEST KITCHEN TIP

For a change of flavor, use cherry-flavored cranberries instead of regular. You can also soak the cranberries in orange juice or liqueur just until plump, then proceed with the recipe.

PEACHY SERRANO
PEPPER WINGS

HEAVENLY APPLESAUCE

Every year my husband and I take our two daughters to an orchard to pick apples, so we can make this luscious applesauce for family and neighbors.
—Jennifer Purcell, Vermilion, OH

PREP: 25 min. • **COOK:** 6 hours
MAKES: 8 servings

- 5 lbs. apples, peeled and sliced (about 13 cups)
- ¾ cup packed light brown sugar
- ⅔ cup unsweetened apple juice
- 2 tsp. ground cinnamon
- 1 tsp. pumpkin pie spice
- 1 Tbsp. vanilla extract

1. In a 5- or 6-qt. slow cooker, combine apples, sugar, juice, cinnamon and pie spice. Cook, covered, on low 6-8 hours or until apples are soft.
2. Add vanilla; stir to break up apples. Serve warm or cold.
FREEZE OPTION: Freeze the cooled applesauce in freezer containers. To use, thaw in refrigerator overnight.
⅔ CUP: 211 cal., 1g fat (0 sat. fat), 0 chol., 7mg sod., 54g carb. (48g sugars, 4g fiber), 0 pro.

SLOW COOKER CAPONATA

This Italian eggplant dips preps quickly and actually gets better as it stands. Serve it warm or at room temperature. Try adding a little leftover caponata to scrambled eggs for a savory breakfast.
—Nancy Beckman, Helena, MT

PREP: 20 min. • **COOK:** 5 hours
MAKES: 6 cups

- 2 medium eggplants, cut into ½-in. pieces
- 1 medium onion, chopped
- 1 can (14½ oz.) diced tomatoes, undrained
- 12 garlic cloves, sliced
- ½ cup dry red wine
- 3 Tbsp. extra virgin olive oil
- 2 Tbsp. red wine vinegar
- 4 tsp. capers, undrained
- 5 bay leaves
- 1½ tsp. salt
- ¼ tsp. coarsely ground pepper
  French bread baguette slices, toasted
  Fresh basil leaves, toasted pine nuts and additional olive oil, optional

Place first eleven ingredients in a 6-qt. slow cooker (do not stir). Cook, covered, on high for 3 hours. Stir gently; replace cover. Cook on high until vegetables are tender, 2 hours longer. Cool slightly; discard bay leaves. Serve with toasted baguette slices. If desired, serve with toppings.
¼ CUP: 34 cal., 2g fat (0 sat. fat), 0 chol., 189mg sod., 4g carb. (2g sugars, 2g fiber), 1g pro.

SLOW COOKER CAPONATA

**CARAMEL PECAN
PUMPKIN CAKE**

SAUSAGE JALAPENO DIP

This creamy dip cooks up like a dream in the slow cooker. Scoop it up with crunchy tortilla chips or raw veggies.

—Gina Fensler, Cincinnati, OH

PREP: 15 min. • **COOK:** 5½ hours
MAKES: 6 cups

- 1 lb. bulk Italian sausage
- 2 large sweet red peppers, finely chopped
- 3 jalapeno peppers, finely chopped
- 1 cup whole milk
- 2 pkg. (8 oz. each) cream cheese, softened
- 1 cup shredded part-skim mozzarella cheese
  Tortilla chips

1. In a large skillet, cook the sausage over medium heat 6-8 minutes or until no longer pink, breaking into crumbles; drain.
2. Place red peppers, jalapenos and sausage in a 3-qt. slow cooker; add milk. Cook, covered, on low 5-6 hours or until peppers are tender.
3. Stir in cheeses. Cook, covered, on low 30 minutes longer or until cheese is melted. Serve with tortilla chips.
NOTE: Wear disposable gloves when cutting hot peppers; the oils can burn skin. Avoid touching your face.
¼ CUP: 137 cal., 12g fat (6g sat. fat), 33mg chol., 211mg sod., 3g carb. (2g sugars, 0 fiber), 5g pro.

CARAMEL PECAN PUMPKIN CAKE

Think slow cooker as cake-maker for some seriously yummy dessert. This cake is easy enough for Sunday brunch and tasty enough for Thanksgiving Day—and frees up oven space on holidays, too.

—Julie Peterson, Crofton, MD

PREP: 15 min.
COOK: 2 hours
MAKES: 10 servings

- 1 cup butter, softened
- 1¼ cups sugar
- 4 large eggs
- 2 cups all-purpose flour
- 2 tsp. baking powder
- 1 tsp. baking soda
- 1 tsp. pumpkin pie spice or ground cinnamon
- ½ tsp. salt
- 1 can (15 oz.) pumpkin
- ½ cup caramel sundae syrup
- ½ cup chopped pecans

1. In large bowl, cream butter and sugar until light and fluffy. Add the eggs, one at a time, beating well after each addition. In another bowl, whisk together the next five ingredients; add to creamed mixture alternately with the pumpkin, beating well after each addition.
2. Line a 5-qt. round slow cooker with heavy duty foil extending over sides; spray with cooking spray. Spread the batter evenly into slow cooker. Cook, covered, on high, until a toothpick inserted in center comes out clean, about 2 hours. To avoid scorching, rotate slow cooker insert one-half turn midway through cooking, lifting carefully with oven mitts. Turn off the slow cooker; let stand, uncovered, for 10 minutes. Using foil, carefully lift the cake out of the slow cooker and invert onto a serving plate.
3. Drizzle caramel syrup over cake; top with pecans. Serve warm.
1 SLICE: 473 cal., 25g fat (13g sat. fat), 123mg chol., 561mg sod., 59g carb. (35g sugars, 2g fiber), 7g pro.

OVERNIGHT
DOUGHNUT BAKE

OVERNIGHT DOUGHNUT BAKE

This extravagant dish will be the star of the brunch table. Try serving it with sausage, fresh berries and yogurt.

—*Taste of Home* Test Kitchen

PREP: 15 min.
COOK: 4 hours + standing
MAKES: 12 servings

24 cake doughnuts, cut into bite-sized pieces
2 apples, peeled and chopped
1 cup heavy whipping cream
4 large eggs
1 Tbsp. vanilla extract
½ cup packed brown sugar
1 tsp. ground cinnamon
Whipped cream, fresh berries, optional

1. Line inside of 5-qt slow cooker with a double layer of heavy duty foil; spray the insert and foil with cooking spray. Layer half the doughnut pieces in the slow cooker; top with half the apples. Repeat with remaining doughnuts and apples. In large bowl, whisk the cream, eggs, and vanilla; pour over doughnut and apples. In a small bowl, mix the brown sugar and cinnamon; sprinkle over the doughnut mixture.

2. Cook, covered on low until set, for 4-5 hours. Remove slow cooker insert. Let stand, uncovered, 20 minutes. If desired, serve with whipped cream and fresh berries.

1 SERVING: 609 cal., 36g fat (17g sat. fat), 95mg chol., 547mg sod., 64g carb. (32g sugars, 2g fiber), 8g pro.

TEST KITCHEN TIP
This recipe is similar to bread pudding, with an even more sticky and rich consistency.

SLOW COOKER COCONUT GRANOLA

Here's a versatile treat with a taste of the tropics. Mix it up by substituting dried pineapple or tropical fruits for the cherries.

—Rashanda Cobbins, Milwaukee, WI

PREP: 15 min.
COOK: 3½ hours + cooling
MAKES: 6 cups

- 4 cups old-fashioned oats
- 1 cup sliced almonds
- 1 cup unsweetened coconut flakes
- 1 tsp. ground cinnamon
- 1 tsp. ground ginger
- ¼ tsp. salt
- ½ cup coconut oil, melted
- ½ cup maple syrup
- 1 cup dried cherries

1. Combine oats, almonds, coconut, cinnamon, ginger and salt in a 3-qt. slow cooker. In small bowl, whisk oil and maple syrup. Pour into the slow cooker; stir to combine. Cook, covered, on low, stirring occasionally, for 3½ to 4 hours. Stir in cherries.
2. Transfer mixture to a baking sheet; let stand until cool.
½ **CUP:** 343 cal., 19g fat (12g sat. fat), 0 chol., 55mg sod., 41g carb. (18g sugars, 5g fiber), 6g pro.

SLOW COOKER
COCONUT GRANOLA

PEAR CIDER

This perfectly spiced pear cider will warm you from head to toe. It's a pleasant twist on traditional hot apple cider.

—*Taste of Home* Test Kitchen

PREP: 5 min. • **COOK:** 3 hours
MAKES: 20 servings (¾ cup each)

- 12 cups unsweetened apple juice
- 4 cups pear nectar
- 8 cinnamon sticks (3 in.)
- 1 Tbsp. whole allspice
- 1 Tbsp. whole cloves

1. In a 6-qt. slow cooker, combine juice and nectar. Place spices on a double thickness of cheesecloth; bring up the corners of cloth and tie with string to form a bag. Place in slow cooker.
2. Cover and cook on low for 3-4 hours or until heated through. Discard spice bag. Serve warm cider in mugs.
¾ **CUP:** 100 cal., 0 fat (0 sat. fat), 0 chol., 6mg sod., 25g carb. (24g sugars, 0 fiber), 0 pro.

TURKEY A LA KING
PAGE 110

Stovetop Suppers

Here are the good, simple meals to fuel your everyday life—just reach for a pan and whip up one of these comforting dinners in no time flat. From classic tuna melts and creamy pastas to adventurous brown rice bowls and stir-fry dishes, you'll find 104 quick, satisfying recipes to reach for time and again.

Beef &
Ground Beef

TASTY BURRITOS

TASTY BURRITOS

My cousin is of Mexican heritage, and I've watched her make this crunchy beef burrito recipe for years. The first time I made them for my own family, they instantly became a favorite meal. They're even better warmed up the next day in the microwave.
—Debi Lane, Chattanooga, TN

TAKES: 30 min. • **MAKES:** 6 servings

- 1 lb. ground beef
- 1 envelope taco seasoning
- 1 can (16 oz.) refried beans
- 6 flour tortillas (12 in.), warmed
- 1 cup shredded Colby-Monterey Jack cheese
- 4 tsp. canola oil
  Sour cream and salsa

1. In a large skillet, cook the beef over medium heat until no longer pink; drain. Stir in taco seasoning. In a small saucepan, cook the refried beans over medium-low heat for 2-3 minutes or until heated through.

2. Spoon about ⅓ cup of the beans off-center on each tortilla; top with ¼ cup beef mixture. Sprinkle with cheese. Fold sides and ends of tortillas over filling and roll up.

3. In a large skillet over medium-high heat, brown burritos in oil on all sides. Serve with sour cream and salsa.

FREEZE OPTION: Individually wrap the cooled burritos in paper towels and foil; freeze in resealable plastic freezer bag. To use, remove the foil and place the paper towel-wrapped burrito on a microwave-safe plate. Microwave on high for 3-4 minutes or until heated through, turning once. Let stand for 20 seconds.

1 BURRITO: 519 cal., 24g fat (10g sat. fat), 63mg chol., 1539mg sod., 49g carb. (1g sugars, 8g fiber), 27g pro.

MUSHROOM STEAK SALAD WITH WALNUT VINAIGRETTE

When I want to have a romantic dinner with my husband, I fix this elegant yet easy salad. Paired with good bread—and a glass of wine—it makes a perfect meal.
—Candace McMenamin, Lexington, SC

TAKES: 30 min. • **MAKES:** 2 servings

- 8 oz. boneless beef sirloin steak (¾ in. thick)
- 3 Tbsp. olive oil, divided
- 1 cup each sliced fresh baby portobello, shiitake and button mushrooms
- 2 Tbsp. balsamic vinegar
- 1 Tbsp. minced fresh thyme or 1 tsp. dried thyme
- 2 Tbsp. walnut oil
- 2 Tbsp. finely chopped walnuts
- 3 cups torn mixed salad greens
- 1 shallot, sliced
- 2 Tbsp. crumbled goat cheese

1. In a large skillet over medium heat, cook the steak in 1 Tbsp. olive oil for 3-4 minutes on each side or until meat reaches desired doneness (for medium-rare, a thermometer should read 135°; medium, 140°; medium-well, 145°). Remove from the skillet; let meat stand for 5 minutes before slicing.
2. Meanwhile, in the same skillet, saute mushrooms until tender. In a small bowl, combine vinegar and thyme. Whisk in walnut oil and remaining olive oil. Stir in walnuts.
3. Divide salad greens and shallot between two serving bowls. Cut steak into slices. Top salads with steak and mushrooms. Drizzle with dressing; sprinkle with cheese.
1 SERVING: 602 cal., 48g fat (9g sat. fat), 75mg chol., 151mg sod., 14g carb. (5g sugars, 4g fiber), 31g pro.

EASY CUBAN PICADILLO

EASY CUBAN PICADILLO

My girlfriend gave me this fabulous recipe years ago. I've made it ever since for family and friends. My daughter says it's the best dish I make and loves to take leftovers to school for lunch the next day.
—Marie Wielgus, Wayne, NJ

TAKES: 25 min. • **MAKES:** 4 servings

- 1 lb. lean ground beef (90% lean)
- 1 small green pepper, chopped
- ¼ cup chopped onion
- 1 can (8 oz.) tomato sauce
- ½ cup sliced pimiento-stuffed olives
- ¼ cup raisins
- 1 Tbsp. cider vinegar
- 2 cups hot cooked rice
  Fresh cilantro leaves, optional

1. In a large skillet, cook and crumble beef with pepper and onion over medium-high heat until no longer pink, 5-7 minutes. Stir in tomato sauce, olives, raisins and vinegar; bring to a boil. Reduce heat; simmer, uncovered, until raisins are softened, 5-6 minutes.
2. Serve with rice. If desired, top with fresh cilantro to serve.
1 CUP BEEF MIXTURE WITH ½ CUP RICE : 354 cal., 12g fat (3g sat. fat), 56mg chol., 697mg sod., 36g carb. (7g sugars, 2g fiber), 25g pro. **DIABETIC EXCHANGES:** 3 lean meat, 1½ starch, 1 vegetable, 1 fat, ½ fruit.

ITALIAN SWISS STEAK

This Swiss steak supper combines tender beef and veggies with a tangy Italian sauce and melted mozzarella. For a classic combo, add a salad and warm garlic bread.

—Janice Lyhane, Marysville, KS

PREP: 20 min. • **COOK:** 1½ hours
MAKES: 6-8 servings

- 3 Tbsp. all-purpose flour
- 2 lbs. boneless beef top round steak, cut into serving-sized pieces
- ¼ cup butter, cubed
- 1 can (14½ oz.) diced tomatoes, undrained
- 1½ tsp. salt
- ¼ tsp. dried basil
- ⅛ tsp. pepper
- ½ cup chopped green pepper
- ½ cup chopped onion
- 1 cup shredded part-skim mozzarella cheese

1. Place the flour in a large resealable plastic bag. Add beef, a few pieces at a time, and shake to coat. Remove the meat from bag; pound to flatten.
2. In a large skillet over medium-high heat, brown steak on both sides in butter. Add the tomatoes, salt, basil and pepper; bring to a boil. Reduce heat; cover and simmer for 45 minutes.
3. Add green pepper and onion. Cook, covered, 30-45 minutes or until meat and vegetables are tender. Sprinkle with the cheese; cook for 2 minutes or until melted.
1 SERVING: 254 cal., 12g fat (6g sat. fat), 87mg chol., 664mg sod., 7g carb. (3g sugars, 1g fiber), 30g pro.

PIZZA POTATO TOPPERS

Not only is this recipe easy to make, but it's an economical dinner as well. I don't know of a more satisfying way to stretch a half pound of meat!

—Sheila Friedrich, Antelope, MT

TAKES: 25 min.
MAKES: 4 servings

- 4 medium baking potatoes
- ½ lb. ground beef
- ½ cup chopped green pepper
- 1 small onion, chopped
- 1 tomato, chopped
- ½ to ¾ cup pizza sauce
- 1 cup shredded part-skim mozzarella cheese
  Fresh oregano, basil or parsley, optional

1. Prick potatoes with fork; cook in a microwave until tender. Meanwhile, in a large skillet, cook beef and green pepper with onion until meat is no longer pink; drain. Stir in tomato and pizza sauce; heat through.
2. Split potatoes lengthwise; flake potato centers with a fork. Spoon meat mixture onto each potato half; top with mozzarella cheese. Sprinkle with herbs if desired.
1 SERVING: 486 cal., 11g fat (5g sat. fat), 44mg chol., 325mg sod., 74g carb. (10g sugars, 7g fiber), 26g pro.

"I made one with sweet potato as well because my husband prefers sweet potatoes. The whole family enjoyed this, even the teenager."
—SKIMBA, TASTEOFHOME.COM

PIZZA POTATO TOPPERS

BEEF & MUSHROOMS WITH SMASHED POTATOES

HEARTY PITA TACOS

You don't need to skimp on fun and flavor when trying to eat healthy. Our 9-year-old daughter enjoys making these tasty tacos with us—and enjoys eating them even more.
—Jamie Valocchi, Mesa, AZ

TAKES: 30 min. • **MAKES:** 6 servings

- 1 lb. lean ground beef (90% lean)
- 1 small sweet red pepper, chopped
- 2 green onions, chopped
- 1 can (16 oz.) kidney beans, rinsed and drained
- ¾ cup frozen corn
- ⅔ cup taco sauce
- 1 can (2¼ oz.) sliced ripe olives, drained
- ½ tsp. garlic salt
- ¼ tsp. onion powder
- ¼ tsp. dried oregano
- ¼ tsp. paprika
- ¼ tsp. pepper
- 6 whole wheat pita pocket halves
- 6 Tbsp. shredded reduced-fat cheddar cheese
  Sliced avocado and additional taco sauce, optional

1. In a large skillet, cook the beef, red pepper and onions over medium heat until meat is no longer pink; drain. Stir in the beans, corn, taco sauce, olives and seasonings; heat through.
2. Spoon ¾ cup beef mixture into each pita half. Sprinkle with cheese. Serve with avocado and additional taco sauce if desired.

1 SERVING: 339 cal., 10g fat (4g sat. fat), 52mg chol., 787mg sod., 38g carb. (4g sugars, 8g fiber), 26g pro. **DIABETIC EXCHANGES:** 3 lean meat, 2½ starch.

BEEF & MUSHROOMS WITH SMASHED POTATOES

I was inspired to make this after I couldn't stop thinking of a similar dish served in my elementary school cafeteria! It goes together quickly and makes people happy outside the cafeteria, too.
—Ronna Farley, Rockville, MD

TAKES: 30 min.
MAKES: 4 servings

- 1½ lbs. red potatoes (about 6 medium), cut into 1½-in. pieces
- 1 lb. ground beef
- ½ lb. sliced fresh mushrooms
- 1 medium onion, halved and sliced
- 3 Tbsp. all-purpose flour
- ¾ tsp. pepper, divided
- ½ tsp. salt, divided
- 1 can (14½ oz.) beef broth
- 2 Tbsp. butter, softened
- ½ cup half-and-half cream
- ½ cup french-fried onions

1. Place potatoes in a large saucepan; add water to cover. Bring to a boil. Reduce the heat to medium; cook, uncovered, until tender, 10-15 minutes.
2. Meanwhile, in a large skillet, cook and crumble beef with mushrooms and onion over medium-high heat until no longer pink, for 6-8 minutes; drain. Stir in flour, ½ tsp. pepper and ¼ tsp. salt until blended. Gradually stir in broth; bring to a boil. Reduce heat; simmer, uncovered, until thickened, about 5 minutes, stirring occasionally.
3. Drain the potatoes; return to pan. Mash potatoes to desired consistency, adding butter, cream and remaining salt and pepper. Spoon into bowls; top with beef mixture. Sprinkle with fried onions.

1 SERVING: 517 cal., 26g fat (12g sat. fat), 100mg chol., 896mg sod., 40g carb. (5g sugars, 4g fiber), 28g pro.

ORANGE BEEF
LETTUCE WRAPS

ORANGE BEEF LETTUCE WRAPS

This is a lighter version of restaurant fare. I also recommend trying these wraps with ground chicken or turkey.
—Robin Haas, Cranston, RI

PREP: 20 min. • **COOK:** 15 min.
MAKES: 8 servings

SAUCE
- ¼ cup rice vinegar
- 3 Tbsp. water
- 3 Tbsp. orange marmalade
- 1 Tbsp. sugar
- 1 Tbsp. reduced-sodium soy sauce
- 2 garlic cloves, minced
- 1 tsp. Sriracha Asian hot chili sauce

WRAPS
- 1½ lbs. lean ground beef (90% lean)
- 2 garlic cloves, minced
- 2 tsp. minced fresh gingerroot
- ¼ cup reduced-sodium soy sauce
- 2 Tbsp. orange juice
- 1 Tbsp. sugar
- 1 Tbsp. orange marmalade
- ¼ tsp. crushed red pepper flakes
- 2 tsp. cornstarch
- ¼ cup cold water
- 8 Bibb or Boston lettuce leaves
- 2 cups cooked brown rice
- 1 cup shredded carrots
- 3 green onions, thinly sliced

1. In a small bowl, combine sauce ingredients.
2. In a large skillet, cook beef, garlic and ginger over medium heat for 8-10 minutes or until the meat is no longer pink, breaking into crumbles; drain. Stir in the soy sauce, orange juice, sugar, marmalade and pepper flakes. In a small bowl, mix cornstarch and water; stir into pan. Cook and stir 1-2 minutes or until sauce is thickened.
3. Serve in lettuce leaves with rice. Top with carrots and green onions; drizzle with sauce.
1 WRAP: 250 cal., 8g fat (3g sat. fat), 53mg chol., 462mg sod., 26g carb. (11g sugars, 2g fiber), 19g pro. **DIABETIC EXCHANGES:** 2 starch, 2 lean meat.

BARLEY BEEF SKILLET

BARLEY BEEF SKILLET

Even my 3-year-old loves this family favorite. It's satisfying, inexpensive and full with veggies. Spice it up even more with chili powder, cayenne or a dash of hot pepper sauce.
—Kit Tunstall, Boise, ID

PREP: 20 min. • **COOK:** 1 hour
MAKES: 4 servings

- 1 lb. lean ground beef (90% lean)
- ¼ cup chopped onion
- 1 garlic clove, minced
- 1 can (14½ oz.) reduced-sodium beef broth
- 1 can (8 oz.) tomato sauce
- 1 cup water
- 2 small carrots, chopped
- 1 small tomato, seeded and chopped
- 1 small zucchini, chopped
- 1 cup medium pearl barley
- 2 tsp. Italian seasoning
- ¼ tsp. salt
- ⅛ tsp. pepper

In a large skillet, cook beef and onion over medium heat until meat is no longer pink. Add garlic; cook 1 minute longer. Drain. Add the broth, tomato sauce and water; bring to a boil. Stir in the remaining ingredients. Reduce heat; cover and simmer until barley is tender, 45-50 minutes.
1½ CUPS: 400 cal., 10g fat (4g sat. fat), 73mg chol., 682mg sod., 48g carb. (4g sugars, 10g fiber), 30g pro.

"Loved this recipe! To be healthier, substituted ground turkey for ground beef. Also, took the submitter's advice and added some chili powder and Tabasco. Delish! Definitely will make again, probably with more veggies."
—SWANKAIT, TASTEOFHOME.COM

FIESTA RAVIOLI

FIESTA RAVIOLI

These ravioli taste like mini enchiladas.
I serve them with a Mexican-inspired
salad and scoop pineapple sherbet
for dessert.
—Debbie Purdue, Westland, MI

TAKES: 20 min. • **MAKES:** 6 servings

- 1 pkg. (25 oz.) frozen beef ravioli
- 1 can (10 oz.) enchilada sauce
- 1 cup salsa
- 2 cups shredded Monterey
     Jack cheese
- 1 can (2¼ oz.) sliced ripe
     olives, drained

1. Cook ravioli according to package
directions. Meanwhile, in a large
skillet, combine enchilada sauce and
salsa. Cook and stir over medium heat
until heated through.

2. Drain ravioli; add to sauce and gently
stir to coat. Top with cheese and olives.
Cover and cook over low heat for 3-4
minutes or until cheese is melted.
1 SERVING: 470 cal., 20g fat (9g sat. fat),
74mg chol., 1342mg sod., 48g carb. (4g
sugars, 6g fiber), 23g pro.

STEAKS WITH MOLASSES-
GLAZED ONIONS

Steak is our favorite, but I wanted
something a little different using
ingredients I had in the pantry. This
one makes us smile.
—Marie Rizzio, Interlochen, MI

TAKES: 25 min. • **MAKES:** 2 servings

- 2   bacon strips, diced
- 2   beef top sirloin steaks (6 oz. each)
- ½ tsp. salt, divided
- ½ tsp. pepper, divided
- 1   large sweet onion, thinly sliced
- 1½ tsp. balsamic vinegar
- ½ tsp. molasses

1. In a large skillet, cook bacon over
medium heat until crisp. Remove to
paper towels with a slotted spoon;
drain, reserving 1½ tsp. drippings in
skillet and 1½ tsp. drippings in a small
bowl. Set bowl aside.

2. Sprinkle steaks with ¼ tsp. salt and
¼ tsp. pepper. In skillet, cook steaks
over medium heat for 3-4 minutes
on each side or until meat reaches
desired doneness (for medium-rare,
a thermometer should read 135°;
medium, 140°; medium-well, 145°).
Remove and keep warm.

3. Add onion and reserved drippings
to the skillet; saute until tender. Add
vinegar, molasses and remaining salt
and pepper; heat through. Serve
onion mixture with steaks; sprinkle
with bacon.
1 SERVING: 370 cal., 16g fat (6g sat. fat),
82mg chol., 837mg sod., 15g carb. (10g
sugars, 2g fiber), 40g pro.

HAMBURGER STEW

There's nothing fancy to this recipe—
it's just bursting with old-fashioned
goodness and hearty flavor.
—Margery Bryan, Moses Lake, WA

PREP: 15 min. • **COOK:** 55 min.
MAKES: 6-8 servings

- 1 lb. ground beef
- 1 envelope onion soup mix
- 1 can (14½ oz.) diced
     tomatoes, undrained
- 1 cup diced carrot
- 1 cup diced peeled potato
- 1 cup chopped cabbage
- 2 cups frozen corn
- 1 can (16 oz.) cut green beans or
     lima beans, drained
- 1 cup uncooked long grain rice
- 2 cups water or tomato or
     vegetable juice

1. In a large skillet, cook beef over
medium heat until no longer pink;
drain. Stir in soup mix and tomatoes;
simmer, uncovered, for 10 minutes.
Add the carrot, potato, cabbage, corn
and beans. Cover and simmer about
20 minutes.
2. Add rice and water or juice; bring
to a boil. Reduce heat and simmer,
covered, for 20 minutes or until rice
is cooked and vegetables are tender.
1 SERVING: 264 cal., 6g fat (2g sat. fat),
28mg chol., 616mg sod., 39g carb. (5g
sugars, 4g fiber), 15g pro.

EASY BEEF GOULASH

I found this stovetop goulash recipe
several years ago in an old cookbook.
It really hits the spot with home-baked
bread and a dish of cold applesauce.
—Phyllis Pollock, Erie, PA

TAKES: 30 min. • **MAKES:** 6 servings

- 1½ cups uncooked spiral pasta
- 1 lb. boneless beef sirloin steak,
     cut into ⅛-in.-thick strips
- 1 Tbsp. vegetable oil
- 1 medium onion, chopped
- 1 medium green pepper, chopped
- 1 can (14½ oz.) diced
     tomatoes, undrained
- 1½ cups water
- 1 cup reduced-sodium beef broth
- 1½ tsp. red wine vinegar
- 1 to 2 tsp. paprika
- 1 tsp. sugar
- ½ tsp. salt
- ¼ tsp. caraway seeds
- ¼ tsp. pepper
- 2 Tbsp. all-purpose flour
- ¼ cup cold water

1. Cook pasta according to package
directions.
2. In a large nonstick skillet, stir-fry the
beef in oil for 4-5 minutes or until no
longer pink. Add the onion and green
pepper; cook and stir for 2 minutes.
Stir in tomatoes, water, broth, vinegar
and seasonings. Bring to boil. Reduce
heat; cover and simmer for 15 minutes.
3. In a small bowl, combine the flour
and cold water until smooth. Add to
skillet. Bring to a boil; cook and stir
about 2 minutes or until thickened.
Drain the pasta; stir into beef mixture.
1 CUP: 272 cal., 7g fat (2g sat. fat), 45mg
chol., 371mg sod., 29g carb. (0 sugars, 2g
fiber), 22g pro. **DIABETIC EXCHANGES:**
2 starch, 2 lean meat.

HAMBURGER STEW

ORANGE BEEF & BROCCOLI STIR-FRY

I found this marvelous recipe in *The Jamestown Sun*. Sometimes we will substitute venison for beef. Either way, it's sure to please.

—Arly M. Schnabel, Ellendale, ND

TAKES: 30 min. • **MAKES:** 4 servings

- 1 lb. beef top sirloin steak, cut into thin strips
- 4 tsp. soy sauce
- 2 tsp. minced fresh gingerroot
- 1 tsp. finely grated orange zest
- 1 Tbsp. canola oil
- 2 cups fresh broccoli florets
- 1 small sweet red pepper, cut into strips
- ⅔ cup picante sauce
- ½ tsp. sugar, optional
- 1 Tbsp. cornstarch
- ⅓ cup orange juice
- 3 green onions with tops, cut diagonally into 1-in. pieces
  Sliced almonds, optional
  Hot cooked rice

1. Toss meat with soy sauce, ginger and orange zest; set aside for 10 minutes.
2. Heat oil in a wok or large skillet on high. Stir-fry mixture just until meat is no longer pink; remove. Add broccoli, pepper, picante sauce and sugar to skillet. Cover; reduce heat to simmer. Cook until vegetables are crisp-tender, about 3 minutes.
3. Combine cornstarch and orange juice until smooth; add to skillet with meat and onions. Cook and stir for 1 minute or until sauce is thickened. Sprinkle with almonds if desired. Serve with rice.
1 SERVING: 230 cal., 8g fat (2g sat. fat), 46mg chol., 663mg sod., 11g carb. (5g sugars, 2g fiber), 27g pro. **DIABETIC EXCHANGES:** 3 lean meat, 1 vegetable, 1 fat, ½ starch.

CHICKEN-FRIED STEAK & GRAVY

CHICKEN-FRIED STEAK & GRAVY

 As a child, I learned from my grandmother how to make this chicken-fried steak. I taught my own daughters, and when my granddaughters are bigger, I'll show them, too.

—Donna Cater, Fort Ann, NY

TAKES: 30 min. • **MAKES:** 4 servings

- 1¼ cups all-purpose flour, divided
- 2 large eggs
- 1½ cups 2% milk, divided
- 4 beef cube steaks (6 oz. each)
- 1¼ tsp. salt, divided
- 1 tsp. pepper, divided
  Oil for frying
- 1 cup water

1. Place 1 cup flour in a shallow bowl. In a separate shallow bowl, whisk eggs and ½ cup milk until blended. Sprinkle the steaks with ¾ tsp. each salt and pepper. Dip in flour to coat both sides; shake off excess. Dip in egg mixture, then again in flour.
2. In a large skillet, heat ¼ in. oil over medium heat. Add the steaks; cook for 4-6 minutes on each side or until golden brown and a thermometer reads 160°. Remove from pan; drain on paper towels. Keep warm.
3. Remove all but 2 Tbsp. oil from pan. Stir in remaining ¼ cup flour, ½ tsp. salt and ¼ tsp. pepper until smooth; cook and stir over medium heat for 3-4 minutes or until golden brown. Gradually whisk in water and remaining milk. Bring to a boil, stirring constantly; cook and stir 1-2 minutes or until thickened. Serve with steaks.
1 STEAK WITH ⅓ CUP GRAVY: 563 cal., 28g fat (5g sat. fat), 148mg chol., 839mg sod., 29g carb. (4g sugars, 1g fiber), 46g pro.t

GREEN PEPPER STEAK

For a delicious, fast meal, try this flavorful beef dinner loaded with tomatoes and peppers—and all the better if the vegetables are fresh from the garden.

—Emmalee Thomas, Laddonia, MO

TAKES: 30 min. • **MAKES:** 4 servings

- 1 Tbsp. cornstarch
- ¼ cup reduced-sodium soy sauce
- ¼ cup water
- 2 Tbsp. canola oil, divided
- 1 lb. beef top sirloin steak, cut into ¼-in.-thick strips
- 2 small onions, cut into thin wedges
- 2 celery ribs, sliced diagonally
- 1 medium green pepper, cut into 1-in. pieces
- 2 medium tomatoes, cut into wedges
  Hot cooked rice

1. Mix cornstarch, soy sauce and water until smooth. In a large skillet, heat 1 Tbsp. oil over medium-high heat; stir-fry the beef until browned, for 2-3 minutes. Remove from pan.
2. Stir-fry onions, celery and pepper in remaining oil for 3 minutes. Stir the cornstarch mixture; add to pan. Bring to a boil; cook and stir until thickened and bubbly, for 1-2 minutes. Stir in the tomatoes and beef; heat through. Serve with rice.
1 SERVING: 259 cal., 12g fat (2g sat. fat), 46mg chol., 647mg sod., 10g carb. (4g sugars, 2g fiber), 27g pro. **DIABETIC EXCHANGES:** 3 lean meat, 2 vegetable, 1½ fat.

BEEFY BARBECUE MACARONI

I developed this dish while visiting a friend. She came home late from work and didn't have time to grocery shop. I threw together this all-in-one skillet dish using pantry staples. Now she makes it for her family every week.

—Mary Cokenour, Monticello, UT

TAKES: 15 min. • **MAKES:** 4 servings

- ¾ lb. ground beef
- ½ cup chopped onion
- 3 garlic cloves, minced
- 3½ cups cooked elbow macaroni
- ¾ cup barbecue sauce
- ¼ tsp. pepper
  Dash cayenne pepper
- ¼ cup whole milk
- 1 Tbsp. butter
- 1 cup shredded sharp cheddar cheese
  Additional cheddar cheese, optional

1. In a large skillet, cook the beef, onion and garlic over medium heat for 5-6 minutes or until meat is no longer pink, breaking into crumbles; drain. Add the macaroni, barbecue sauce, pepper and cayenne.
2. In a small saucepan, heat milk and butter over medium heat until butter is melted. Stir in cheese until melted. Pour over the macaroni mixture and gently toss to coat. Sprinkle with additional cheese if desired.
1 SERVING: 456 cal., 21g fat (12g sat. fat), 81mg chol., 647mg sod., 39g carb. (9g sugars, 2g fiber), 28g pro.

GREEN PEPPER STEAK

BEEF TENDERLOIN IN MUSHROOM SAUCE

When our kids are visiting Grandma, I make this recipe for just my husband, Derek, and me. It's a recipe that my mother-in-law has been using for more than 30 years. I especially look forward to preparing it as part of a special Valentine's Day menu.
—Denise McNab, Warminster, PA

TAKES: 25 min. • **MAKES:** 2 servings

- 4 Tbsp. butter, divided
- 1 tsp. canola oil
- 2 beef tenderloin steaks (1 in. thick and 4 oz. each)
- 1 cup sliced fresh mushrooms
- 1 Tbsp. chopped green onion
- 1 Tbsp. all-purpose flour
- ⅛ tsp. salt
  Dash pepper
- ⅔ cup chicken or beef broth
- ⅛ tsp. browning sauce, optional

1. In a large skillet, heat 2 Tbsp. butter and oil over medium-high heat; cook the steaks to desired doneness (for medium-rare, a thermometer should read 135°; medium, 140°), 5-6 minutes per side. Remove from pan, reserving drippings; keep warm.
2. In the same pan, heat drippings and remaining butter over medium-high heat; saute the mushrooms and green onion until tender. Stir in flour, salt and pepper until blended; gradually stir in broth and, if desired, browning sauce. Bring to a boil, stirring constantly; cook and stir until thickened, 1-2 minutes. Serve with steaks.

1 SERVING: 417 cal., 32g fat (17g sat. fat), 112mg chol., 659mg sod., 5g carb. (1g sugars, 1g fiber), 26g pro.

"Very good sauce! I actually used cube steak because of cost—beef tenderloin is an expensive cut of meat. The cube steak was tender and the sauce delicious."
—HOMEMADEWITHLOVE, TASTEOFHOME.COM

FANTASTIC BEEF FAJITAS

The first time I made these beef fajitas, my family couldn't get enough, and the next time I made a double batch for everyone. With their colorful pepper and avocado, these would be good choice for entertaining.
—Marla Brenneman, Goshen, IN

PREP: 15 min. + marinating
COOK: 10 min. • **MAKES:** 4 servings

- 1 lb. beef top sirloin steak or flank steak, trimmed and cut against the grain into ¼-in. strips

MARINADE
- 3 Tbsp. canola oil
- 2 Tbsp. lemon juice
- 1 tsp. dried oregano
- 1 garlic clove, minced
- ¼ tsp. salt
- ¼ tsp. pepper

FAJITAS
- ½ medium onion, sliced
- 1 medium sweet red pepper, sliced into thin strips
- 2 Tbsp. canola oil, divided
- 8 flour tortilla shells, warmed
- 2 avocados, peeled and sliced
  Salsa
  Sour cream

1. In a large resealable bag, combine marinade ingredients; add beef. Seal bag and refrigerate for 3-6 hours or overnight, turning several times.
2. Discard marinade. In a skillet, saute onion and pepper in 1 Tbsp. oil until crisp tender; remove from pan. Add remaining oil and saute meat until no longer pink, about 4 minutes. Add the vegetables to pan and heat through.
3. To assemble, place a spoonful of meat and vegetable mixture on a warmed tortilla and top with avocado, salsa and sour cream. Roll the tortilla around filling.

2 FAJITAS: 731 cal., 38g fat (6g sat. fat), 46mg chol., 674mg sod., 64g carb. (2g sugars, 9g fiber), 35g pro.

BEEF TENDERLOIN IN MUSHROOM SAUCE

BEEFY RED PEPPER PASTA

Filled with veggies and gooey with cheese, this hearty one-dish meal will warm the whole family to their toes! Pureed roasted red peppers add zing and color to the sauce.
—Marge Werner, Broken Arrow, OK

PREP: 20 min. • **COOK:** 25 min.
MAKES: 6 servings

- 1 jar (12 oz.) roasted sweet red peppers, drained
- 1 lb. lean ground beef (90% lean)
- 1 small onion, chopped
- 1 can (14½ oz.) diced tomatoes, undrained
- 2 garlic cloves, minced
- 1 tsp. dried oregano
- 1 tsp. dried basil
- ¾ tsp. salt
- 8 oz. uncooked ziti or small tube pasta
- 1½ cups cut fresh green beans
- 1½ cups shredded part-skim mozzarella cheese

1. Place peppers in a food processor; cover and process until smooth. In a large skillet, cook beef and onion until meat is no longer pink; drain. Stir in the pepper puree, tomatoes, garlic, oregano, basil and salt. Bring to a boil. Reduce heat; simmer, uncovered, for 15 minutes.
2. Meanwhile, in a Dutch oven, cook pasta according to package directions, adding green beans during the last 5 minutes of cooking. Cook until pasta and green beans are tender; drain. Stir in meat sauce. Sprinkle with cheese; stir until melted.
1⅔ CUPS: 362 cal., 11g fat (5g sat. fat), 53mg chol., 739mg sod., 38g carb. (7g sugars, 4g fiber), 28g pro. **DIABETIC EXCHANGES:** 3 lean meat, 2 starch, 1 vegetable.

CHUCK WAGON TORTILLA STACK

I make this skillet specialty on nights when I'm craving southwestern fare. It's easy to cut and remove the slices from the pan.
—Bernice Janowski, Stevens Point, WI

PREP: 15 min. • **COOK:** 40 min.
MAKES: 6 servings

- 1 lb. ground beef
- 2 to 3 garlic cloves, minced
- 1 can (16 oz.) baked beans
- 1 can (14½ oz.) stewed tomatoes, undrained
- 1 can (11 oz.) whole kernel corn, drained
- 1 can (4 oz.) chopped green chilies
- ¼ cup barbecue sauce
- 4½ tsp. chili powder
- 1½ tsp. ground cumin
- 4 flour tortillas (10 in.)
- 1⅓ cups shredded pepper jack cheese

Shredded lettuce, chopped red onion, sour cream and chopped tomatoes, optional

1. In a large skillet, cook beef until meat is no longer pink; drain. Add the garlic, beans, tomatoes, corn, chilies, barbecue sauce, chili powder and cumin. Bring to a boil. Reduce heat; simmer, uncovered, for 10-12 minutes or until liquid is reduced.
2. Coat a large deep skillet with cooking spray. Place one tortilla in skillet; spread with 1½ cups meat mixture. Sprinkle with ⅓ cup cheese. Repeat layers three times. Cover and cook on low for 15 minutes or until cheese is melted and tortillas are heated through. Cut into wedges. Serve with toppings of your choice.
1 SLICE: 539 cal., 23g fat (10g sat. fat), 79mg chol., 1383mg sod., 56g carb. (12g sugars, 9g fiber), 30g pro.

CHUCK WAGON
TORTILLA STACK

POTATO-TOPPED GROUND BEEF SKILLET

3. Meanwhile, place potatoes in a large saucepan; add water to cover. Bring to a boil. Reduce heat; cook, uncovered, until tender, for 10-12 minutes. Drain; cool slightly.

4. Preheat broiler. Arrange potatoes over the stew, overlapping slightly; brush lightly with oil. Sprinkle with salt and pepper, then cheese. Broil 5-6 in. from heat until the potatoes are lightly browned, 6-8 minutes. Let stand for 5 minutes. If desired, sprinkle the top with parsley.

1¼ CUPS: 313 cal., 14g fat (5g sat. fat), 74mg chol., 459mg sod., 18g carb. (4g sugars, 3g fiber), 26g pro. **DIABETIC EXCHANGES:** 3 lean meat, 1 vegetable, ½ starch, ½ fat.

SKILLET STEAK & CORN

This skillet dish combines canned vegetables and meat in a savory sauce. The thin strips of steak cook up in minutes. If you like, substitute slices of chicken breast for the steak.
—Ruth Taylor, Greeneville, TN

PREP: 10 min. • **COOK:** 30 min.
MAKES: 4 servings

- 1 lb. boneless beef top round steak, cut into strips
- 1 medium onion, cut into ¼-in. wedges
- ½ tsp. dried thyme
- 2 Tbsp. canola oil
- ¾ cup red wine or beef broth
- 1 can (14½ oz.) diced tomatoes, undrained
- 2 cans (11 oz. each) Mexicorn, drained
  Hot cooked rice

In a large skillet, cook steak, onion and thyme over medium-high heat in oil until meat is no longer pink; drain. Add wine; simmer, uncovered, for 10 minutes or until the liquid has evaporated. Stir in tomatoes; cover and simmer 15 minutes longer. Add corn and heat through. Serve with rice.

1 SERVING: 386 cal., 12g fat (0 sat. fat), 70mg chol., 975mg sod., 36g carb. (0 sugars, 0 fiber), 32g pro.

POTATO-TOPPED GROUND BEEF SKILLET

The depth of flavor in this recipe is amazing. I love recipes that I can cook and serve in the same skillet, including for potlucks. Coarsely ground beef for chili lends an extra-meaty texture.
—Fay Moreland, Wichita Falls, TX

PREP: 25 min.
COOK: 45 min.
MAKES: 8 servings

- 2 lbs. lean ground beef (90% lean)
- ½ tsp. salt
- ¼ tsp. pepper
- 1 Tbsp. olive oil
- 1 large onion, chopped
- 4 medium carrots, sliced
- ½ pound sliced fresh mushrooms
- 4 garlic cloves, minced
- 2 Tbsp. all-purpose flour
- 2 tsp. herbes de Provence
- 1¼ cups dry red wine or reduced-sodium beef broth
- 1 can (14½ oz.) reduced-sodium beef broth

TOPPING
- 1¼ lbs. red potatoes (about 4 medium), cut into ¼-in. slices
- 1 Tbsp. olive oil
- ¼ tsp. salt
- ⅛ tsp. pepper
- ⅓ cup shredded Parmesan cheese
  Minced fresh parsley, optional

1. In a broiler-safe 12-in. skillet, cook and crumble beef over medium-high heat until no longer pink, 6-8 minutes. Stir in salt and pepper; remove from the pan.

2. In the same pan, heat oil over medium-high heat; saute the onion, carrots, mushrooms and garlic until onion is tender, 4-6 minutes. Stir in flour and herbs; cook 1 minute. Stir in wine; bring to a boil. Cook for 1 minute, stirring to loosen browned bits from pan. Add beef and beef broth; return to a boil. Reduce the heat; simmer, covered, until flavors are blended, about 30 minutes, stirring occasionally. Remove from the heat.

ARTICHOKE
BEEF STEAKS

CILANTRO BEEF TACOS

When I have leftover steak, it's time to make tacos. Set out bowls of lettuce, tomatoes, sour cream, avocado and salsa for topping. That's a fiesta!
—Patti Rose, Tinley Park, IL

TAKES: 30 min. • **MAKES:** 4 servings

- 1   beef flank steak (1 lb.)
- ½   tsp. salt
- ¼   tsp. pepper
- 4   tsp. olive oil, divided
- 1   medium onion, halved and sliced
- 1   jalapeno pepper, seeded and finely chopped
- 1   garlic clove, minced
- ½   cup salsa
- ¼   cup minced fresh cilantro
- 2   tsp. lime juice
     Dash hot pepper sauce
- 8   flour tortillas (6 in.), warmed
     Optional toppings: salsa, cilantro, shredded lettuce and sour cream

1. Sprinkle steak with salt and pepper. In a large skillet, heat 2 tsp. oil over medium-high heat. Add steak; cook for 5-7 minutes on each side or until meat reaches desired doneness (for medium-rare, a thermometer should read 135°; medium, 140°; medium-well, 145°). Remove from pan.
2. In same skillet, heat remaining oil over medium heat. Add onion; cook and stir 4-5 minutes or until tender. Add jalapeno and garlic; cook about 2 minutes longer. Stir in the salsa, cilantro, lime juice and pepper sauce; heat through.
3. Thinly slice steak across the grain; stir into onion mixture. Serve in tortillas; top as desired.
NOTE: Wear disposable gloves when cutting hot peppers; the oils can burn skin. Avoid touching your face.
2 TACOS: 451 cal., 20g fat (7g sat. fat), 54mg chol., 884mg sod., 38g carb. (3g sugars, 4g fiber), 27g pro.

ARTICHOKE BEEF STEAKS

Light green artichokes and vibrant pimientos dress up these delectable steaks. If weather permits, grill the steaks outside and prepare the topping in a skillet as directed.
—*Taste of Home* Test Kitchen

TAKES: 25 min. • **MAKES:** 4 servings

- 1   jar (6½ oz.) marinated artichoke hearts
- 4   beef ribeye steaks (¾ in. thick and about 8 oz. each)
- ½   tsp. salt
- 2   Tbsp. butter
- 1   small onion, sliced and separated into rings
- 1   garlic clove, minced
- 1   jar (2 oz.) sliced pimientos, drained

1. Drain artichokes, reserving 1 Tbsp. marinade. Coarsely chop artichokes; set aside. Sprinkle steaks with salt.
2. In a large skillet, cook steaks in butter over medium-high heat for 3 minutes on each side or until the meat reaches desired doneness (for medium-rare, a thermometer should read 135°; medium, 140°; medium-well, 145°). Remove the steaks to a serving platter; keep warm.
3. In same skillet, saute onion and garlic in reserved marinade about 3 minutes. Add the artichokes and pimientos; heat through. Serve with ribeye steaks.
1 SERVING: 631 cal., 49g fat (20g sat. fat), 150mg chol., 618mg sod., 5g carb. (1g sugars, 1g fiber), 41g pro.

CILANTRO
BEEF TACOS

MINI CHEESE
MEAT LOAVES

MINI CHEESE MEAT LOAVES

Here's a stovetop recipe for meatloaf just as tasty as traditional meatloaf— and no long wait for oven-baking.
—Betty Claycomb, Alverton, PA

PREP: 20 min. • **COOK:** 25 min.
MAKES: 6 servings

- 1   large egg, beaten
- 1   cup soft bread cubes
- ¼   cup whole milk
- 1½ tsp. onion salt
- 1   tsp. dried parsley flakes
      Dash pepper
- 1½ lbs. lean ground beef (90% lean)
- 6   sticks (2½x½ in. each) cheddar or mozzarella cheese

SAUCE

- 2   cans (15 oz. each) tomato sauce
- ½   cup chopped onion
- 1   Tbsp. dried parsley flakes
- ½   tsp. dried oregano
- ¼   tsp. garlic salt

1. In a bowl, combine egg, bread, milk and seasonings. Mix in beef. Divide into six portions. Shape each portion around a cheese stick and form into a loaf. Set aside.
2. In a large skillet, combine all sauce ingredients. Add loaves and spoon sauce over each. Cover and bring to a boil. Reduce heat to simmer; cook until a thermometer reads 160°, about 20 minutes.

1 SERVING: 342 cal., 19g fat (10g sat. fat), 122mg chol., 1152mg sod., 9g carb. (3g sugars, 1g fiber), 32g pro.

"I gave this recipe to my two sons to make as they need simple meals to cook. They and their friends LOVED it. In fact, they said it might be their new favorite recipe."
—DTALLMAN, TASTEOFHOME.COM

SKILLET BBQ BEEF POTPIE

Beef potpie is a classic comfort food, but who has time to see it through? This version is not only speedy but uses up leftover stuffing.
—Priscilla Yee, Concord, CA

TAKES: 25 min. • **MAKES:** 4 servings

- 1 lb. lean ground beef (90% lean)
- ⅓ cup thinly sliced green onions, divided
- 2 cups frozen mixed vegetables, thawed
- ½ cup salsa
- ½ cup barbecue sauce
- 3 cups cooked cornbread stuffing
- ½ cup shredded cheddar cheese
- ¼ cup chopped sweet red pepper

1. In a large skillet, cook beef and ¼ cup green onions over medium heat 6-8 minutes or until beef is no longer pink, breaking into crumbles; drain. Stir in mixed vegetables, salsa and barbecue sauce; cook, covered, over medium-low heat 4-5 minutes or until heated through.

2. Layer cornbread stuffing over the beef; sprinkle with cheese, pepper and remaining green onion. Cook, covered, 3-5 minutes longer or until heated through and cheese is melted.

1½ CUPS: 634 cal., 27g fat (9g sat. fat), 85mg chol., 1372mg sod., 62g carb. (19g sugars, 9g fiber), 33g pro.

HAMBURGER STEAKS WITH MUSHROOM GRAVY

Cozy up to a meat-and-potatoes meal that no one will want to miss.
—Denise Wheeler, Newaygo, MI

TAKES: 25 min. • **MAKES:** 4 servings

- 1 large egg
- ½ cup dry bread crumbs
- 1 envelope onion soup mix, divided
  Dash pepper
- 1 lb. ground beef
- 3 Tbsp. all-purpose flour
- 1¾ cups cold water
- 1 tsp. Worcestershire sauce
- 1 jar (4½ oz.) whole mushrooms, drained
  Hot cooked mashed potatoes

1. In a large bowl, combine the egg, bread crumbs, 2 Tbsp. soup mix and pepper. Crumble beef over mixture and mix well. Shape into four patties.

2. In a large skillet, cook patties over medium heat for 4-5 minutes on each side or until a thermometer reads 160° and juices run clear. Set aside and keep warm.

3. Stir flour, water, Worcestershire sauce and remaining soup mix until blended; stir into skillet. Add whole mushrooms. Bring to a boil; cook and stir for 5 minutes or until thickened. Serve with hamburger steak patties and mashed potatoes.

1 SERVING: 325 cal., 15g fat (6g sat. fat), 123mg chol., 920mg sod., 20g carb. (2g sugars, 2g fiber), 25g pro.

SKILLET BBQ BEEF POTPIE

EASY MEATBALL STROGANOFF

MUSHROOM PEPPER STEAK

Pick this one for a stir-fry with lots of fresh veggies and rich flavor. It's perfect over rice.

—Billie Moss, Walnut Creek, CA

PREP: 15 min. + marinating
COOK: 15 min. • **MAKES:** 4 servings

- 6 Tbsp. reduced-sodium soy sauce, divided
- ⅛ tsp. pepper
- 1 lb. beef top sirloin steak, cut into thin strips
- 1 Tbsp. cornstarch
- ½ cup reduced-sodium beef broth
- 1 garlic clove, minced
- ½ tsp. minced fresh gingerroot
- 3 tsp. canola oil, divided
- 1 cup julienned sweet red pepper
- 1 cup julienned green pepper
- 2 cups sliced fresh mushrooms
- 2 medium tomatoes, cut into wedges
- 6 green onions, sliced
  Hot cooked rice, optional

1. In a large resealable plastic bag, combine 3 Tbsp. soy sauce and pepper; add beef. Seal bag and turn to coat the meat; refrigerate for 30-60 minutes. In a small bowl, combine the cornstarch, broth and remaining soy sauce until smooth; set aside.
2. Drain and discard marinade from beef. In a large nonstick skillet or wok, stir-fry the garlic and ginger in 2 tsp. oil for 1 minute. Add the beef; stir-fry for 4-6 minutes or until no longer pink. Remove beef and keep warm.
3. Stir-fry the peppers in remaining oil for 1 minute. Add mushrooms; stir-fry 2 minutes longer or until peppers are crisp-tender. Stir the broth mixture and add to vegetable mixture. Bring to a boil; cook and stir for 2 minutes or until thickened. Return beef to pan; add tomatoes and onions. Cook about 2 minutes or until heated through. Serve over rice if desired.
1 SERVING: 241 cal., 10g fat (3g sat. fat), 64mg chol., 841mg sod., 13g carb. (5g sugars, 3g fiber), 25g pro. **DIABETIC EXCHANGES:** 3 lean meat, 2 vegetable, 1 fat.

EASY MEATBALL STROGANOFF

This recipe has fed not only my own family but many neighborhood kids! It's a reliable supper you can throw together after work on a busy day.

—Julie May, Hattiesburg, MS

TAKES: 30 min.
MAKES: 4 servings

- 3 cups uncooked egg noodles
- 1 Tbsp. olive oil
- 1 pkg. (12 oz.) frozen fully cooked Italian meatballs, thawed
- 1½ cups beef broth
- 1 tsp. dried parsley flakes
- ¾ tsp. dried basil
- ½ tsp. salt
- ½ tsp. dried oregano
- ¼ tsp. pepper
- 1 cup heavy whipping cream
- ¾ cup sour cream

1. Cook the egg noodles according to package directions for al dente; drain.
2. Meanwhile, in a large skillet, heat oil over medium-high heat. Brown the meatballs; remove from pan. Add the broth, stirring to loosen browned bits from pan. Add seasonings. Bring to a boil; cook 5-7 minutes or until liquid is reduced to ½ cup.
3. Add meatballs, noodles and cream. Bring to a boil. Reduce heat; simmer, covered, 3-5 minutes or until slightly thickened. Stir in the sour cream and heat through.
1 SERVING: 717 cal., 57g fat (30g sat. fat), 172mg chol., 1291mg sod., 31g carb. (5g sugars, 2g fiber), 20g pro.

MUSHROOM
PEPPER STEAK

Poultry

TURKEY A LA KING

TURKEY A LA KING
This is a smart way to use up leftover turkey. You might want to make a double batch!
—Mary Gaylord, Balsam Lake, WI

TAKES: 25 min. • **MAKES:** 6 servings

- 1 medium onion, chopped
- ¾ cup sliced celery
- ¼ cup diced green pepper
- ¼ cup butter, cubed
- ¼ cup all-purpose flour
- 1 tsp. sugar
- 1½ cups chicken broth
- ¼ cup half-and-half cream
- 3 cups cubed cooked turkey or chicken
- 1 can (4 oz.) sliced mushrooms, drained
- 6 slices bread, toasted

1. In a large skillet, saute the onion, celery and green pepper in butter until tender. Stir in flour and sugar until a paste forms.
2. Gradually stir in broth. Bring to a boil; boil 1 minute or until thickened. Reduce heat. Add the cream, turkey and mushrooms; heat through. Serve with toast.
1 SERVING: 297 cal., 13g fat (7g sat. fat), 98mg chol., 591mg sod., 21g carb. (4g sugars, 2g fiber), 24g pro.

DID YOU KNOW?
The term "a la king" applies to any variety of dishes—usually chicken or turkey—served in a cream sauce with mushrooms and either pimientos or green peppers.

CHICKEN & SPANISH CAULIFLOWER "RICE"

SPICY TURKEY TACOS

So easy, so healthy and so good—I love these whenever I'm in the mood for a little Mexican food. With a hint of cinnamon, these tacos have an unusual blend of seasonings that's exotic and mouthwatering.
—Kendra Doss, Colorado Springs, CO

TAKES: 25 min. • **MAKES:** 4 servings

- 8 taco shells
- 1 lb. extra-lean ground turkey
- 1 small red onion, finely chopped
- 1 cup salsa
- ½ tsp. dried oregano
- ½ tsp. paprika
- ½ tsp. ground cinnamon
- ½ tsp. ground cumin
- 2 cups shredded lettuce
- ½ cup shredded pepper jack cheese
- ¼ cup fat-free sour cream
    Cubed avocado and additional salsa, optional

1. Heat taco shells according to package directions.
2. Meanwhile, in a large nonstick skillet, cook turkey and onion over medium heat until meat is no longer pink. Stir in salsa and spices; heat through.
3. To serve, fill each taco shell with ⅓ cup turkey mixture. Serve with lettuce, cheese, sour cream and, if desired, optional ingredients.
FREEZE OPTION: Freeze cooled meat mixture in freezer containers for up to 3 months. To use, partially thaw in refrigerator overnight. Heat through in a saucepan, stirring occasionally and adding a little water if necessary. Serve as directed.
2 TACOS: 324 cal., 11g fat (4g sat. fat), 63mg chol., 502mg sod., 23g carb. (4g sugars, 2g fiber), 35g pro. **DIABETIC EXCHANGES:** 4 lean meat, 1 starch, 1 vegetable, 1 fat.

CHICKEN & SPANISH CAULIFLOWER "RICE"

I learned about the paleo diet from some friends who now have tons of energy and are super fit. Since then, I've changed my eating habits, too. Everyone from my dad to my little nephew loves this riced cauliflower.
—Megan Schmoldt, Westminster, CO

TAKES: 30 min. • **MAKES:** 4 servings

- 1 large head cauliflower
- 1 lb. boneless skinless chicken breasts, cut into ½-in. cubes
- ½ tsp. salt
- ½ tsp. pepper
- 1 Tbsp. canola oil
- 1 medium green pepper, chopped
- 1 small onion, chopped
- 1 garlic clove, minced
- ½ cup tomato juice
- ¼ tsp. ground cumin
- ¼ cup chopped fresh cilantro
- 1 Tbsp. lime juice

1. Core and cut cauliflower into 1-in. pieces. In batches, pulse cauliflower in a food processor until it resembles rice (do not overprocess).
2. Toss chicken with salt and pepper. In a large skillet, heat oil over medium-high heat; saute chicken until lightly browned, about 5 minutes. Add green pepper, onion and garlic; cook and stir 3 minutes.
3. Stir in tomato juice and cumin; bring to a boil. Add cauliflower; cook, covered, over medium heat until cauliflower is tender, 7-10 minutes, stirring occasionally. Stir in cilantro and lime juice.
1½ CUPS: 227 cal., 7g fat (1g sat. fat), 63mg chol., 492mg sod., 15g carb. (6g sugars, 5g fiber), 28g pro. **DIABETIC EXCHANGES:** 3 lean meat, 1 starch, ½ fat.

HEALTHY CHICKEN STROGANOFF

When I prepare this meal, I often tell people it's beef Stroganoff. Because of its convincing appearance and taste, they're surprised when I later reveal that it's actually chicken.
—Lori Borrowman, Schenectady, NY

TAKES: 30 min. • **MAKES:** 6 servings

- 1 lb. fresh mushrooms, sliced
- 1 large onion, chopped
- 2 Tbsp. butter
- 1½ lbs. boneless skinless chicken breasts, cut into 2-in. strips
- ¼ cup browning sauce
- 1⅓ cups reduced-sodium beef broth, divided
- 1 cup white wine or additional reduced-sodium beef broth
- 2 Tbsp. ketchup
- 2 garlic cloves, minced
- 1 tsp. salt
- 3 Tbsp. all-purpose flour
- 1 cup (8 oz.) fat-free sour cream
- 6 cups cooked no-yolk noodles

1. In a large nonstick skillet, saute mushrooms and onion in butter until tender. Remove and set aside. In the same skillet, cook the chicken with browning sauce until browned. Add 1 cup broth, wine, ketchup, garlic and salt. Bring to a boil. Reduce heat; cover and simmer chicken for 15 minutes or until no longer pink.

2. Combine flour and remaining ⅓ cup broth until smooth; stir into chicken mixture. Add reserved mushroom mixture. Bring to a boil; cook and stir for 2 minutes or until thickened. Reduce heat to low. Stir in the sour cream; heat through (do not boil). Serve over noodles.

1 CUP: 535 cal., 7g fat (3g sat. fat), 80mg chol., 1339mg sod., 66g carb. (0 sugars, 4g fiber), 41g pro.

TURKEY THYME RISOTTO

EAT SMART

TURKEY THYME RISOTTO

This satisfying risotto is a wonderful way to reinvent leftover turkey. I use Romano cheese, garlic and plenty of fresh mushrooms to create it.
—Sunny McDaniel, Cary, NC

PREP: 10 min. • **COOK:** 35 min.
MAKES: 4 servings

- 2¾ to 3¼ cups reduced-sodium chicken broth
- 1 Tbsp. olive oil
- 2 cups sliced fresh mushrooms
- 1 small onion, chopped
- 1 garlic clove, minced
- 1 cup uncooked arborio rice
- 1 tsp. minced fresh thyme or ¼ tsp. dried thyme
- ½ cup white wine or additional broth
- 1½ cups cubed cooked turkey breast
- 2 Tbsp. shredded Romano cheese
- ¼ tsp. salt
- ¼ tsp. pepper

1. In a small saucepan, bring broth to a simmer; keep hot. In a large nonstick skillet, heat oil over medium-high heat; saute mushrooms, onion and garlic until tender, about 3 minutes. Add rice and thyme; cook and stir 2 minutes.

2. Stir in wine. Reduce heat to maintain a simmer; cook and stir until wine is absorbed. Add hot broth, ½ cup at a time, cooking and stirring until the broth has been absorbed after each addition, rice is tender but firm to the bite, and risotto is creamy. (This will take about 20 minutes.)

3. Add the remaining ingredients; cook and stir until heated through. Serve immediately.

1 CUP: 337 cal., 6g fat (2g sat. fat), 43mg chol., 651mg sod., 44g carb. (2g sugars, 1g fiber), 24g pro. **DIABETIC EXCHANGES:** 3 starch, 2 lean meat, ½ fat.

SMOTHERED CHICKEN BREASTS

After trying this chicken dish in a restaurant, I decided to re-create it at home. Topped with bacon, caramelized onions and zippy shredded cheese, it comes together in no time with ingredients I usually have on hand. Plus, it cooks in one skillet, so it's a cinch to clean up!
—Brenda Carpenter, Warrensburg, MO

TAKES: 30 min. • **MAKES:** 4 servings

- 4 boneless skinless chicken breast halves (6 oz. each)
- ¼ tsp. salt
- ¼ tsp. lemon-pepper seasoning
- 1 Tbsp. canola oil
- 8 bacon strips
- 1 medium onion, sliced
- ¼ cup packed brown sugar
- ½ cup shredded Colby-Monterey Jack cheese

1. Sprinkle chicken with salt and lemon pepper. In a large skillet, heat oil over medium heat; cook chicken until a thermometer reads 165°, 6-8 minutes per side. Remove from the pan and keep warm.
2. In same skillet, cook bacon over medium heat until crisp. Remove bacon to paper towels; pour off all but 2 Tbsp. drippings.
3. In drippings, saute onion with brown sugar over medium heat until tender and golden brown. Top chicken with bacon, onion mixture and cheese.
1 SERVING: 560 cal., 34g fat (12g sat. fat), 143mg chol., 710mg sod., 17g carb. (15g sugars, 0 fiber), 45g pro.

CHICKEN BREASTS WITH MELON RELISH

The topping is sweet and very flavorful in this tropical-tasting melon relish recipe. It tastes so good with the tender chicken breasts. Here is a perfect recipe for summer.
—Roxanne Chan, Albany, CA

TAKES: 30 min. • **MAKES:** 4 servings

- ¼ tsp. salt
- ¼ tsp. ground ginger
- ¼ tsp. ground nutmeg
- ¼ tsp. pepper
- 4 boneless skinless chicken breast halves (6 oz. each)
- 1 Tbsp. canola oil

RELISH
- 1 cup diced cantaloupe
- ¼ cup finely chopped celery
- 1 green onion, chopped
- 2 Tbsp. minced fresh mint
- 1 Tbsp. chopped crystallized ginger
- 1 Tbsp. lime juice
- 1 Tbsp. honey
- ½ tsp. grated lime peel

1. In a small bowl, combine the salt, ginger, nutmeg and pepper. Rub over both sides of chicken. In a large skillet, cook chicken in oil over medium heat until a thermometer inserted in chicken reads 165°, 6-8 minutes on each side.
2. Meanwhile, in a small bowl, combine relish ingredients. Serve with chicken.
1 SERVING: 260 cal., 8g fat (2g sat. fat), 94mg chol., 243mg sod., 12g carb. (9g sugars, 1g fiber), 35g pro. **DIABETIC EXCHANGES:** 4 lean meat, 1 starch, ½ fat.

SMOTHERED CHICKEN BREASTS

CONFETTI KIELBASA SKILLET

Here's one of my husband's favorite dishes. When it's in season, substitute fresh corn for frozen. Add a dash of cayenne pepper if you like a little heat.
—Sheila Gomez, Shawnee, KS

TAKES: 30 min. • **MAKES:** 4 servings

- 1   Tbsp. canola oil
- 7   oz. smoked turkey kielbasa, cut into ¼-in. slices
- 1   medium onion, halved and sliced
- ½   cup sliced baby portobello mushrooms
- 2   garlic cloves, minced
- ½   cup reduced-sodium chicken broth
- ¾   tsp. Mrs. Dash Garlic & Herb seasoning blend
- 1   can (15 oz.) no-salt-added black beans, rinsed and drained
- 1   pkg. (8.8 oz.) ready-to-serve brown rice
- 1   cup frozen corn
- ½   cup chopped roasted sweet red peppers
- 4   tsp. minced fresh cilantro

1. In a large skillet, heat oil over medium-high heat. Add kielbasa, onion and mushrooms; cook and stir 4-6 minutes or until the vegetables are tender. Add the garlic; cook 1 minute longer.

2. Add broth and seasoning blend, stirring to loosen browned bits from pan. Bring to a boil; cook 2-3 minutes or until liquid is almost evaporated. Stir in the remaining ingredients and heat through.

1¼ CUPS: 347 cal., 9g fat (1g sat. fat), 31mg chol., 692mg sod., 45g carb. (4g sugars, 7g fiber), 18g pro. **DIABETIC EXCHANGES:** 3 starch, 2 lean meat, ½ fat.

TURKEY-CRANBERRY MONTE CRISTO

TURKEY-CRANBERRY MONTE CRISTO

Every year, my husband and I look forward to Thanksgiving leftovers just so we can make this sandwich. Once you try it, I'm sure you will agree that this is the best turkey sandwich ever!
—Cleo Gonske, Redding, CA

TAKES: 30 min. • **MAKES:** 4 servings

- 8   slices egg bread
- 3   Tbsp. Dijon mustard
- 10 oz. thinly sliced cooked turkey
- 6   oz. smoked Gouda cheese, thinly sliced
- ½   cup whole-berry cranberry sauce
- 3   large eggs
- ⅓   cup 2% milk
- ¼   tsp. salt
- ¼   tsp. pepper
- 3   tsp. butter
- 3   tsp. canola oil

1. Preheat oven to 350°. Spread four slices of bread with mustard. Layer with the turkey and cheese. Spread remaining bread with cranberry sauce; place on cheese.

2. In a shallow bowl, whisk eggs, milk, salt and pepper. In a large skillet, heat 1½ tsp. each butter and oil over medium heat until butter is melted. Dip two sandwiches in egg mixture; add to the skillet. Cook until golden brown, 2-3 minutes per side. Repeat with the remaining butter, oil and sandwiches.

3. Transfer sandwiches to a baking sheet. Bake until cheese is melted, 4-5 minutes.

1 SANDWICH: 674 cal., 30g fat (13g sat. fat), 297mg chol., 1282mg sod., 56g carb. (12g sugars, 2g fiber), 44g pro.

CHORIZO BURRITO BOWLS

I'm always on the hunt for fast and filling meals. Chicken sausage makes an awesome one-dish dinner by itself or served with brown rice in a burrito.

—Elisabeth Larsen, Pleasant Grove, UT

TAKES: 25 min. • **MAKES:** 4 servings

- 2 tsp. canola oil
- 1 pkg. (12 oz.) fully cooked jalapeno or chorizo chicken sausage links, sliced
- 1 medium onion, chopped
- 1 can (15 oz.) no-salt-added black beans, rinsed and drained
- 1 can (10 oz.) diced tomatoes and green chilies, undrained
- 1 cup fresh or frozen corn
- 1 pkg. (8.8 oz.) ready-to-serve brown rice
- 2 cups fresh baby spinach
- ¼ cup crumbled queso fresco or shredded Monterey Jack cheese
  Chopped fresh cilantro

1. In a large skillet, heat oil over medium heat. Add sausage; cook and stir until lightly browned. Remove from pan.
2. Add onion to same skillet; cook and stir 3-5 minutes or until tender. Stir in beans, tomatoes, corn and sausage; bring to a boil. Reduce heat; simmer, uncovered, 5 minutes. Stir in rice and spinach; cook 2-3 minutes or until heated through and spinach is wilted. Sprinkle with cheese and cilantro.

1⅓ CUPS: 425 cal., 14g fat (3g sat. fat), 70mg chol., 1275mg sod., 52g carb. (7g sugars, 8g fiber), 27g pro.

CHORIZO BURRITO BOWLS

TORTILLA CRUNCH TURKEY CUTLETS

I was inspired to create more southwestern-flavored foods from our travels the region. This is a creative way to use leftover chips and salsa. You can substitute chicken cutlets for the turkey if you like.

—Lisa Varner, El Paso, TX

TAKES: 25 min. • **MAKES:** 4 servings

- 2 large eggs
- 2 Tbsp. water
- 3 tsp. ground cumin
- 1 tsp. garlic salt
- ½ tsp. pepper
- 1¾ cups crushed tortilla chips
- 1 pkg. (17.6 oz.) turkey breast cutlets
- 2 Tbsp. canola oil
- ½ cup pico de gallo
  Sour cream and chopped fresh cilantro, optional

1. In a shallow bowl, whisk together first five ingredients. Place crushed chips in another shallow bowl. Dip cutlets in egg mixture, then in chips, pressing to help adhere.
2. In a large skillet, heat oil over medium-high heat. In batches, cook turkey cutlets until golden brown, 2-3 minutes per side. Serve with pico de gallo and, if desired, sour cream and cilantro.

1 SERVING: 343 cal., 15g fat (2g sat. fat), 136mg chol., 603mg sod., 17g carb. (1g sugars, 1g fiber), 34g pro.

**SOUTHWEST
TURKEY BURGERS**

SOUTHWEST TURKEY BURGERS

I made these turkey burgers with corn, green chilies and taco spice for my parents. They originally weren't sold on an untraditional burger, but they absolutely loved them! People gobble up these burgers every time.

—Katie Ring, Menasha, WI

TAKES: 30 min. • **MAKES:** 6 servings

- ½ cup seasoned bread crumbs
- ½ cup frozen corn, thawed
- 1 can (4 oz.) chopped green chilies
- 1 Tbsp. reduced-sodium taco seasoning
- 1 lb. lean ground turkey
- 6 whole wheat hamburger buns, split
- 6 wedges The Laughing Cow queso fresco chipotle cheese, halved
  Lettuce leaves, optional

1. Preheat broiler. Mix the first four ingredients. Add turkey; mix lightly but thoroughly. Shape into six ½-in.-thick patties.
2. In a large nonstick skillet coated with cooking spray, cook burgers in batches over medium heat until a thermometer reads 165°, 4-6 minutes per side. Keep warm.
3. Meanwhile, place buns on a baking sheet, cut side up. Broil 3-4 in. from heat until toasted, about 30 seconds. Spread the tops with cheese. Serve burgers in buns, with lettuce if desired.
FREEZE OPTION: Place uncooked patties on a plastic wrap-lined baking sheet; cover and freeze until firm. Remove from pan and transfer to a large resealable plastic bag; return to freezer. To use, cook frozen patties in a nonstick skillet coated with cooking spray over medium-low heat until a thermometer reads 165°, 6-8 minutes per side.
1 BURGER: 316 cal., 10g fat (3g sat. fat), 57mg chol., 812mg sod., 35g carb. (6g sugars, 4g fiber), 22g pro. **DIABETIC EXCHANGES:** 3 lean meat, 2 starch, ½ fat.

CHORIZO SPAGHETTI SQUASH SKILLET

CHORIZO SPAGHETTI SQUASH SKILLET

Get your noodle fix minus the pasta with this spiced-up meal you can make in one skillet. The healthy, satisfying dinner is also low in calories—a weeknight winner!

—Sherrill Oake, Springfield, MA

TAKES: 30 min. • **MAKES:** 4 servings

- 1 small spaghetti squash (about 2 lbs.)
- 1 Tbsp. canola oil
- 1 pkg. (12 oz.) fully cooked chorizo chicken sausage links or flavor of choice, sliced
- 1 medium sweet yellow pepper, chopped
- 1 medium sweet onion, halved and sliced
- 1 cup sliced fresh mushrooms
- 1 can (14½ oz.) no-salt-added diced tomatoes, undrained
- 1 Tbsp. reduced-sodium taco seasoning
- ¼ tsp. pepper
  Chopped green onions, optional

1. Halve squash lengthwise; discard seeds. Place squash on a microwave-safe plate, cut side down; microwave on high until tender, about 15 minutes. Cool slightly.
2. Meanwhile, in a large skillet, heat 1 Tbsp. oil over medium-high heat; saute sausage, yellow pepper, onion and mushrooms until onion is tender, about 5 minutes.
3. Separate strands of squash with a fork; add to skillet. Stir in tomatoes and seasonings; bring to a boil. Reduce heat; simmer, uncovered, until flavors are blended, about 5 minutes. If desired, top with green onions.
1½ CUPS: 299 cal., 12g fat (3g sat. fat), 65mg chol., 725mg sod., 34g carb. (12g sugars, 6g fiber), 18g pro. **DIABETIC EXCHANGES:** 2 starch, 2 lean meat, 1 vegetable, 1 fat.

TEST KITCHEN TIP
One 8-ounce container of sliced mushrooms contains about 3½ cups. If you're not planning on using mushrooms later in the week, just grab 1 cup from the grocery store salad bar.

JEZEBEL CHICKEN THIGHS

On busy weeknights, this sweet and spicy chicken is our standby.
—Judy Armstrong, Prairieville, LA

TAKES: 25 min. • **MAKES:** 4 servings

- 4   bone-in chicken thighs
- ½   tsp. salt
- ½   tsp. paprika
- ¼   tsp. pepper
- 1   Tbsp. olive oil
- 1   shallot, finely chopped
- 2   garlic cloves, minced
- ½   cup apricot preserves
- ¼   cup chicken broth
- 1   to 2 Tbsp. horseradish sauce
- 4   green onions, sliced, divided

1. Sprinkle chicken with seasonings. In a large nonstick skillet, heat oil over medium-high heat; brown chicken on both sides, beginning skin side down. Remove from pan, reserving drippings.
2. In same pan, saute shallot and garlic in drippings over medium-high heat until tender, 1-2 minutes. Stir in the preserves, broth, horseradish sauce and half of the green onions. Add the chicken; cook, covered, over medium heat until a thermometer reads 170°-175°, about 10-12 minutes.
3. To serve, spoon sauce over chicken; sprinkle with remaining green onions.
1 CHICKEN THIGH WITH 2 TBSP. SAUCE: 380 cal., 19g fat (5g sat. fat), 82mg chol., 474mg sod., 30g carb. (19g sugars, 1g fiber), 23g pro.

QUICK CHICKEN & BROCCOLI STIR-FRY

This Asian stir-fry is a suppertime best bet. The spicy sauce goes well with beef, chicken, pork or seafood. Add whatever veggies you have on hand.
—Kristin Rimkus, Snohomish, WA

TAKES: 25 min. • **MAKES:** 4 servings

- 2   Tbsp. rice vinegar
- 2   Tbsp. mirin (sweet rice wine)
- 2   Tbsp. chili garlic sauce
- 1   Tbsp. cornstarch
- 1   Tbsp. reduced-sodium soy sauce
- 2   tsp. fish sauce or additional soy sauce
- ½   cup reduced-sodium chicken broth, divided
- 2   cups instant brown rice
- 2   tsp. sesame oil
- 4   cups fresh broccoli florets
- 2   cups cubed cooked chicken
- 2   green onions, sliced

1. In a small bowl, mix the first six ingredients and ¼ cup chicken broth until smooth. Cook rice according to package directions.
2. Meanwhile, in a large skillet, heat oil over medium-high heat. Add broccoli; stir-fry 2 minutes. Add the remaining broth; cook 1-2 minutes or until the broccoli is crisp-tender. Stir the sauce mixture and add to pan. Bring to a boil; cook and stir 1-2 minutes or until sauce is thickened.
3. Stir in chicken and green onions; heat through. Serve with rice.
1 CUP CHICKEN MIXTURE WITH ½ CUP RICE: 387 cal., 9g fat (2g sat. fat), 62mg chol., 765mg sod., 45g carb. (6g sugars, 4g fiber), 28g pro. **DIABETIC EXCHANGES:** 3 lean meat, 2½ starch, 1 vegetable, ½ fat.

QUICK CHICKEN & BROCCOLI STIR-FRY

CHILI
CHICKEN
STRIPS

CHILI CHICKEN STRIPS

Instead of ordinary bread crumbs, seasoned crushed corn chips coat these slightly crunchy chicken fingers. If your family likes food with some heat, use the full 1½ teaspoons of chili powder.

—*Taste of Home* Test Kitchen

TAKES: 25 min. • **MAKES:** 6 servings

- ¾ cup crushed corn chips
- 2 Tbsp. dry bread crumbs
- 1 Tbsp. all-purpose flour
- 1 to 1½ tsp. chili powder
- ½ tsp. seasoned salt
- ½ tsp. poultry seasoning
- ¼ tsp. pepper
- ¼ tsp. paprika
- 1 large egg
- 1½ lbs. boneless skinless chicken breasts, cut into ½-in. strips
- 4 Tbsp. butter

1. In a shallow bowl, combine the first eight ingredients. In another shallow bowl, beat egg. Dip chicken in egg, then roll in corn chip mixture.
2. In a large skillet, cook half of the chicken in 2 Tbsp. butter 8-10 minutes or until the meat is no longer pink. Repeat with the remaining chicken and butter.

1 SERVING: 265 cal., 12g fat (6g sat. fat), 119mg chol., 381mg sod., 14g carb. (0 sugars, 1g fiber), 25g pro.

EASY SANTA FE CHICKEN

My day is busy from start to finish, so quick-prep main dishes like this one are a lifesaver.

—Debra Cook, White Deer, TX

PREP: 10 min. • **COOK:** 30 min.
MAKES: 4 servings

- 1 large onion, chopped
- 1 Tbsp. butter
- 1¼ cups chicken broth
- 1 cup salsa
- 1 cup uncooked long grain rice
- ⅛ tsp. garlic powder
- 4 boneless skinless chicken breast halves (4 oz. each)
- ¾ cup shredded cheddar cheese
  Chopped fresh cilantro, optional

1. In a large skillet, saute onion in butter until tender. Add broth and salsa; bring to a boil. Stir in rice and garlic powder. Place chicken over rice; cover and simmer for 10 minutes.
2. Turn chicken; cook 10-15 minutes longer or until a thermometer reads 165°. Remove from the heat. Sprinkle with the cheese; cover and let stand for 5 minutes. Garnish with cilantro if desired.

1 SERVING: 339 cal., 10g fat (7g sat. fat), 46mg chol., 744mg sod., 43g carb. (5g sugars, 3g fiber), 15g pro.

PEPPERY HERBED TURKEY TENDERLOIN

I won the North Carolina Turkey Cook-Off one year with these tenderloins in rich sauce. Marinating the turkey in wine, garlic, rosemary and thyme gives it a fantastic taste.
—Virginia Anthony, Jacksonville, FL

PREP: 10 min. + marinating
COOK: 15 min. • **MAKES:** 6 servings

- 3 turkey breast tenderloins (12 oz. each)
- 1 cup dry white wine or apple juice
- 3 green onions, chopped
- 3 Tbsp. minced fresh parsley
- 6 tsp. olive oil, divided
- 1 Tbsp. finely chopped garlic
- ¾ tsp. dried rosemary, crushed
- ¾ tsp. dried thyme
- 1 tsp. coarsely ground pepper
- ¾ tsp. salt, divided
- 4 tsp. cornstarch
- 1 cup reduced-sodium chicken broth

1. Pat tenderloins dry; flatten to ¾-in. thickness. In a small bowl, combine the wine or juice, onions, parsley, 4 tsp. oil, garlic, rosemary and thyme. Pour ¾ cup marinade into a large resealable plastic bag; add turkey. Seal bag and turn to coat; refrigerate for at least 4 hours, turning occasionally. Cover and refrigerate remaining marinade.
2. Drain turkey, discarding marinade. Sprinkle turkey with pepper and ½ tsp. salt. In a large nonstick skillet, cook turkey in remaining oil for 5-6 minutes on each side or until turkey reaches 165°. Remove and keep warm.
3. In a small bowl, combine cornstarch, broth, reserved marinade and remaining salt until smooth; pour into skillet. Bring to a boil; cook and stir for 1-2 minutes or until thickened. Slice turkey; serve with sauce.

5 OZ.: 258 cal., 5g fat (1g sat. fat), 116mg chol., 476mg sod., 4g carb. (0 sugars, 0 fiber), 41g pro. **DIABETIC EXCHANGES:** 6 lean meat, 1 fat.

MANGO CHUTNEY CHICKEN CURRY

My father invented this recipe while we were traveling together. Adjust the amount of curry according to your taste and the level of heat desired.
—Dina Moreno, Seattle, WA

TAKES: 25 min. • **MAKES:** 4 servings

- 1 Tbsp. canola oil
- 1 lb. boneless skinless chicken breasts, cubed
- 1 Tbsp. curry powder
- 2 garlic cloves, minced
- ¼ tsp. salt
- ¼ tsp. pepper
- ½ cup mango chutney
- ½ cup half-and-half cream

1. In a large skillet, heat oil over medium-high heat; brown chicken. Stir in curry powder, garlic, salt and pepper; cook 1-2 minutes longer or until aromatic.
2. Stir in chutney and cream. Bring to boil. Reduce heat; simmer, uncovered, 4-6 minutes or until the chicken is no longer pink, stirring occasionally.
½ CUP: 320 cal., 9g fat (3g sat. fat), 78mg chol., 558mg sod., 30g carb. (19g sugars, 1g fiber), 24g pro.

PEPPERY HERBED TURKEY TENDERLOIN

BUFFALO CHICKEN SALAD

RED BEANS & RICE WITH TURKEY SAUSAGE

I adapted this recipe from a cookbook to eliminate time-consuming steps like browning the sausage and soaking and boiling beans. Red pepper flakes add zest to this satisfying dish that's chock-full of beans and sausage.
—Brenda Leonard, Missoula, MT

TAKES: 30 min. • **MAKES:** 10 servings

- 3 celery ribs, chopped
- 1 medium onion, chopped
- 6 green onions, thinly sliced
- 2 garlic cloves, minced
- 1¾ cups water
- 1 can (16 oz.) light red kidney beans, rinsed and drained
- 1 can (16 oz.) dark red kidney beans, rinsed and drained
- ½ tsp. dried oregano
- ½ tsp. dried thyme
- ¼ tsp. crushed red pepper flakes
- ¼ tsp. pepper
- ¼ lb. fully cooked smoked turkey sausage, halved and cut into ½-in. pieces
- 4 cups hot cooked rice

1. In a large skillet that has been coated with cooking spray, saute celery, onions and garlic until tender. Add water, beans, oregano, thyme, red pepper flakes and pepper. Bring to a boil; reduce heat. Simmer, uncovered, for 10 minutes, stirring occasionally.
2. Remove about 1½ cups of bean mixture and mash with a fork. Return to skillet. Add the sausage; bring to a boil. Boil for 5 minutes or until bean mixture reaches desired thickness. Serve over rice.
½ CUP: 197 cal., 2g fat (0 sat. fat), 7mg chol., 116mg sod., 35g carb. (0 sugars, 0 fiber), 9g pro. **DIABETIC EXCHANGES:** 2 starch, ½ meat, ½ vegetable.

EAT SMART

BUFFALO CHICKEN SALAD

This salad is delicious, and even better—quick! Buffalo Chicken Salad is a summer staple at our house. Sometimes we cook the chicken on the grill, then sprinkle the hot sauce over it with the dressing, because you've gotta have that kick!
—Cori Cooper, Boise, ID

TAKES: 25 min. • **MAKES:** 4 servings

- 1 Tbsp. olive oil
- 1 lb. boneless skinless chicken breasts, cut into ¾-in. cubes
- 2 Tbsp. Louisiana-style hot sauce
- ¼ tsp. salt
- ¼ tsp. pepper
- 1 bunch romaine, chopped (about 5 cups)
- 2 celery ribs, chopped
- 1 cup shredded carrots
- ½ cup fat-free ranch salad dressing

1. In a large skillet, heat the oil over medium-high heat. In batches, saute the chicken until no longer pink, 3-4 minutes; remove to a bowl. Stir in hot sauce, salt and pepper.
2. On a platter, combine romaine, celery and carrots. Top with chicken. Serve with dressing.
1 SERVING: 229 cal., 7g fat (1g sat. fat), 63mg chol., 644mg sod., 16g carb. (4g sugars, 3g fiber), 25g pro. **DIABETIC EXCHANGES:** 3 lean meat, 1 starch, 1 vegetable, ½ fat.

DID YOU KNOW?

Ranch dressing was created by Nebraska cowboy-turned-cook Steve Henson more than 60 years ago. While cooking for a work crew in Alaska in the 1940s, Steve perfected his recipe for buttermilk salad dressing. It later became the house dressing at Hidden Valley Ranch, a dude ranch he bought with his wife, Gayle, outside Santa Barbara, California.

CHICKEN ARTICHOKE SKILLET

This quick chicken entree features artichokes and olives for an authentic Greek flair. Seasoned with lemon juice and oregano, the chicken always turns out flavorful and tender.
—Carol Latimore, Arvada, CO

TAKES: 25 min. • **MAKES:** 4 servings

4 boneless skinless chicken breast halves (4 oz. each)
¼ tsp. salt
¼ tsp. pepper
2 tsp. olive oil
1 can (14 oz.) water-packed quartered artichoke hearts, rinsed and drained
⅔ cup reduced-sodium chicken broth
¼ cup halved pimiento-stuffed olives
¼ cup halved pitted Greek olives
2 Tbsp. minced fresh oregano or 2 tsp. dried oregano
1 Tbsp. lemon juice

1. Sprinkle chicken with salt and pepper. In a large skillet, heat oil over medium-high heat; brown chicken on both sides.
2. Add remaining ingredients; bring to a boil. Reduce heat; simmer, covered, until a thermometer inserted in the chicken reads 165°, 4-5 minutes.
1 SERVING: 225 cal., 9g fat (1g sat. fat), 63mg chol., 864mg sod., 9g carb. (0 sugars, 0 fiber), 26g pro.
DIABETIC EXCHANGES: 3 lean meat, 1 vegetable.

TEST KITCHEN TIP
Common olive oil works better for cooking at high heat than virgin or extra virgin oil. These higher grades have ideal flavor for cold foods, but they smoke at lower temperatures.

SIMPLE SAUSAGE PASTA TOSS

SIMPLE SAUSAGE PASTA TOSS

For a flash of tasty inspiration, grab a skillet and stir up turkey sausage with tomatoes, garlic and olives. Toss everything with spaghetti, and sprinkle with Parmesan.
—*Taste of Home* Test Kitchen

TAKES: 25 min. • **MAKES:** 5 servings

8 oz. uncooked multigrain spaghetti
¼ cup seasoned bread crumbs
1 tsp. olive oil
¾ lb. Italian turkey sausage links, cut into ½-in. slices
1 garlic clove, minced
2 cans (14½ oz. each) no-salt-added diced tomatoes, undrained
1 can (2¼ oz.) sliced ripe olives, drained

1. Cook spaghetti according to package directions; drain. Meanwhile, in a large skillet, toss bread crumbs with oil; cook and stir over medium heat until toasted. Remove from pan.
2. Add sausage to same pan; cook and stir over medium heat until no longer pink. Add garlic; cook 30-60 seconds longer. Stir in tomatoes and olives; heat through. Add spaghetti and toss to combine. Sprinkle with toasted bread crumbs before serving.
1⅔ CUPS: 340 cal., 10g fat (2g sat. fat), 41mg chol., 689mg sod., 44g carb. (6g sugars, 6g fiber), 21g pro. **DIABETIC EXCHANGES:** 3 lean meat, 2 starch, 1 vegetable, ½ fat.

CHICKEN
ARTICHOKE
SKILLET

GOAT CHEESE-STUFFED CHICKEN WITH APRICOT GLAZE

My original version of this recipe used several tablespoons of butter versus the tablespoon of oil. With a few more tweaks, this special entree for two is now under 350 calories.

—David Dahlman, Chatsworth, CA

PREP: 20 min. • **COOK:** 20 min.
MAKES: 2 servings

- 2   boneless skinless chicken breast halves (6 oz. each)
- ¼   tsp. salt
- ¼   tsp. pepper
- 2   Tbsp. goat cheese
- 2   Tbsp. part-skim ricotta cheese
- 4   Tbsp. chopped shallots, divided
- 1   tsp. olive oil
- ⅔   cup reduced-sodium chicken broth
- 2   Tbsp. apricot spreadable fruit
- 1   Tbsp. lemon juice
- 1   tsp. spicy brown mustard
- 1   tsp. minced fresh parsley

1. Flatten chicken to ¼-in. thickness; sprinkle with the salt and pepper. Combine the goat cheese, ricotta and 1 Tbsp. shallots; spread over the center of each chicken breast. Roll up and secure with toothpicks.
2. In a small nonstick skillet, brown chicken in oil on all sides. Remove and keep warm.
3. In the same skillet, saute remaining shallots until tender. Stir in the broth, spreadable fruit, lemon juice and mustard. Bring to a boil; cook until liquid is reduced by half.
4. Return the chicken to the pan; cook, covered until a thermometer inserted in the chicken reads 165°, 6-7 minutes. Discard toothpicks. Serve chicken with cooking liquid. Sprinkle with parsley.
1 SERVING: 340 cal., 12g fat (5g sat. fat), 110mg chol., 695mg sod., 16g carb. (10g sugars, 0 fiber), 41g pro.

HEARTY CHICKEN GYROS

EAT SMART
HEARTY CHICKEN GYROS

I love reinventing classic recipes to fit our taste and healthy lifestyle. This recipe is quick to prepare and can be served with oven fries or on its own. You can add Greek olives, omit the onion, or even use cubed pork tenderloin for a new taste.

—Kayla Douthitt, Elizabethtown, KY

PREP: 30 min. + marinating
COOK: 5 min. • **MAKES:** 6 servings

- 1½ lbs. boneless skinless chicken breasts, cut into ½-in. cubes
- ½   cup salt-free lemon-pepper marinade
- 3   Tbsp. minced fresh mint

SAUCE
- ½   cup fat-free plain Greek yogurt
- 2   Tbsp. lemon juice
- 1   tsp. dill weed
- ½   tsp. garlic powder

ASSEMBLY
- 1   medium cucumber, seeded and chopped
- 1   medium tomato, chopped
- ¼   cup finely chopped onion
- 6   whole wheat pita pocket halves, warmed
- ⅓   cup crumbled feta cheese

1. Place chicken, marinade and mint in a large resealable plastic bag; seal bag and turn to coat. Refrigerate up to 6 hours.
2. Drain chicken, discarding marinade. Place a large nonstick skillet over medium-high heat. Add the chicken; cook and stir 4-6 minutes or until no longer pink.
3. In a small bowl, mix the sauce ingredients. In another bowl, combine cucumber, tomato and onion. Serve chicken in pita pockets with sauce, vegetable mixture, and cheese.
1 GYRO: 248 cal., 4g fat (2g sat. fat), 66mg chol., 251mg sod., 22g carb. (4g sugars, 3g fiber), 30g pro. **DIABETIC EXCHANGES:** 3 lean meat, 1½ starch, ½ fat.

TURKEY MEDALLIONS WITH TOMATO SALAD

In this quick meal, turkey medallions with a crisp coating are enhanced by the bright, summery flavors of a garden tomato salad.

—Gilda Lester, Millsboro, DE

PREP: 30 min. • **COOK:** 15 min.
MAKES: 6 servings

- 2 Tbsp. olive oil
- 1 Tbsp. red wine vinegar
- ½ tsp. sugar
- ¼ tsp. dried oregano
- ¼ tsp. salt
- 1 medium green pepper, coarsely chopped
- 1 celery rib, coarsely chopped
- ¼ cup chopped red onion
- 1 Tbsp. thinly sliced fresh basil
- 3 medium tomatoes

TURKEY
- 1 large egg
- 2 Tbsp. lemon juice
- 1 cup panko (Japanese) bread crumbs
- ½ cup grated Parmesan cheese
- ½ cup finely chopped walnuts
- 1 tsp. lemon-pepper seasoning
- 1 pkg. (20 oz.) turkey breast tenderloins
- ¼ tsp. salt
- ¼ tsp. pepper
- 3 Tbsp. olive oil
  Additional fresh basil

1. Whisk together the first five ingredients. Stir in green pepper, celery, onion and basil. Cut tomatoes into wedges; cut wedges in half. Stir into pepper mixture.
2. In a shallow bowl, whisk together egg and lemon juice. In another shallow bowl, toss bread crumbs with cheese, walnuts and lemon pepper.
3. Cut tenderloins crosswise into 1-in. slices; flatten slices with a meat mallet to ½-in. thickness. Sprinkle with salt and pepper. Dip in egg mixture, then in crumb mixture, patting to adhere.
4. In a large skillet, heat 1 Tbsp. oil over medium-high heat. Add a third of the turkey; cook until golden brown, 2-3 minutes per side. Repeat twice with the remaining oil and turkey. Serve with tomato mixture; sprinkle with basil.
1 SERVING: 351 cal., 21g fat (3g sat. fat), 68mg chol., 458mg sod., 13g carb. (4g sugars, 2g fiber), 29g pro.

GARLIC CHICKEN WITH POTATOES

People like the sweet garlic flavor of this dish. I like being able to cook the entire meal—meat and potatoes—in one pan!

—Joni Palmer, Walla Walla, WA

PREP: 15 min. • **COOK:** 50 min.
MAKES: 2 servings

- 6 small red potatoes
- 2 chicken leg quarters
- 1 Tbsp. canola oil
- 1 cup chicken broth
- 12 garlic cloves, minced
- ½ tsp. minced fresh rosemary or ¼ tsp. dried rosemary, crushed
- ¼ tsp. minced fresh thyme or dash dried thyme

1. Remove a thin strip of peel around the center of each potato; set aside.
2. With a sharp knife, cut leg quarters at the joints if desired. In a large skillet, brown chicken in oil on both sides. Add the potatoes, broth, garlic, rosemary and thyme. Bring to a boil. Reduce heat to low; cook, covered, until a thermometer inserted in chicken reads 175°, 40-45 minutes.
1 SERVING: 494 cal., 24g fat (5g sat. fat), 105mg chol., 390mg sod., 34g carb. (2g sugars, 3g fiber), 36g pro.

TURKEY MEDALLIONS WITH TOMATO SALAD

Pork

**FIG-GLAZED
PORK TENDERLOIN**

FIG-GLAZED PORK TENDERLOIN

I like to experiment with different flavors and try to make the food look photo-worthy. But for my husband, the dish just has to taste good. Here's a supper that makes us both happy.
—Jean Gottfried, Upper Sandusky, OH

TAKES: 30 min. • **MAKES:** 4 servings

- 1 pork tenderloin (1 lb.), cut into 8 slices
- ½ tsp. salt
- ½ tsp. pepper
- 1 Tbsp. olive oil
- ⅓ cup fig preserves
- 3 Tbsp. apple juice
- 2 Tbsp. cider vinegar
- 1½ tsp. Worcestershire sauce
- 1 garlic clove, minced
- ¾ tsp. curry powder

1. Sprinkle pork with salt and pepper. In a large skillet, heat oil over medium-high heat. Brown pork on both sides; remove from pan.

2. Add the preserves, juice, vinegar, Worcestershire sauce, garlic and curry powder to same pan; bring to a boil. Return pork to pan. Reduce heat; simmer, covered, until a thermometer inserted in pork reads 145°, about 5-7 minutes. Let pork stand 5 minutes before serving.

2 PORK SLICES WITH 2 TBSP. SAUCE: 239 cal., 7g fat (2g sat. fat), 63mg chol., 509mg sod., 20g carb. (18g sugars, 0 fiber), 23g pro.

TEST KITCHEN TIP
This recipe is flexible, so try it with different juices and jams that you have on hand. Orange juice and marmalade would also work deliciously here! Apple jelly is another great stand-in.

PORK VEGGIE STIR-FRY

A colorful combination of vegetables, tender pork, seasonings and crunchy peanuts, this main dish appeals even to kids. When it's served over rice, it doesn't really need any side dishes.
—Laurel Reisinger, Saskatoon , SK

TAKES: 20 min. • **MAKES:** 6 servings

- 3 cups sliced cauliflower
- 3 Tbsp. vegetable oil, divided
- 2 medium carrots, julienned
- 1 can (15 oz.) whole baby corn, rinsed and drained
- ½ cup frozen peas, thawed
- 1 lb. boneless pork, cut into thin strips
- 2 green onions, thinly sliced
- 2 garlic cloves, minced
- 1 Tbsp. minced fresh gingerroot
- ½ to 1 tsp. chili powder
- 1 cup water
- ¼ cup soy sauce
- 4 tsp. honey
- 2 tsp. chicken bouillon granules
- 4 tsp. cornstarch
- 2 Tbsp. cold water
- ¼ cup salted peanuts
  Hot cooked rice, optional

1. In a skillet or wok, stir-fry cauliflower in 2 Tbsp. oil for 3 minutes. Add the carrots; stir-fry for 2 minutes. Add corn and peas; stir-fry until vegetables are crisp-tender. Remove; keep warm.
2. Stir-fry pork in remaining oil for 2 minutes. Add onions, garlic, ginger and chili powder; stir-fry until pork is no longer pink. Remove; keep warm.
3. Combine water, soy sauce, honey and bouillon in same pan. Combine cornstarch and cold water; gradually add to pan. Bring to a boil; cook and stir for 2 minutes or until thickened.
4. Return vegetables and pork mixture to pan; heat through. Stir in peanuts. If desired, serve with rice.
1 SERVING: 277 cal., 14g fat (3g sat. fat), 45mg chol., 1131mg sod., 16g carb. (8g sugars, 4g fiber), 22g pro.

SESAME RAMEN SALAD

SESAME RAMEN SALAD

This spicy sausage and ramen noodle salad is equally good for lunch or a potluck.
—Denese Johnson, Chico, TX

TAKES: 30 min. • **MAKES:** 8 servings

- 3 pkg. (3 oz. each) shrimp ramen noodles
- 6 cups hot water
- 1 lb. bulk spicy pork sausage
- ¾ cup Asian toasted sesame salad dressing
- ¾ cup sliced green onions (about 6 medium), divided
- ½ cup chopped fresh cilantro
- ½ tsp. grated lime zest
- 3 Tbsp. lime juice
- 3 cups fresh snow peas, halved diagonally (about 8 oz.)
- 1½ cups julienned carrots
- 4 Tbsp. chopped dry roasted peanuts, divided

1. Break ramen noodles into quarters and place in a large bowl; reserve one seasoning packet. Cover noodles with hot water; let stand until softened, about 5 minutes.
2. Drain the noodles; rinse with cold water. Drain well and return to bowl.
3. In a large skillet, cook and crumble sausage over medium heat until no longer pink, 5-7 minutes. Drain on paper towels.
4. Mix salad dressing, ½ cup green onions, cilantro, lime zest, lime juice and contents of reserved seasoning packet; add to noodles. Toss with the snow peas, carrots, 3 Tbsp. peanuts and sausage. Sprinkle with remaining green onions and peanuts.
1 CUP: 402 cal., 25g fat (8g sat. fat), 31mg chol., 972mg sod., 33g carb. (8g sugars, 2g fiber), 12g pro.

PORK LO MEIN WITH SPAGHETTI

This irresistible stir-fry is sure to bring rave reviews from your family. Ginger, sesame oil, red pepper flakes and soy sauce jazz up the combination of snow peas, sweet pepper and pork. Serve it with rice as an alternative to the pasta for a change of pace.
—Linda Trainor, Phoenix, AZ

PREP: 10 min. + marinating
COOK: 10 min. • **MAKES:** 4 servings

- 1   pork tenderloin (1 lb.)
- ¼   cup reduced-sodium soy sauce
- 3   garlic cloves, minced
- 1   tsp. minced fresh gingerroot
- ¼   tsp. crushed red pepper flakes
- 2   cups fresh snow peas
- 1   medium sweet red pepper, julienned
- 3   cups cooked thin spaghetti
- ⅓   cup reduced-sodium chicken broth
- 2   tsp. sesame oil

1. Cut tenderloin in half lengthwise. Cut each half widthwise into ¼-in. slices; set aside. In a large resealable plastic bag, combine the soy sauce, garlic, ginger and pepper flakes; add the pork. Seal bag and turn to coat; refrigerate for 20 minutes.
2. In a large nonstick skillet or wok coated with cooking spray, stir-fry pork and marinade for 4-5 minutes or until meat is no longer pink. Add peas and red pepper; stir-fry for 1 minute. Stir in spaghetti and broth; cook 1 minute longer. Remove from the heat; stir in sesame oil.

1½ CUPS: 343 cal., 7g fat (2g sat. fat), 74mg chol., 716mg sod., 37g carb. (0 sugars, 3g fiber), 31g pro. **DIABETIC EXCHANGES:** 3 lean meat, 2 starch, 1 vegetable.

BRAISED PORK LOIN CHOPS

EAT SMART
BRAISED PORK LOIN CHOPS

An easy herb rub gives sensational flavor to these pork chops. The meat turns out tender as well as delicious.
—Marilyn Larsen, Port Orange, FL

TAKES: 30 min. • **MAKES:** 4 servings

- 1   garlic clove, minced
- 1   tsp. rubbed sage
- 1   tsp. dried rosemary, crushed
- ½   tsp. salt
- ⅛   tsp. pepper
- 4   boneless pork loin chops (½ in. thick and 4 oz. each)
- 1   Tbsp. butter
- 1   Tbsp. olive oil
- ¾   cup dry white wine or apple juice
- 1   Tbsp. minced fresh parsley

1. Mix first five ingredients; rub over both sides of pork chops. In a large nonstick skillet, heat butter and oil over medium-high heat; brown chops on both sides. Remove from pan.
2. In same pan, bring wine to a boil, stirring to loosen browned bits from pan. Cook, uncovered, until liquid is reduced to ½ cup. Add pork chops; return to a boil. Reduce heat; simmer, covered, until pork is tender, about 6-8 minutes. Sprinkle with parsley.

1 PORK CHOP WITH 2 TBSP. SAUCE: 218 cal., 13g fat (5g sat. fat), 62mg chol., 351mg sod., 3g carb. (2g sugars, 0 fiber), 22g pro. **DIABETIC EXCHANGES:** 3 lean meat, 1½ fat.

BLACK BEAN
PORK BURRITOS

I love the zesty freshness of my own homemade salsa in these burritos, but you can certainly speed up your dinner prep with salsa from the deli or a jar.

—Fiona Seels, Pittsburgh, PA

PREP: 35 min. + marinating
COOK: 5 min. • **MAKES:** 6 servings

- ¾ cup thawed limeade concentrate
- 1 Tbsp. olive oil
- 2 tsp. salt, divided
- 1½ tsp. pepper, divided
- 1 lb. boneless pork loin, cut into thin strips
- 2 cups chopped seeded plum tomatoes
- 1 small green pepper, chopped
- 1 small onion, chopped
- ¼ cup plus ⅓ cup minced fresh cilantro, divided
- 1 jalapeno pepper, seeded and chopped
- 1 Tbsp. lime juice
- ¼ tsp. garlic powder
- 1 cup uncooked long grain rice
- 2 cups shredded Monterey Jack cheese
- 6 flour tortillas (10 in.), warmed
- 1 can (15 oz.) black beans, rinsed and drained

1. In a large resealable plastic bag, combine the limeade concentrate, oil, 1 tsp. salt and ½ tsp. pepper; add pork. Seal bag and turn to coat; refrigerate for at least 20 minutes.

2. For salsa, in a small bowl, combine the tomatoes, green pepper, onion, ¼ cup cilantro, jalapeno, lime juice, garlic powder and remaining salt and pepper. Set aside.

3. Meanwhile, cook rice according to package directions. Stir in remaining cilantro; keep warm. Drain and discard marinade. In a large nonstick skillet, saute pork for 5-6 minutes or until no longer pink; drain.

4. Sprinkle ⅓ cup cheese off-center on each tortilla. Layer each tortilla with about ½ cup pork and ¼ cup salsa; top with ½ cup rice mixture and ¼ cup black beans. Fold sides and ends over filling. Serve with remaining salsa.

NOTE: Wear disposable gloves when cutting hot peppers; the oils can burn skin. Avoid touching your face.

1 SERVING: 678 cal., 21g fat (10g sat. fat), 70mg chol., 1425mg sod., 78g carb. (10g sugars, 11g fiber), 36g pro.

HAM & SALAMI
JAMBALAYA

This all-in-one dish is packed with flavor in every bite. With two types of meat, lots of celery, tomatoes and rice, you'll find that this hearty meal will satisfy just about anybody.

—Carol A. Gawronski, Lake Wales, FL

TAKES: 30 min. • **MAKES:** 8 servings

- 2½ cups water
- 2 cups sliced celery
- 2 cups cubed fully cooked ham
- 1 can (14½ oz.) diced tomatoes, undrained
- 1 cup uncooked long grain rice
- ¼ lb. thinly sliced hard salami, julienned
- ¾ cup chopped onion
- 2 Tbsp. butter
- ½ tsp. dried parsley flakes
- ½ tsp. dried thyme
- ½ tsp. minced garlic
- ¼ tsp. pepper
- 2 bay leaves

In a Dutch oven, combine all the ingredients. Bring to a boil. Reduce heat; cover and simmer 15-20 minutes or until rice and vegetables are tender. Discard bay leaves.

1 CUP: 227 cal., 9g fat (4g sat. fat), 42mg chol., 814mg sod., 24g carb. (3g sugars, 2g fiber), 14g pro.

"This is very easy to make and everyone liked it—even the young grandkids."
—CRIS9, TASTEOFHOME.COM

**BLACK BEAN
PORK BURRITOS**

NO-FUSS PORK CHOPS

These tender chops taste like sweet-and-sour pork, but require little attention or time. I prepare them year-round, whenever I'm on a tight schedule but still want something scrumptious and homemade.
—Sally Jones, Lancaster, NH

TAKES: 30 min. • **MAKES:** 4 servings

- ½ cup pineapple juice
- 2 Tbsp. brown sugar
- 2 Tbsp. cider vinegar
- ½ tsp. salt
- 2 Tbsp. olive oil, divided
- 4 boneless pork loin chops (5 oz. each)
- 2 medium onions, chopped
  Hot cooked noodles and sliced green onions, optional

1. Mix first four ingredients. In a large skillet, heat 1 Tbsp. oil over medium heat; brown pork chops on both sides. Remove from pan.

2. In same pan, saute the onions in remaining oil over medium heat until tender. Add juice mixture; bring to a boil. Reduce heat; simmer, covered, 10 minutes. Add pork chops; cook, covered, until a thermometer inserted in pork reads 145°, 2-3 minutes. Let stand, covered, for 5 minutes before serving. If desired, serve over noodles and top with green onions.

1 PORK CHOP: 315 cal., 15g fat (4g sat. fat), 68mg chol., 340mg sod., 16g carb. (12g sugars, 1g fiber), 28g pro.

EAT SMART

HAM & SPINACH COUSCOUS

A simple way to dress up couscous, this foolproof dish makes a tasty meal when time is tight.
—Lisa Shannon, Cullman, AL

TAKES: 20 min. • **MAKES:** 4 servings

- 2 cups water
- 1 cup chopped fully cooked ham
- 1 cup chopped fresh spinach
- ½ tsp. garlic salt
- 1 cup uncooked couscous
- ¼ cup shredded cheddar cheese

In a large saucepan, combine the water, ham, spinach and garlic salt. Bring to a boil. Stir in the couscous. Remove from the heat; cover and let stand for 5-10 minutes or until water is absorbed. Fluff with a fork. Sprinkle with cheese.

1 CUP: 248 cal., 6g fat (3g sat. fat), 26mg chol., 727mg sod., 36g carb. (1g sugars, 2g fiber), 14g pro. **DIABETIC EXCHANGES:** 2 starch, 1 lean meat, 1 fat.

NO-FUSS
PORK CHOPS

BERNIE'S PORK CHOP
SANDWICHES

BERNIE'S PORK CHOP SANDWICHES

My aunt worked in Butte, Montana, and whenever we visited we had pork chop sandwiches. This recipe is a take on that old favorite and a super nice change from burgers.
—Jeanette Kotecki, Billings, MT

TAKES: 25 min. • **MAKES:** 4 servings

- ¾ cup cornmeal
- 1 cup all-purpose flour
- ½ tsp. onion powder
- ½ tsp. garlic powder
- ½ tsp. dry mustard
- ½ tsp. paprika
- 1 cup fat-free milk
- 4 boneless pork loin chops (3 oz. each)
- ½ tsp. salt
- ¼ tsp. pepper
- 2 Tbsp. canola oil
- 4 whole wheat hamburger buns, split and warmed
  Optional toppings: thinly sliced onion, pickle slices, prepared mustard

1. Place cornmeal in a shallow bowl. In another bowl, mix flour and spices; add milk, stirring just until dry ingredients are moistened. Pound chops with a meat mallet to ¼-in. thickness; season with salt and pepper.

2. In two batches, heat oil in a large skillet over medium heat. Lightly coat chops with cornmeal. Dip in batter, allowing excess to drip off; place in skillet. Cook until golden brown, 2-4 minutes per side. Drain on paper towels. Serve in buns, topping with remaining ingredients as desired.

1 SANDWICH: 476 cal., 15g fat (3g sat. fat), 42mg chol., 564mg sod., 60g carb. (6g sugars, 5g fiber), 26g pro.

PEACHY PORK WITH RICE

Pork tenderloin does an awesome job of showing off my homemade peach preserves, though you can certainly use store-bought in the recipe. Tweak the heat level by using mild or spicy salsa and taco seasonings.

—Melissa Molaison, Hawkinsville, GA

TAKES: 30 min. • **MAKES:** 4 servings

- 1½ cups uncooked instant brown rice
- 1 pound pork tenderloin, cut into 1-in. cubes
- 2 Tbsp. olive oil
- 2 Tbsp. reduced-sodium taco seasoning
- 1 cup salsa
- 3 Tbsp. peach preserves

1. Cook rice according to the package directions. Meanwhile, place pork in a large bowl; drizzle with oil. Sprinkle with taco seasoning; toss to coat.
2. Place a large nonstick skillet coated with cooking spray over medium heat. Add pork; cook and stir 8-10 minutes or until no longer pink. Stir in the salsa and preserves; heat through. Serve with rice.

1 CUP PORK WITH ½ CUP RICE: 387 cal., 12g fat (2g sat. fat), 63mg chol., 540mg sod., 42g carb. (13g sugars, 2g fiber), 25g pro. **DIABETIC EXCHANGES:** 3 lean meat, 2½ starch, 1½ fat.

SIMPLE GLAZED PORK TENDERLOIN

These cutlets are a little bit savory and a little bit sweet, and best of all, they taste grilled even though you made them on the stovetop.

—Debra Arone, Fort Collins, CO

TAKES: 20 min. • **MAKES:** 4 servings

- 1 pork tenderloin (1 lb.)
- ¼ cup packed brown sugar
- 4 garlic cloves, minced
- 1 Tbsp. Montreal steak seasoning
- 2 Tbsp. butter

1. Cut pork into four pieces and pound with a meat mallet to ¼-in. thickness. In a shallow bowl, mix brown sugar, garlic and steak seasoning. Dip pork in brown sugar mixture, patting to help coating adhere.
2. In a large skillet, heat butter over medium-high heat. Add the pork; cook about 2-3 minutes on each side or until tender.
1 SERVING: 236 cal., 10g fat (5g sat. fat), 78mg chol., 585mg sod., 14g carb. (13g sugars, 0 fiber), 23g pro.

PEACHY PORK WITH RICE

ITALIAN SAUSAGE WITH
ARTICHOKES & FETA

ASIAN PORK TENDERLOIN SALAD

Look for the salad mix in the produce section near other bagged salad blends. If you can't find it, pick up mixed greens, snow peas, shredded carrots, chow mein noodles and a bottle of sesame-ginger or Asian-style salad dressing.
—*Taste of Home* Test Kitchen

PREP: 10 min. + marinating
COOK: 5 min. • **MAKES:** 4 servings

- 1   can (15 oz.) apricot halves
- ¼ cup reduced-sodium soy sauce
- 1   Tbsp. brown sugar
- 1   Tbsp. canola oil
- ½ tsp. ground ginger
- ½ tsp. minced garlic
- ¼ tsp. ground mustard
- 1   pound pork tenderloin, thinly sliced
- 2   pkg. (9¾ oz. each) Asian crunch salad mix

1. Drain apricots, reserving ½ cup juice; set apricots aside. In a large resealable plastic bag, combine soy sauce, brown sugar, oil, ginger, garlic, mustard and reserved apricot juice; add pork. Seal bag and turn to coat; refrigerate at least 1 hour.
2. Drain and discard marinade. In a large skillet or wok, stir-fry pork for 4-5 minutes or until juices run clear. Prepare salad mixes according to package directions; top with apricots and pork.

1½ CUPS: 361 cal., 15g fat (3g sat. fat), 63mg chol., 580mg sod., 24g carb. (12g sugars, 4g fiber), 26g pro.

ITALIAN SAUSAGE WITH ARTICHOKES & FETA

To impress dinner guests, I add some marinated artichoke hearts to my favorite sausage and pasta. This dish tastes like a gourmet masterpiece.
—Aysha Schurman, Ammon, ID

TAKES: 25 min. • **MAKES:** 4 servings

- 1   lb. bulk Italian sausage
- 1   small red onion, finely chopped
- 1   garlic clove, minced
- 1   jar (7½ oz.) marinated quartered artichoke hearts, drained and coarsely chopped
- ½ cup tomato sauce
- ¼ cup dry red wine or chicken broth
- ½ tsp. Italian seasoning
- ½ cup crumbled feta cheese
  Minced fresh parsley, optional
  Hot cooked gemelli or spiral pasta

1. In a large skillet, cook the sausage, onion and garlic over medium heat 6-8 minutes or until the sausage is no longer pink and the onion is tender, breaking sausage into crumbles; drain.
2. Stir in the artichoke hearts, tomato sauce, wine and Italian seasoning; heat through. Gently stir in the cheese. If desired, sprinkle with parsley. Serve with pasta.

FREEZE OPTION: Freeze cooled sausage mixture in freezer containers. To use, partially thaw in refrigerator overnight. Place sausage mixture in a saucepan; heat through, stirring occasionally and adding a little broth, wine or water if necessary.

1 SERVING: 435 cal., 35g fat (11g sat. fat), 69mg chol., 1149mg sod., 9g carb. (5g sugars, 1g fiber), 16g pro.

CARAMELIZED
PORK SLICES

CARAMELIZED PORK SLICES

This easy treatment for pork caught my eye when I was thumbing through a cookbook and saw "caramelized," always a good sign. I like to serve the slices over noodles or rice, or alongside mashed potatoes.

—Elisa Lochridge, Beaverton, OR

TAKES: 25 min. • **MAKES:** 4 servings

1   pork tenderloin (1 lb.)
2   tsp. canola oil, divided
2   garlic cloves, minced
2   Tbsp. brown sugar
1   Tbsp. orange juice
1   Tbsp. molasses
½   tsp. salt
¼   tsp. pepper

1. Cut tenderloin into eight slices; pound each with a meat mallet to ½-in. thickness. In a nonstick skillet, heat 1 tsp. oil over medium-high heat; brown pork on both sides. Remove from pan.
2. In same skillet, heat remaining oil over medium-high heat; saute garlic 1 minute. Stir in remaining ingredients. Add the pork, turning to coat; cook, uncovered, until a thermometer inserted in pork reads 145°, about 3-4 minutes. Let stand 5 minutes before serving.

2 PORK SLICES: 198 cal., 6g fat (2g sat. fat), 64mg chol., 344mg sod., 12g carb. (11g sugars, 0 fiber), 23g pro. **DIABETIC EXCHANGES:** 3 lean meat, ½ starch.

PEAR PORK CHOPS

PEAR PORK CHOPS

You'll be tempted to eat this main dish straight out of the pan. But save some for your guests! It's sure to wow them at the dinner table.

—*Taste of Home* Test Kitchen

TAKES: 30 min. • **MAKES:** 4 servings

1   pkg. (6 oz.) corn bread stuffing mix
4   boneless pork loin chops (6 oz. each)
½   tsp. pepper
¼   tsp. salt
2   Tbsp. butter
2   medium pears, chopped
1   medium sweet red pepper, chopped
2   green onions, thinly sliced

1. Prepare stuffing mix according to package directions. Meanwhile, sprinkle chops with pepper and salt. In a large skillet, brown pork chops in butter. Sprinkle with pears and red pepper.
2. Top with stuffing and onions. Cook, uncovered, over medium heat until a thermometer inserted in pork reads 145°, 8-10 minutes.

1 PORK CHOP WITH ¾ CUP STUFFING MIXTURE: 603 cal., 28g fat (14g sat. fat), 127mg chol., 1094mg sod., 47g carb. (14g sugars, 5g fiber), 38g pro.

PULLED PORK GRILLED CHEESE

PULLED PORK GRILLED CHEESE

My family combined two of our favorite things, pulled pork and grilled cheese, in these sandwiches. The recipe is super fast and easy when you use store-bought pulled pork.

—Crystal Jo Bruns, Iliff, CO

TAKES: 30 min. • **MAKES:** 4 servings

- 1   carton (16 oz.) refrigerated fully cooked barbecued shredded pork
- 1   garlic clove, minced
- 8   slices country white bread
- 6   oz. sliced manchego cheese or 8 slices Monterey Jack cheese
- 1   small red onion, thinly sliced
- ¼   cup mayonnaise

1. Heat shredded pork according to package directions. Stir in garlic. Layer four slices of bread with cheese, onion, pork mixture and remaining bread. Spread the outsides of sandwiches with mayonnaise.

2. In a large nonstick skillet, toast sandwiches in batches over medium-low heat until golden brown and cheese is melted, 2-3 minutes per side.

1 SANDWICH: 605 cal., 29g fat (13g sat. fat), 74mg chol., 1406mg sod., 53g carb. (22g sugars, 2g fiber), 29g pro.

"I made these last night and my family really liked them. I used leftover homemade pulled pork, but the biggest revelation was the mayo on the outside instead of butter. Who knew you could do that? It was the best, most crispy grilled cheese ever!"

—ANGELA32, TASTEOFHOME.COM

ITALIAN-STYLE PORK CHOPS

One of the first recipes I tried making in the early years of my marriage was an Italian-style version of pork chops. I've changed it over the years to make it healthier by reducing the oil and fat and by adding some vegetables. The chops also work well over hot rice.
—Traci Hoppes, Spring Valley, CA

TAKES: 30 min. • **MAKES:** 4 servings

- 2 medium green peppers, cut into ¼-in. strips
- ½ lb. sliced fresh mushrooms
- 1 Tbsp. plus 1½ tsp. olive oil, divided
- 4 boneless pork loin chops (6 oz. each)
- ¾ tsp. salt, divided
- ¾ tsp. pepper, divided
- 2 cups marinara or spaghetti sauce
- 1 can (3½ oz.) sliced ripe olives, drained

1. In a large skillet, saute peppers and mushrooms in 1 Tbsp. oil until tender. Remove and keep warm.
2. Sprinkle chops with ¼ tsp. salt and ¼ tsp. pepper. In the same skillet, brown chops in remaining oil. Add the marinara sauce, olives, remaining salt and pepper and the reserved pepper mixture. Bring to a boil. Reduce heat; cover and simmer until a thermometer inserted in pork reads 145°, for about 10-15 minutes. Let stand for 5 minutes before serving.

1 PORK CHOP WITH ¾ CUP SAUCE: 397 cal., 18g fat (5g sat. fat), 82mg chol., 930mg sod., 22g carb. (12g sugars, 5g fiber), 37g pro.

EAT SMART
PROSCIUTTO-PEPPER PORK CHOPS

Here's a dish that's simple, fast and most importantly, delicious. It's easy to adjust the recipe for two, six or eight. Serve these chops with pasta salad for a light and satisfying meal.
—Donna Prisco, Randolph, NJ

TAKES: 20 min. • **MAKES:** 4 servings

- 4 boneless pork loin chops (4 oz. each)
- ⅛ tsp. garlic powder
- ⅛ tsp. pepper
- 2 tsp. canola oil
- 4 thin slices prosciutto or deli ham
- ½ cup julienned roasted sweet red peppers
- 2 slices reduced-fat provolone cheese, cut in half

1. Sprinkle pork chops with garlic powder and pepper. In a large nonstick skillet, cook chops in oil over medium heat, until a thermometer inserted in pork reads 145°, 4-5 minutes on each side.
2. Top each pork chop with prosciutto, red peppers and cheese. Cover and cook for 1-2 minutes or until cheese is melted. Let stand for 5 minutes before serving.

1 PORK CHOP: 237 cal., 12g fat (4g sat. fat), 72mg chol., 483mg sod., 1g carb. (1g sugars, 0 fiber), 28g pro. **DIABETIC EXCHANGES:** 4 lean meat, ½ fat.

ITALIAN-STYLE PORK CHOPS

CREAMY HAM PENNE

BLUE CHEESE PORK MEDALLIONS

This pork dish comes together fast and seems fancy, thanks to the creamy sauce kicked up a notch by blue cheese. So I love to serve it to guests, who can't get enough.
—Lynne German, Woodland Hill, CA

TAKES: 25 min. • **MAKES:** 4 servings

- 1 pork tenderloin (1 lb.)
- 2 tsp. Montreal steak seasoning
- 2 Tbsp. butter
- ½ cup heavy whipping cream
- ¼ cup crumbled blue cheese
- 1 Tbsp. minced fresh parsley

1. Cut pork into 12 slices; sprinkle with steak seasoning. In a large skillet, heat butter over medium heat. Add pork; cook, covered, until pork is tender, 3-5 minutes per side. Remove from pan; keep warm.
2. Add cream to skillet; bring to a boil, stirring to loosen browned bits from pan. Cook until cream is slightly thickened, 2-3 minutes. Stir in cheese until melted. Serve with pork. Sprinkle with parsley.
3 MEDALLIONS WITH 2 TBSP. SAUCE: 317 cal., 23g fat (13g sat. fat), 126mg chol., 539mg sod., 1g carb. (1g sugars, 0 fiber), 25g pro.

EAT SMART
CREAMY HAM PENNE

Mixing spreadable cheese with whole wheat pasta, broccoli and fat-free milk for a main dish is a healthier use of this convenient product than simply smearing it on crackers.
—Barbara Pletzke, Herndon, VA

TAKES: 30 min. • **MAKES:** 4 servings

- 2 cups uncooked whole wheat penne pasta
- 2 cups fresh broccoli florets
- 1 cup fat-free milk
- 1 pkg. (6½ oz.) reduced-fat garlic-herb spreadable cheese
- 1 cup cubed fully cooked ham
- ¼ tsp. pepper

In a large saucepan, cook the penne according to package directions, adding broccoli during the last 5 minutes of cooking; drain. Set aside. In the same pan, combine milk and spreadable cheese. Cook and stir over medium heat for 3-5 minutes or until cheese is melted. Add ham, pepper and penne mixture; heat through.
1¼ CUPS: 371 cal., 8g fat (5g sat. fat), 47mg chol., 672mg sod., 49g carb. (5g sugars, 7g fiber), 25g pro.

TEST KITCHEN TIP
For best results, buy a wedge of blue cheese and crumble it yourself for the pork recipe. Tubs of ready-made crumbles are convenient for salads, but they are expensive and may have additives that will affect their creaminess and melting ability.

**BLUE CHEESE
PORK MEDALLIONS**

BARBECUE PORK SALAD

All it takes is a little bit of barbecue seasoning to put a tasty, unexpected twist on this simple main-dish salad.

—*Taste of Home* Test Kitchen

TAKES: 30 min. • **MAKES:** 4 servings

- 1 pork tenderloin (1 lb.), cut into 1-in. cubes
- 1 tsp. barbecue seasoning
- ⅛ tsp. salt
- 2 tsp. olive oil
- 1 bunch romaine, torn
- 1 cup cherry tomatoes, quartered
- ¾ cup canned black beans

VINAIGRETTE
- ½ cup cider vinegar
- ¼ cup olive oil
- 2 green onions, sliced
- 1 tsp. barbecue seasoning
- ⅛ tsp. salt
- ⅛ tsp. pepper

1. Toss pork with barbecue seasoning and salt. In a large skillet, saute pork in oil until no longer pink; set aside.
2. In a large bowl, combine the romaine, tomatoes, black beans and pork. In a small bowl, combine the vinaigrette ingredients; drizzle over salad and toss to coat.
2 CUPS: 339 cal., 20g fat (3g sat. fat), 63mg chol., 757mg sod., 12g carb. (2g sugars, 4g fiber), 27g pro.

QUICK GINGER PORK

QUICK GINGER PORK

My husband and I are empty nesters. It was a challenge learning to cook for just two again, but recipes like this give us delicious scaled-down dinners.

—Esther Johnson Danielson, Lawton, PA

TAKES: 20 min. • **MAKES:** 2 servings

- ½ lb. pork tenderloin, cut into thin strips
- 1 Tbsp. canola oil
- 1 garlic clove, minced
- 2 Tbsp. reduced-sodium soy sauce
- ¼ tsp. sugar
- ⅛ to ¼ tsp. ground ginger
- ½ cup cold water
- 1½ tsp. cornstarch
  Optional: hot cooked rice, thinly sliced green onions, toasted sesame seeds

1. In a large skillet or wok, stir-fry pork in oil until no longer pink. Add garlic; cook 1 minute longer.
2. In a small bowl, combine the soy sauce, sugar and ginger; add to skillet. Combine water and cornstarch until smooth; add to skillet. Bring to a boil; cook and stir for 2 minutes or until thickened. If desired, serve with; top with green onions and sesame seeds.
1 SERVING: 216 cal., 11g fat (2g sat. fat), 64mg chol., 621mg sod., 4g carb. (1g sugars, 0 fiber), 24g pro. **DIABETIC EXCHANGES:** 3 lean meat, 1½ fat, ½ starch.

PORK TENDERLOIN WITH THREE-BERRY SALSA

My husband came home from a work meeting that had served pork with a spicy blueberry salsa. He was amazed at how tasty it was, so I came up with my own rendition without seeing or tasting what he had. It took several tries, but this is the delicious result.
—Angie Phillips, Tarzana, CA

PREP: 30 min. + standing
COOK: 25 min. • **MAKES:** 6 servings

1¼ cups fresh or frozen blackberries (about 6 oz.), thawed and drained

1¼ cups fresh or frozen raspberries (about 6 oz.), thawed and drained
1 cup fresh or frozen blueberries (about 6 oz.), thawed
1 medium sweet red pepper, finely chopped
1 jalapeno pepper, seeded and minced
½ medium red onion, finely chopped
¼ cup lime juice
3 Tbsp. minced fresh cilantro
¼ tsp. salt
PORK
2 pork tenderloins (¾ lb. each), cut into ¾-in. slices
1 tsp. salt
½ tsp. pepper
2 Tbsp. olive oil, divided
½ cup white wine or chicken broth
2 shallots, thinly sliced
½ cup chicken stock

1. Place the first five ingredients in a bowl; toss lightly to combine. Reserve 1 cup berry mixture for sauce. For salsa, gently stir onion, lime juice, cilantro and salt into remaining mixture; let stand 30 minutes.

2. Meanwhile, sprinkle pork with salt and pepper. In a large skillet, heat 1 Tbsp. oil over medium-high heat. Add half of the pork and cook until a thermometer inserted in pork reads 145°, 2-4 minutes on each side. Remove from pan. Repeat with remaining pork and oil.

3. In same pan, add wine, shallots and reserved berry mixture, stirring to loosen browned bits from pan. Bring to a boil; cook 4-6 minutes or until liquid is reduced to 1 Tbsp. Stir in stock; cook 5 minutes longer or until shallots are tender, stirring occasionally. Return pork to pan; heat through. Serve with the salsa.

3 OZ. COOKED PORK WITH ⅔ CUP SALSA AND 3 TBSP. SAUCE: 239 cal., 9g fat (2g sat. fat), 64mg chol., 645mg sod., 15g carb. (7g sugars, 5g fiber), 25g pro. **DIABETIC EXCHANGES:** 3 lean meat, ½ starch, ½ fruit.

DID YOU KNOW?

A member of the onion family, shallots are more delicately flavored than onions and also taste a bit like garlic—another relative. Since the shallots in this sauce are cooked, you can substitute ⅓-½ cup chopped Vidalia, Walla Walla or other sweet onion. In uncooked dishes where raw onion would be too strong, a good substitute for shallots is chopped green onions.

PORK TENDERLOIN WITH THREE-BERRY SALSA

SKILLET BARBECUED PORK CHOPS

On days I volunteer at church or shuttle between after-school activities, I'm glad this dinner comes together in one skillet. The sauce makes the chops so moist and tender. I also simmer it up with other meats like chicken, beef or venison steaks.

—Tammy Messing, Ruth, MI

PREP: 10 min. • **COOK:** 25 min.
MAKES: 4 servings

- 4 boneless pork loin chops (½ in. thick)
- 1 tsp. seasoned salt
- 1 Tbsp. butter
- 1 medium onion, chopped
- ½ cup water
- ½ cup packed brown sugar
- 1 cup honey barbecue sauce
- 1 Tbsp. Worcestershire sauce
- 2 tsp. cornstarch
- 1 Tbsp. cold water

1. Sprinkle pork chops with seasoned salt. In a large skillet, brown chops on both sides in butter over medium-high heat. Remove chops.
2. In the drippings, saute onion until golden brown. Add the water, brown sugar, barbecue and Worcestershire sauces. Return chops to the skillet. Bring to a boil. Reduce the heat; cover and simmer 15 minutes or until a thermometer inserted in pork reads 145°. Remove chops; keep warm.
3. Combine cornstarch and cold water until smooth; gradually stir into skillet. Bring to a boil; cook and stir 2 minutes or until thickened. Serve with pork.
1 SERVING: 423 cal., 9g fat (4g sat. fat), 62mg chol., 1214mg sod., 58g carb. (51g sugars, 1g fiber), 22g pro.

HAM & MANGO QUESADILLAS FOR TWO

If you like the ease of quesadillas, especially on busy weeknights, you'll really love this fresh and fruity variation featuring salsa that starts in a jar: just add mango and cilantro.

—*Taste of Home* Test Kitchen

TAKES: 25 min. • **MAKES:** 2 servings

- 1½ tsp. butter
- 2 flour tortillas (8 in.)
- 1 cup shredded Monterey Jack cheese
- ⅔ cup chopped peeled mango, divided
- 2 oz. thick sliced deli ham, cut into ½-in. strips
- 3 tsp. minced fresh cilantro, divided
- ⅓ cup salsa
  Sour cream, optional

1. Spread butter over one side of each tortilla. Place the tortillas, butter side down, on a griddle. Sprinkle each with ½ cup cheese, 3 Tbsp. mango, ¼ cup ham and 1 tsp. cilantro. Fold over and cook over low heat for 1-2 minutes on each side or until cheese is melted. Cut into wedges.
2. Combine the salsa and remaining mango and cilantro; serve with the quesadillas. If desired, garnish with sour cream.
1 SERVING: 460 cal., 24g fat (13g sat. fat), 70mg chol., 998mg sod., 38g carb. (10g sugars, 1g fiber), 24g pro.

HAM & MANGO QUESADILLAS FOR TWO

SAVORY
BEER PORK CHOPS

SAVORY BEER PORK CHOPS

These tender chops in savory sauce are perfect for a hectic weeknight because they're so easy to prep, and they use only five ingredients. Try them with hot buttery noodles.
—Jana Christian, Farson, WY

TAKES: 20 min. • **MAKES:** 4 servings

- 4 boneless pork loin chops (4 oz. each)
- ½ tsp. salt
- ½ tsp. pepper
- 1 Tbsp. canola oil
- 3 Tbsp. ketchup
- 2 Tbsp. brown sugar
- ¾ cup beer or nonalcoholic beer

1. Sprinkle pork chops with salt and pepper. In a large skillet, heat oil over medium heat; brown the chops on both sides.
2. Mix ketchup, brown sugar and beer; pour over pork chops. Bring to a boil. Reduce heat; simmer, uncovered, until a thermometer inserted in pork reads 145°, 4-6 minutes. Let stand 5 minutes before serving.

FREEZE OPTION: Place pork chops in freezer containers; top with sauce. Cool and freeze. To use, partially thaw in refrigerator overnight. Heat through in a covered saucepan, gently stirring sauce and adding a little water if necessary.

1 PORK CHOP: 239 cal., 10g fat (3g sat. fat), 55mg chol., 472mg sod., 11g carb. (11g sugars, 0 fiber), 22g pro. **DIABETIC EXCHANGES:** 3 lean meat, 1 fat, ½ starch.

BLT SKILLET SUPPER

Chunks of bacon and tomato adorn this weeknight meal that's a pasta lover's take on the beloved BLT. (The L stands for linguine!)
—Edrie O'Brien, Denver, CO

TAKES: 30 min. • **MAKES:** 4 servings

- 8 oz. uncooked linguine or whole wheat linguine
- 8 bacon strips, cut into 1½-in. pieces
- 2 plum tomatoes, cut into 1-in. pieces
- 2 garlic cloves, minced
- 1 Tbsp. lemon juice
- ½ tsp. salt
- ½ tsp. pepper
- ¼ cup grated Parmesan cheese
- 2 Tbsp. minced fresh parsley

1. Cook linguine according to package directions. Meanwhile, in a large skillet, cook bacon over medium heat until crisp. Remove to paper towels; drain, reserving 2 tsp. drippings.
2. In the drippings, cook and stir the tomatoes and garlic 2-3 minutes or until heated through. Stir in bacon, lemon juice, salt and pepper.
3. Drain the linguine; add to skillet. Sprinkle with cheese and parsley; toss to coat.

1½ CUPS: 335 cal., 11g fat (4g sat. fat), 23mg chol., 685mg sod., 44g carb. (3g sugars, 2g fiber), 15g pro.

SPICY RICE
CASSEROLE

SPICY RICE CASSEROLE

Stirring up pork sausage, wild rice and jalapeno to taste makes this a terrific side. Or make it a main dish and serve it with cornbread. It's easy to prepare ahead and reheat in a microwave for a potluck meal.

—Debbie Terenzini-Wilkerson, Lusby, MD

TAKES: 30 min. • **MAKES:** 4 servings

- 1 lb. mild bulk pork sausage
- 1 tsp. ground cumin
- ½ tsp. garlic powder
- 2 medium onions, chopped
- 2 medium green peppers, chopped
- 2 tsp. reduced-sodium beef bouillon granules
- 2 cups boiling water
- 1 to 2 jalapeno peppers, seeded and finely minced
- 1 pkg. (6.20 oz.) fast-cooking long grain and wild rice mix

1. In a large skillet, cook the sausage, cumin and garlic powder over medium heat until the meat is no longer pink; drain. Add onions and green peppers; saute until crisp-tender.
2. Dissolve bouillon in water; add to skillet. Stir in jalapenos, rice and rice seasoning packet; bring to a boil. Reduce heat and simmer, uncovered, until water is absorbed, 5-10 minutes.
NOTE: Wear disposable gloves when cutting hot peppers; the oils can burn skin. Avoid touching your face.
1½ CUPS: 473 cal., 25g fat (58g sat. fat), 61mg chol., 1365mg sod., 45g carb. (5g sugars, 3g fiber), 18g pro.

TEST KITCHEN TIP
Green peppers are unripened versions of the red, yellow or orange peppers. They are less expensive because they're quicker to get to market. Use colored peppers in recipes for more sweetness.

PENNE
ALLA
VODKA

PENNE ALLA VODKA

This easy but impressive pasta is always on the menu when my husband and I invite first-time guests over for dinner. Many friends have asked me to make the recipe again years after they first tried it.

—Cara Langer, Overland Park, KS

TAKES: 30 min. • **MAKES:** 6 servings

- 1 pkg. (16 oz.) penne pasta
- 3 Tbsp. butter
- 2 garlic cloves, minced
- 4 oz. thinly sliced prosciutto, cut into strips
- 1 can (28 oz.) whole plum tomatoes, drained and chopped
- ¼ cup vodka
- ½ tsp. salt
- ½ tsp. crushed red pepper flakes
- ½ cup heavy whipping cream
- ½ cup shredded Parmesan cheese

1. Cook the pasta according to the package directions.
2. Meanwhile, in a large skillet, heat butter over medium-high heat. Add garlic; cook and stir 1 minute. Add prosciutto; cook 2 minutes longer. Stir in tomatoes, vodka, salt and pepper flakes. Bring to a boil. Reduce heat; simmer, uncovered, 5 minutes. Stir in the cream; cook 2-3 minutes longer, stirring occasionally.
3. Drain pasta. Add pasta and cheese to sauce; toss to combine.
1⅓ CUPS: 504 cal., 19g fat (11g sat. fat), 64mg chol., 966mg sod., 62g carb. (6g sugars, 4g fiber), 19g pro.

Fish & Seafood

EAT SMART

FISH TACOS WITH GUACAMOLE

Fish tacos are my new favorite thing—lighter and healthier than beef tacos smothered in cheese. Try adding chopped tomatoes, green onions and jalapeno on top.
—Deb Perry, Traverse City, MI

PREP: 25 min. • **COOK:** 10 min.
MAKES: 4 servings

 2 cups angel hair coleslaw mix
1½ tsp. canola oil
1½ tsp. lime juice
GUACAMOLE
 1 medium ripe avocado, peeled
   and quartered
 2 Tbsp. fat-free sour cream
 1 Tbsp. finely chopped onion
 1 Tbsp. minced fresh cilantro
 ⅛ tsp. salt
   Dash pepper
TACOS
 1 lb. tilapia fillets, cut into
   1-in. pieces
 ¼ tsp. salt
 ⅛ tsp. pepper
 2 tsp. canola oil
 8 corn tortillas (6 in.), warmed
   Optional toppings: hot pepper
   sauce, chopped tomatoes, green
   onions and jalapeno pepper

1. In a small bowl, toss coleslaw mix with oil and lime juice; refrigerate until serving. In another bowl, mash avocado with a fork; stir in sour cream, onion, cilantro, salt and pepper.
2. Sprinkle tilapia with salt and pepper. In a large nonstick skillet coated with cooking spray, heat oil over medium-high heat. Add tilapia; cook until fish just begins to flake easily with a fork, 3-4 minutes on each side. Serve in tortillas with coleslaw, guacamole and desired toppings.
2 TACOS: 308 cal., 12g fat (2g sat. fat), 56mg chol., 299mg sod., 28g carb. (2g sugars, 6g fiber), 25g pro. **DIABETIC EXCHANGES:** 3 lean meat, 2 starch, 2 fat.

FISH TACOS WITH GUACAMOLE

CHIVE CRAB CAKES

SALMON WITH POLENTA

My husband was of Italian-Swiss descent, and one of his favorite dishes was salmon or bass with tomato sauce served over polenta. I still prepare this recipe for my son and his family.
—Rena Pilotti, Ripon, CA

PREP: 20 min. + simmering
COOK: 25 min. • **MAKES:** 6 servings

- 2 celery ribs, chopped
- 1 medium onion, chopped
- 2 Tbsp. olive oil, divided
- 1 can (28 oz.) diced tomatoes, undrained
- 1 can (8 oz.) tomato sauce
- ¼ cup minced fresh parsley
- 1½ tsp. salt, divided
- 1 tsp. Italian seasoning
- ½ tsp. dried thyme
- ½ tsp. dried basil
- ½ tsp. pepper
- 6 cups water
- 2 cups cornmeal
- ¼ cup all-purpose flour
- 6 salmon fillets (6 oz. each)

1. In a Dutch oven, saute celery and onion in 1 Tbsp. oil until tender. Add the tomatoes, tomato sauce, parsley, ½ tsp. salt, Italian seasoning, thyme, basil and pepper. Cover and simmer for 1 hour, stirring occasionally.
2. In a large heavy saucepan, bring water and remaining salt to a boil. Reduce heat to a gentle boil; slowly whisk in cornmeal. Cook and stir with a wooden spoon for 15-20 minutes or until polenta is thickened and pulls away cleanly from the sides of the pan.
3. Place flour in a large shallow bowl; coat salmon on both sides. In a large skillet, brown salmon in remaining oil. Transfer salmon to tomato mixture; cook, uncovered, until fish just begins to flake with a fork, 3-5 minutes. Serve salmon and sauce with polenta.
1 SERVING: 583 cal., 24g fat (4g sat. fat), 100mg chol., 1068mg sod., 50g carb. (7g sugars, 7g fiber), 40g pro.

CHIVE CRAB CAKES

These tasty crab cakes are perfect for appetizers, or try them with a salad for a light meal.
—Cindy Worth, Lapwai, ID

PREP: 20 min. + chilling
COOK: 10 min./batch
MAKES: 6 servings

- 4 large egg whites
- 1 large egg
- 2 cups panko (Japanese) bread crumbs, divided
- 6 Tbsp. minced fresh chives
- 3 Tbsp. all-purpose flour
- 1 to 2 tsp. hot pepper sauce
- 1 tsp. baking powder
- ½ tsp. salt
- ¼ tsp. pepper
- 4 cans (6 oz. each) crabmeat, drained, flaked and cartilage removed
- 2 Tbsp. canola oil
  Lemon wedges, optional

1. In a large bowl, lightly beat the egg whites and egg. Add ¾ cup bread crumbs, chives, flour, pepper sauce, baking powder, salt and pepper; mix well. Fold in crab. Cover and refrigerate for at least 2 hours.
2. Place remaining bread crumbs in a shallow bowl. Drop crab mixture by scant ¼ cupfuls into crumbs. Gently coat and shape into ½-in.-thick patties. **3.** In a large nonstick skillet, cook crab cakes in oil in batches over medium-high heat for 3-4 minutes on each side or until golden brown. If desired, serve with lemon wedges.
2 CRAB CAKES: 238 cal., 6g fat (0 sat. fat), 142mg chol., 1018mg sod., 16g carb. (0 sugars, 0 fiber), 26g pro.

LEMON SHRIMP WITH PARMESAN RICE

I grew up in Biloxi, Mississippi, where rice, garlic and seafood are staples in Gulf Coast cuisine. This easy dish is a longtime family favorite that's ready in minutes.
—Amie Overby, Reno, NV

TAKES: 20 min. • **MAKES:** 4 servings

- 2 cups chicken broth
- 2 cups uncooked instant rice
- 1 lb. uncooked medium shrimp, peeled and deveined
- ½ cup chopped green onions
- 2 Tbsp. butter
- 2 Tbsp. olive oil
- 2 tsp. minced garlic
- 3 Tbsp. lemon juice
- ¼ tsp. pepper
- ½ cup grated Parmesan cheese
- 2 Tbsp. minced fresh parsley

1. In a small saucepan, bring broth to a boil. Stir in rice; cover and remove from the heat. Let stand for 5 minutes.
2. Meanwhile, in a large skillet, cook shrimp and onions in butter and oil over medium heat for 4-5 minutes. Add garlic and cook 1 minute longer or until garlic is tender and shrimp turn pink. Stir in lemon juice and pepper.
3. Stir cheese and parsley into rice; serve with shrimp.
1 SERVING: 438 cal., 17g fat (7g sat. fat), 191mg chol., 908mg sod., 43g carb. (2g sugars, 1g fiber), 27g pro.

SPICY TILAPIA RICE BOWL

I love eating well, and tilapia is a staple in my kitchen. Fresh vegetables are always good but take more prep time, so I like the frozen veggie blend here.
—Rosalin Johnson, Tupelo, MS

TAKES: 30 min. • **MAKES:** 4 servings

- 4 tilapia fillets (4 oz. each)
- 1¼ tsp. Cajun seasoning
- 3 Tbsp. olive oil, divided
- 1 medium yellow summer squash, halved lengthwise and sliced
- 1 pkg. (16 oz.) frozen pepper and onion stir-fry blend
- 1 can (14½ oz.) diced tomatoes, drained
- 1 envelope fajita seasoning mix
- 1 can (15 oz.) black beans, rinsed and drained
- ⅛ tsp. salt
- ⅛ tsp. pepper
- 3 cups hot cooked brown rice

Optional toppings: cubed avocado, sour cream and salsa

1. Sprinkle fillets with Cajun seasoning. In a large skillet, heat 2 Tbsp. oil over medium heat. Add fillets; cook until fish just begins to flake easily with a fork, 4-6 minutes on each side. Remove from pan and keep warm. Wipe pan clean.
2. In same skillet, heat remaining oil. Add squash; cook and stir 3 minutes. Add the stir-fry blend and tomatoes; cook until the vegetables are tender, 6-8 minutes longer. Stir in the fajita seasoning mix; cook and stir until slightly thickened, 1-2 minutes longer.
3. In a small bowl, mix beans, salt and pepper. Divide the rice among four serving bowls; layer with beans, vegetables and fillets. If desired, serve with toppings.
1 SERVING: 538 cal., 13g fat (2g sat. fat), 55mg chol., 1365mg sod., 71g carb. (11g sugars, 10g fiber), 33g pro.

SPICY TILAPIA RICE BOWL

SHRIMP PASTA
ALFREDO

COCONUT-CRUSTED PERCH

A coconut breading lends tropical taste to tender perch served with a sweet-and-sour sauce for dipping. I've made this dish for my family for years. It's good with any kind of whitefish.
—Norma Thurber, Johnston, RI

PREP: 20 min. • **COOK:** 15 min.
MAKES: 8 servings

- ½ cup apricot preserves
- ¼ cup ketchup
- ¼ cup light corn syrup
- 2 Tbsp. lemon juice
- ¼ tsp. ground ginger
- 2 cups crushed Ritz crackers (about 50 crackers)
- 1 cup sweetened shredded coconut
- 2 large eggs
- 2 Tbsp. evaporated milk
- ½ tsp. salt
- 3 lbs. perch fillets
- 1 cup canola oil, divided

1. For sweet-and-sour sauce, combine the preserves, ketchup, corn syrup, lemon juice and ginger in a small saucepan. Bring to a boil. Reduce heat; simmer, uncovered, for 5 minutes or until slightly thickened. Remove from the heat and keep warm.
2. In a shallow dish, combine the cracker crumbs and coconut. In another shallow dish, whisk the eggs, milk and salt. Dip fillets in egg mixture, then coat with crumb mixture.
3. In a large skillet, cook fish in 3 Tbsp. oil in batches over medium-high heat for 1-2 minutes on each side or until fish just begins to flake with a fork, adding oil as needed. Serve with sweet-and-sour sauce.
5 OZ. COOKED FISH WITH 2 TBSP. SAUCE: 497 cal., 20g fat (6g sat. fat), 201mg chol., 570mg sod., 42g carb. (24g sugars, 1g fiber), 37g pro.

SHRIMP PASTA ALFREDO

My son loves any recipe with Alfredo sauce. When he cooked as a bachelor, shrimp pasta was one of his first recipes. Now his children ask for it.
—Gail Lucas, Olive Branch, MS

TAKES: 25 min. • **MAKES:** 4 servings

- 3 cups uncooked bow tie pasta
- 2 cups frozen peas
- 1 lb. peeled and deveined cooked medium shrimp, tails removed
- 1 jar (15 oz.) Alfredo sauce
- ¼ cup shredded Parmesan cheese

1. In a Dutch oven, cook pasta according to package directions, adding peas during the last 3 minutes of cooking; drain and return to pan.
2. Stir in shrimp and sauce; heat through over medium heat, stirring occasionally. Sprinkle with cheese.
2 CUPS: 545 cal., 16g fat (9g sat. fat), 206mg chol., 750mg sod., 60g carb. (5g sugars, 6g fiber), 41g pro.

"This was so easy to make. Just five ingredients, and it was delicious. I especially liked the way the peas kept their flavor. I shared it with my daughter and she agreed that it was a keeper recipe."
—BUTLERMARY75, TASTEOFHOME.COM

SHRIMP &
NECTARINE
SALAD

SHRIMP & NECTARINE SALAD

For a cool salad on a hot summer day, I combine shrimp, corn, tomatoes and nectarines with a drizzle of tarragon dressing. We love it chilled, but it's delectable warm, too.
—Mary Ann Lee, Clifton Park, NY

TAKES: 30 min. • **MAKES:** 4 servings

⅓ cup orange juice
3 Tbsp. cider vinegar
1½ tsp. Dijon mustard
1½ tsp. honey
1 Tbsp. minced fresh tarragon
SALAD
4 tsp. canola oil, divided
1 cup fresh or frozen corn
1 lb. uncooked shrimp (26-30 per lb.), peeled and deveined
½ tsp. lemon-pepper seasoning
¼ tsp. salt
8 cups torn mixed salad greens
2 medium nectarines, cut into 1-in. pieces
1 cup grape tomatoes, halved
½ cup finely chopped red onion

1. In a small bowl, whisk orange juice, vinegar, mustard and honey until blended. Stir in tarragon.
2. In a large skillet, heat 1 tsp. oil over medium-high heat. Add corn; cook and stir 1-2 minutes or until crisp-tender. Remove from pan.
3. Sprinkle shrimp with lemon pepper and salt. In the same skillet, heat remaining oil over medium-high heat. Add shrimp; cook and stir 3-4 minutes or until shrimp turn pink. Stir in corn.
4. In a large bowl, combine remaining ingredients. Drizzle with ⅓ cup dressing and toss to coat. Divide mixture among four plates. Top with shrimp mixture; drizzle with remaining dressing. Serve immediately.

1 SERVING: 252 cal., 7g fat (1g sat. fat), 138mg chol., 448mg sod., 27g carb. (14g sugars, 5g fiber), 23g pro. **DIABETIC EXCHANGES:** 3 lean meat, 2 vegetable, 1 fat, ½ starch, ½ fruit.

TEST KITCHEN TIP
Many fruit juices and nectars—such as orange, grapefruit, apple, lemon, pomegranate and mango—can be made into light and flavorful vinaigrettes to dress salad greens.

COCONUT CURRY SHRIMP

Here's a shrimp dish with sweet coconut milk, complemented by the spiciness of curry. Jasmine rice makes a fragrant bed for the sumptuous stir-fry.
—Cindy Romberg, Mississauga, ON

TAKES: 25 min. • **MAKES:** 3 servings

- ⅔ cup coconut milk
- 1 Tbsp. fish sauce
- 1½ tsp. curry powder
- 1 tsp. brown sugar
- ¼ tsp. salt
- ¼ tsp. pepper
- 1 lb. uncooked large shrimp, peeled and deveined
- 1 medium sweet red pepper, finely chopped
- 2 green onions, chopped
- ¼ cup minced fresh cilantro
  Hot cooked jasmine rice
  Lime wedges

1. In a small bowl, combine the first six ingredients. In a large skillet or wok, stir-fry shrimp in 2 Tbsp. coconut milk mixture until shrimp turn pink. Remove and keep warm.
2. Add the red pepper, green onions and remaining coconut milk mixture to pan. Bring to a boil; cook and stir for 3-4 minutes or until vegetables are crisp-tender. Add shrimp and cilantro; heat through. Serve with rice and lime wedges.
1 CUP SHRIMP MIXTURE: 256 cal., 13g fat (10g sat. fat), 184mg chol., 841mg sod., 8g carb. (4g sugars, 2g fiber), 27g pro.

SWISS TUNA MELTS

These hot sandwiches pair perfectly with your favorite homemade soup. You'll love the crunch the celery gives to the creamy tuna filling. If you'd like to kick up the flavor a notch, add a pinch of garlic powder and dill relish.
—Karen Owen, Rising Sun, IN

TAKES: 20 min. • **MAKES:** 4 servings

- 1 can (6 oz.) light water-packed tuna, drained and flaked
- ¾ cup shredded Swiss cheese
- ¼ cup chopped onion
- ¼ cup chopped celery
- ½ cup sour cream
- ½ cup mayonnaise
  Pepper to taste
- 8 slices bread
- 2 to 3 Tbsp. butter, softened

1. In a large bowl, combine the tuna, cheese, onion and celery. In a small bowl, combine the sour cream and mayonnaise. Pour over tuna mixture and toss to coat. Spread about ½ cup over four slices of bread; top with remaining bread. Butter the outsides of sandwiches.
2. On a griddle or in a large skillet over medium heat, toast sandwiches for 4-5 minutes on each side or until lightly browned.
1 SANDWICH: 576 cal., 42g fat (15g sat. fat), 58mg chol., 672mg sod., 31g carb. (5g sugars, 2g fiber), 20g pro.

COCONUT
CURRY SHRIMP

TUNA STEAK
ON FETTUCCINE

CARIBBEAN SHRIMP & RICE BOWL

I had a similar rice bowl on vacation and re-created this lighter version at home. It takes me back to the islands every time I make it. Try grilling the shrimp for a more beachy flavor.
—Lauren Katz, Ashburn, VA

TAKES: 20 min. • **MAKES:** 4 servings

- 1 medium ripe avocado, peeled and pitted
- ⅓ cup reduced-fat sour cream
- ¼ tsp. salt
- 1 can (15 oz.) black beans, rinsed and drained
- 1 can (8 oz.) unsweetened crushed pineapple, undrained
- 1 medium mango, peeled and cubed
- ½ cup salsa
- 1 pkg. (8.8 oz.) ready-to-serve brown rice
- 1 lb. uncooked shrimp (31-40 per lb.), peeled and deveined
- 1 tsp. Caribbean jerk seasoning
- 1 Tbsp. canola oil
- 2 green onions, sliced
  Lime wedges, optional

1. For avocado cream, mash avocado with sour cream and salt until smooth. In a small saucepan, combine beans, pineapple, mango and salsa; heat through, stirring occasionally. Prepare rice according to package directions.
2. Toss shrimp with jerk seasoning. In a large skillet, heat oil over medium-high heat. Add shrimp; cook and stir 2-3 minutes or until shrimp turn pink.
3. Divide rice and bean mixture among four bowls. Top with shrimp and green onions. Serve with avocado cream and, if desired, lime wedges.
1 SERVING: 498 cal., 14g fat (2g sat. fat), 145mg chol., 698mg sod., 62g carb. (23g sugars, 9g fiber), 29g pro.

TUNA STEAK ON FETTUCCINE

For something new to do with tuna, I suggest this tangy dish. Although I prefer the marinade on tuna or mahi mahi, it's scrumptious on any fish, grilled, baked or broiled.
—Caren Stearns, Austin, TX

PREP: 10 min. + marinating
COOK: 20 min. • **MAKES:** 2 servings

- 8 Tbsp. white wine or chicken broth, divided
- 3 Tbsp. olive oil, divided
- 1 tsp. dried basil, divided
- 1 tsp. dried oregano, divided
- ¼ tsp. salt, divided
- ⅛ tsp. pepper, divided
- 1 tuna, swordfish or halibut steak (about 10 oz.), cut in half
- ½ cup thinly sliced sweet onion
- 1 cup canned diced tomatoes, undrained
- ¼ tsp. brown sugar
- 3 oz. uncooked fettuccine

1. In a resealable plastic bag, combine 2 Tbsp. wine, 2 Tbsp. oil, ¼ tsp. basil, ¼ tsp. oregano, and half the salt and pepper; add tuna. Seal bag and turn to coat; refrigerate 1 hour.
2. In a large skillet, saute onion in the remaining oil until tender. Add the tomatoes, brown sugar and remaining wine, basil, oregano, salt and pepper. Bring to a boil. Reduce heat; simmer, uncovered, until bubbly and slightly thickened, 4-6 minutes. Meanwhile, cook fettuccine according to the package directions.
3. Drain tuna, discarding marinade. Place tuna over tomato mixture; return to a boil. Reduce heat; simmer, covered, until fish just begins to flake easily with a fork, about 6 minutes. Remove tuna and keep warm. Drain fettuccine; add to tomato mixture and toss to coat. Divide between two plates; top with tuna.
1 SERVING: 505 cal., 17g fat (3g sat. fat), 55mg chol., 518mg sod., 41g carb. (8g sugars, 5g fiber), 42g pro.

CARIBBEAN SHRIMP & RICE BOWL

SALMON WITH SWEET SALSA

After years of not eating salmon, I tasted it one night at a formal dinner, where it was served with a sweet topping that I really liked. After experimenting on my own, I came up with this sweet and spicy combo that's become a favorite. I love to serve it with fried rice I pick up on my way home from work.
—Rebecca Reece, Henderson, NV

TAKES: 15 min. • **MAKES:** 4 servings

- 4 salmon fillets (6 oz. each)
- 4 tsp. Creole seasoning
- 2 Tbsp. olive oil
- ¾ cup salsa
- ½ cup apricot preserves

1. Sprinkle one side of salmon fillets with Creole seasoning. In a large skillet, cook salmon, seasoned side down, in oil over medium-high heat for 2 minutes. Turn salmon; reduce heat to medium and cook until fish just begins to flake easily with a fork, 8-10 minutes.
2. Meanwhile, in a small bowl, combine the salsa and apricot preserves. Serve with salmon.
NOTE: The following spices may be substituted for 1 tsp. of Creole seasoning: ¼ tsp. each salt, garlic powder and paprika; and a pinch each of dried thyme, ground cumin and cayenne pepper.
1 SERVING: 249 cal., 11g fat (2g sat. fat), 25mg chol., 915mg sod., 27g carb. (26g sugars, 2g fiber), 9g pro.

"Delicious! I was afraid the Creole seasoning would be too salty, but the sweet salsa balanced it out nicely. This was a super easy entree for Mother's Day dinner."
—KATLAYDEE3, TASTEOFHOME.COM

CRUMB-COATED RED SNAPPER

CRUMB-COATED RED SNAPPER

I reel in the compliments when I serve these crispy fillets. Heart-healthy omega-3 oils are an added bonus with this simple but delicious entree that's ready in just minutes. It's one of the best red snapper recipes I've found.
—Charlotte Elliott, Neenah, WI

TAKES: 30 min. • **MAKES:** 4 servings

- ½ cup dry bread crumbs
- 2 Tbsp. grated Parmesan cheese
- 1 tsp. lemon-pepper seasoning
- ¼ tsp. salt
- 4 red snapper fillets (6 oz. each)
- 2 Tbsp. olive oil

1. In a shallow bowl, combine the bread crumbs, cheese, lemon pepper and salt; add fillets, one at a time, and turn to coat.
2. In a heavy skillet over medium heat, cook fillets in oil, in batches, until fish just begins to flake easily with a fork, 4-5 minutes on each side.
6 OZ.: 288 cal., 10g fat (2g sat. fat), 62mg chol., 498mg sod., 10g carb. (0 sugars, 0 fiber), 36g pro. **DIABETIC EXCHANGES:** 5 lean meat, 1 fat, ½ starch.

TUNA NOODLE SKILLET

Enjoy the comforting flavor of tuna noodle casserole in minutes with this simple stovetop version. It's easy to make with convenient ingredients like frozen peas and jarred Alfredo sauce.
—Ruth Simon, Buffalo, NY

TAKES: 30 min. • **MAKES:** 6 servings

- 2 jars (16 oz. each) Alfredo sauce
- 1 can (14½ oz.) chicken broth
- 1 pkg. (16 oz.) wide egg noodles
- 1 pkg. (10 oz.) frozen peas
- ¼ tsp. pepper
- 1 can (12 oz.) albacore white tuna in water

1. In a large skillet over medium heat, bring Alfredo sauce and broth to a boil. Add noodles; cover and cook for 7-8 minutes.
2. Reduce heat; stir in peas and pepper. Cover and cook 4 minutes longer or until noodles are tender. Stir in tuna; heat through.
1⅔ CUPS: 620 cal., 21g fat (12g sat. fat), 131mg chol., 1179mg sod., 73g carb. (4g sugars, 6g fiber), 34g pro.

SHRIMP & BROCCOLI BROWN RICE PAELLA

Years ago my husband and I were vacationing in France and came across an open market where a man from Spain was making paella in a skillet; we've been hooked ever since. I love to whip this up for a large group, but if the gathering is small, I know I can easily freeze leftovers for another time.
—Joni Hilton, Rocklin, CA

PREP: 45 min. • **COOK:** 50 min.
MAKES: 8 servings

- 1 Tbsp. olive oil
- 1 medium onion, chopped
- 1 medium sweet red pepper, chopped
- 1 cup sliced fresh mushrooms
- 2 cups uncooked long grain brown rice
- 2 garlic cloves, minced
- 2 tsp. paprika
- ½ tsp. salt
- ½ tsp. cayenne pepper
- ¼ tsp. saffron threads
- 6 cups chicken stock
- 2 lbs. uncooked large shrimp, peeled and deveined
- 1½ cups fresh broccoli florets
- 1 cup frozen peas

1. In a Dutch oven, heat oil over medium-high heat. Add onion, red pepper and mushrooms; cook and stir 6-8 minutes or until tender. Stir in the rice, garlic and seasonings; cook 1-2 minutes longer.
2. Stir in stock; bring to a boil. Reduce heat; simmer, covered, 40-45 minutes or until liquid is absorbed and rice is tender. Add shrimp and broccoli; cook 8-10 minutes longer or until shrimp turn pink. Stir in peas; heat through.
FREEZE OPTION: Place cooled paella in freezer containers. To use, partially thaw in refrigerator overnight. Microwave, covered, on high in a microwave-safe dish until heated through, stirring gently and adding a little stock or water if necessary.
1½ CUPS: 331 cal., 5g fat (1g sat. fat), 138mg chol., 693mg sod., 44g carb. (4g sugars, 4g fiber), 27g pro. **DIABETIC EXCHANGES:** 3 lean meat, 2½ starch.

HONEY-FRIED WALLEYE

We fish on most summer weekends, so we have lots of fresh fillets. Everyone who tries this crisy, golden fish loves it. It's one of my husband's favorite walleye recipes, and I never have leftovers. Honey gives the coating a deliciously different twist.
—Sharon Collis, Colona, IL

TAKES: 15 min. • **MAKES:** 6 servings

- 1 large egg
- 1 tsp. honey
- 1 cup coarsely crushed saltines (about 22 crackers)
- ⅓ cup all-purpose flour
- ¼ tsp. salt
- ¼ tsp. pepper
- 4 to 6 walleye fillets (about 1½ lbs.)
   Canola oil
   Additional honey

1. In a shallow bowl, beat egg and honey. In another bowl, combine the cracker crumbs, flour, salt and pepper. Dip fillets into egg mixture, then coat with crumb mixture.
2. In a large skillet, heat ¼ in. of oil; fry fish in the oil over medium-high heat for 3-4 minutes on each side or until fish just begins to flake easily with a fork. Drizzle with honey.
1 SERVING: 189 cal., 3g fat (1g sat. fat), 133mg chol., 296mg sod., 14g carb. (1g sugars, 1g fiber), 25g pro.

SHRIMP & BROCCOLI BROWN RICE PAELLA

SPICY SALMON PATTIES

Made with canned salmon, these patties are good hot or cold. I usually serve them on buns with slices of ripe tomato, sweet red onion, and red and green bell pepper.

—Barbara Coston, Little Rock, AR

TAKES: 30 min. • **MAKES:** 4 servings

- 2   slices whole wheat bread
- 12 miniature pretzels
- 2   tsp. Italian seasoning
- 2   tsp. salt-free spicy seasoning blend
- ½   tsp. pepper
- 2   large eggs, lightly beaten
- 1   can (14¾ oz.) salmon, drained, bones and skin removed
- ½   cup finely chopped onion
- ⅓   cup finely chopped green pepper
- 1   Tbsp. finely chopped jalapeno pepper
- 2   garlic cloves, minced
- 2   Tbsp. olive oil

1. Place the first five ingredients in a blender or food processor; cover and process until the mixture resembles fine crumbs.

2. In a bowl, combine the eggs, salmon, onion, green pepper, jalapeno, garlic and ½ cup crumb mixture. Shape into eight ½-in.-thick patties. Coat with the remaining crumb mixture.

3. In a large nonstick skillet over medium heat, cook patties in oil for 4-5 minutes on each side or until golden brown.

NOTE: Wear disposable gloves when cutting hot peppers; the oils can burn skin. Avoid touching your face.

2 PATTIES: 339 cal., 18g fat (3g sat. fat), 176mg chol., 607mg sod., 13g carb. (2g sugars, 2g fiber), 30g pro. **DIABETIC EXCHANGES:** 4 lean meat, 2 fat, 1 starch.

TILAPIA & LEMON SAUCE

Serve this dish with any tossed salad full of your favorite vegetables, plus some buttered bread. It's easy, quick and unique. And it's a big hit with company, too.

—Susan Taul, Birmingham, AL

TAKES: 30 min. • **MAKES:** 4 servings

- ¼   cup plus 1 Tbsp. all-purpose flour, divided
- 1   tsp. salt
- 4   tilapia fillets (4 oz. each)
- 2   Tbsp. plus 2 tsp. butter, divided
- ⅓   cup reduced-sodium chicken broth
- 2   Tbsp. white wine or additional reduced-sodium chicken broth
- 1½ tsp. lemon juice
- 1½ tsp. minced fresh parsley
- 2   cups hot cooked rice
- ¼   cup sliced almonds, toasted

1. In a shallow bowl, combine ¼ cup flour and the salt. Dip fillets in the flour mixture.

2. In a large nonstick skillet coated with cooking spray, cook fillets in 2 Tbsp. butter over medium-high heat until fish just begins to flake with a fork, 4-5 minutes on each side. Remove and keep warm.

3. In the same skillet, melt remaining butter. Stir in remaining flour until smooth; gradually add the broth, wine and lemon juice. Bring to a boil; cook and stir for 2 minutes or until thickened. Stir in parsley. Serve fish and sauce with rice; garnish with sliced almonds.

1 FILLET WITH ½ CUP RICE AND 4 TSP. SAUCE: 334 cal., 12g fat (6g sat. fat), 75mg chol., 586mg sod., 30g carb. (1g sugars, 1g fiber), 26g pro. **DIABETIC EXCHANGES:** 3 lean meat, 2 starch, 2 fat.

TILAPIA & LEMON SAUCE

THAI LIME SHRIMP & NOODLES

THAI LIME SHRIMP & NOODLES

The flavors just keep popping in this quick dinner! Use as much lime peel and chili paste as you like. My family is into spicy foods, but I kept the heat moderate in this version.

—Teri Rasey, Cadillac, MI

TAKES: 25 min. • **MAKES:** 6 servings

- 1 cup minced fresh basil
- 3 Tbsp. lime juice
- 4 tsp. Thai red chili paste
- 1 garlic clove, minced
- 1 tsp. minced fresh gingerroot
- 1½ lbs. uncooked shrimp (26-30 per lb.), peeled and deveined
- 12 oz. uncooked angel hair pasta
- 4 tsp. olive oil, divided

- 1 can (14½ oz.) chicken broth
- 1 can (13.66 oz.) coconut milk
- 1 tsp. salt
- 1 Tbsp. cornstarch
- 2 Tbsp. cold water
- 2 Tbsp. grated lime peel

1. Place the first five ingredients in a blender; cover and process until blended. Remove 1 Tbsp. mixture; toss with shrimp.

2. Cook pasta according to package directions. Meanwhile, in a large nonstick skillet, heat 2 tsp. oil over medium-high heat. Add half of the shrimp mixture; stir-fry 2-4 minutes or until shrimp turn pink. Remove from pan; keep warm. Repeat with remaining oil and shrimp mixture.

3. Add broth, coconut milk, salt and remaining basil mixture to same pan. In a small bowl, mix cornstarch and water until smooth. Stir into broth mixture. Bring to a boil; cook and stir 1-2 minutes or until slightly thickened. Stir in lime peel.

4. Drain pasta; add pasta and shrimp to sauce, tossing to coat.

1 SERVING: 486 cal., 20g fat (13g sat. fat), 141mg chol., 865mg sod., 49g carb. (3g sugars, 2g fiber), 28g pro.

COD & ASPARGUS BAKE
PAGE 226

169

206

221

188

Oven Entrees

Nothing warms the heart like a hot-from-the-oven dish. These are the comfort-food superstars: bubbly casseroles, homey potpies, saucy manicotti and family-favorite meat loaves. You'll find 105 oven specialties, including easy sheet-pan suppers, quick broiled dinners and fun, melty sandwiches made to share. Go ahead, dig into oven-fresh goodness.

Beef & Ground Beef

MINI SHEPHERD'S PIES

FREEZE IT
MINI SHEPHERD'S PIES

I'm as confident serving these little freezer-friendly pies to company as I am serving them to my husband and three boys. If I'm not rushed for time, I make these with homemade biscuits and mashed potatoes.
—Ellen Osborne, Clarksville, TN

PREP: 30 min. • **BAKE:** 20 min.
MAKES: 5 servings

- 1 lb. ground beef
- ¼ cup chopped onion
- 1 garlic clove, minced
- ⅓ cup chili sauce or ketchup
- 1 Tbsp. cider vinegar
- 1¼ cups water
- 3 oz. cream cheese, cubed
- 3 Tbsp. butter
- 1¼ cups mashed potato flakes
- 2 tubes (6 oz. each) small refrigerated buttermilk biscuits
- ½ cup crushed potato chips
  Paprika, optional

1. Preheat oven to 375°. In a large skillet, cook and crumble beef with onion and garlic over medium heat until no longer pink, 5-7 minutes; drain. Stir in chili sauce and vinegar.
2. In a small saucepan, combine water, cream cheese and butter; bring to a boil. Remove from heat; stir in the potato flakes.
3. Separate biscuits; press each onto bottom and up sides of a greased muffin cup. Fill with beef mixture; top with mashed potatoes. Sprinkle with potato chips.
4. Bake mini pies until the topping is golden brown, 20-25 minutes. If desired, sprinkle with paprika.
FREEZE OPTION: Freeze cooled pies in a single layer in freezer containers. To use, partially thaw in refrigerator overnight. Reheat on a baking sheet in a preheated 375° oven until heated through, 15-18 minutes.
2 MINI SHEPHERD'S PIES: 612 cal., 36g fat (15g sat. fat), 92mg chol., 1094mg sod., 49g carb. (11g sugars, 2g fiber), 24g pro.

SMOTHERED BURRITOS

TOURTIERES

TOURTIERES

Some time ago, a co-worker brought a meat pie to lunch. The aroma was so familiar—after one taste, I was amazed to discover it was the same pie that my grandmother used to serve when I was a youngster! The co-worker gave me the recipe, and I have been enjoying it ever since.
—Rita Winterberger, Huson, MT

PREP: 20 min. • **BAKE:** 30 min.
MAKES: 2 pies (8 servings each)

- 2 large onions, thinly sliced
- ¼ cup canola oil
- 2 lbs. ground beef
- 2 lbs. ground pork
- 3 cups frozen mixed vegetables
- 2 cups mashed potatoes
- 1 Tbsp. ground allspice
- 2 tsp. salt
- ½ tsp. pepper
  Pastry for two double-crust pies (9 in.)
- 1 large egg, lightly beaten

1. In a Dutch oven, saute onions in oil until tender. Remove and set aside. In the same pan, cook the beef and pork over medium heat until meat is no longer pink; drain. Remove from the heat. Add the onions, vegetables, potatoes and seasonings.
2. Line two 9-in. pie plates with the bottom crusts; trim crust even with edge of plate. Fill each with about 5 cups filling. Roll out remaining crust to fit tops of pies; place over filling. Trim, seal and flute the edges. Cut slits in crust and brush the tops with egg. Bake at 375° for 30-35 minutes or until golden brown.
FREEZE OPTION: Cover and freeze unbaked pies. To use, remove from freezer 30 minutes before baking (do not thaw). Preheat oven to 425°. Bake 15 minutes. Reduce heat to 375°. Cover edges loosely with foil and bake for 35-40 minutes longer or until crusts are golden brown.
1 PIECE: 487 cal., 31g fat (13g sat. fat), 115mg chol., 620mg sod., 26g carb. (2g sugars, 3g fiber), 25g pro.

SMOTHERED BURRITOS

This recipe is quick and easy and will satisfy even the pickiest of eaters. Salsa verde is spicy. You can reduce the amount of salsa verde to make a milder version.
—Kim Kenyon, Greenwood, MO

TAKES: 30 min. • **MAKES:** 4 servings

- 1 can (10 oz.) green enchilada sauce
- ¾ cup salsa verde
- 1 lb. ground beef
- 4 flour tortillas (10 in.)
- 1½ cups shredded cheddar cheese, divided

1. Preheat oven to 375°. In a small bowl, mix enchilada sauce and salsa verde.
2. In a large skillet, cook the beef over medium heat 8-10 minutes or until no longer pink, breaking into crumbles; drain. Stir in ½ cup sauce mixture.
3. Spoon ⅔ cup beef mixture across center of each tortilla; top each with 3 Tbsp. cheese. Fold bottom and sides of tortilla over filling and roll up.
4. Place in a greased 11x7-in. baking dish. Pour remaining sauce mixture over top; sprinkle with remaining ¾ cup cheese. Bake, uncovered, for 10-15 minutes or until cheese is melted.
1 BURRITO: 624 cal., 33g fat (15g sat. fat), 115mg chol., 1470mg sod., 44g carb. (6g sugars, 2g fiber), 36g pro.

"Raves from my husband. I will make this again. It would be easy to substitute leftover rotisserie chicken or holiday turkey. I could easily double or triple it to bring to potluck dinners!"
—CASAPRKY, TASTEOFHOME.COM

CHILI COTTAGE PIE

CHILI COTTAGE PIE

This filling cottage pie is creamy with cheesy potato and loaded with chili flavor. The kids love to help layer it up.
—Jacob Miller, Ledyard, CT

PREP: 25 min. • **BAKE:** 15 min.
MAKES: 8 servings

- 1 lb. ground beef
- ¼ tsp. salt
- ¼ tsp. pepper
- 1 Tbsp. olive oil
- 1 medium red onion, diced
- 6 garlic cloves, minced
- 1 pkg. (16 oz.) frozen mixed vegetables
- 1 can (16 oz.) kidney beans, rinsed and drained
- 1 can (14½ oz.) diced tomatoes
- 1 cup beef stock
- 1 envelope chili seasoning mix
- 1 pkg. (24 oz.) refrigerated mashed potatoes
- 1 cup shredded cheddar-Monterey Jack cheese
- 4 green onions, thinly sliced Grated Parmesan cheese

1. Preheat oven to 350°. In a large skillet, cook and crumble beef, salt and pepper until beef is no longer pink; drain and remove from skillet.
2. In the same skillet, heat oil over medium heat. Add onion; cook and stir until tender, 2-3 minutes. Add garlic, cook 1 minute longer.
3. Add beef, mixed vegetables, kidney beans, tomatoes, beef stock and chili seasoning; bring to a boil. Cook and stir until thickened, about 5 minutes. Transfer to a greased 13x9-in. baking dish. Heat mashed potatoes according to microwave package directions; spread over top of beef mixture.
4. Sprinkle with the cheese; bake until the casserole is bubbly and cheese is melted, 15-20 minutes. Cool for about 5 minutes; sprinkle with green onions and Parmesan cheese.
1 SERVING: 390 cal., 16g fat (8g sat. fat), 58mg chol., 992mg sod., 33g carb. (7g sugars, 7g fiber), 21g pro.

TEST KITCHEN TIP

Cottage pie or shepherd's pie? Traditionally, shepherd's pie is made with lamb, while cottage pie is the same dish but prepared with beef.

NEW-WORLD STUFFED CABBAGE

European immigrants brought their favorite stuffed cabbage recipes to the New World in the 19th century. Here's my take on tradition.

—Katherine Stefanovich, Desert Hot Springs, CA

PREP: 45 min. • **BAKE:** 2 hours
MAKES: 6 servings

- 1   medium head cabbage
- 1   can (16 oz.) sauerkraut, divided
- 3   bacon strips, diced
- 1   cup finely chopped onion
- 2   garlic cloves, minced
- ¼   cup all-purpose flour
- 1   Tbsp. Hungarian paprika
- ¼   tsp. cayenne pepper
- 1   can (16 oz.) crushed tomatoes
- 2   cups beef broth
- 1   cup cooked long grain rice
- 1   lb. ground turkey
- 2   Tbsp. chopped fresh parsley
- 1   tsp. salt
- ½   tsp. pepper
- 1   large egg, beaten

1. Remove core from head of cabbage. Place in a large saucepan and cover with water. Bring to a boil; boil until outer leaves loosen from head. Lift out cabbage; remove the softened leaves. Return head to boiling water to soften more leaves. Repeat until all leaves are removed. Remove tough center stalk from each leaf. Set aside 12 large leaves for the rolls; reserve the balance to use as the recipe directs. Spoon half of the sauerkraut into Dutch oven; set aside.
2. In a heavy saucepan, fry bacon until crisp. Remove to paper towels. In the drippings, saute onion and garlic until tender. Remove half to a bowl to cool. To remaining onion mixture, add the flour, paprika and cayenne pepper. Cook and stir for 1 to 2 minutes. Stir in tomatoes and broth; bring to a boil. Remove from the heat and set aside.

To cooled onion mixture, add rice, turkey, parsley, salt, pepper, egg and bacon; mix well.
3. Place 3-4 Tbsp. of the mixture on each cabbage leaf. Roll up, tucking in sides. Place rolls, seam side down, on sauerkraut in Dutch oven. Cover with remaining sauerkraut. Chop remaining cabbage leaves; place over sauerkraut. Pour tomato mixture over all, adding water to cover if necessary. Cover and bake at 325° for about 2 hours.
2 CABBAGE ROLLS: 352 cal., 13g fat (4g sat. fat), 90mg chol., 1508mg sod., 38g carb. (11g sugars, 9g fiber), 24g pro.

BBQ SHORT RIBS

These short ribs remain popular with good reason. The meat is fork-tender, and the sauce is wonderfully tangy. We're retired now but raised beef for many years. We still put this recipe to good use.

—Margery Bryan, Moses Lake, WA

PREP: 1¼ hours • **BAKE:** 1¼ hours
MAKES: 6 servings

- 3½ to 4 lbs. beef short ribs
- 1½ cups water
- 1   medium onion, sliced
- 1   Tbsp. vinegar

SAUCE
- ½   cup ketchup
- ¼   cup chopped onion
- 2   Tbsp. lemon juice
- 2   garlic cloves, minced
- 1   tsp. sugar
- ½   tsp. salt
- ⅛   tsp. pepper

1. In a Dutch oven, combine the ribs, water, onion and vinegar; bring to a boil. Reduce hat; cover and simmer for 1 hour, turning ribs occasionally. Drain.
2. Place the ribs in a single layer in an ungreased 13-in. x 9-in. baking dish. Combine sauce ingredients; spoon over ribs. Bake at 325°, covered, until meat is tender, about 1¼ hours.
1 SERVING: 241 cal., 12g fat (5g sat. fat), 64mg chol., 475mg sod., 10g carb. (5g sugars, 1g fiber), 22g pro.

NEW-WORLD STUFFED CABBAGE

BAKED MEXICAN LASAGNA

Take lasagna south of the border with big Mexican flavor and corn tortillas instead of noodles. This is a favorite in our Southern home.
—Jeanne Bennett, North Richland Hills, TX

PREP: 20 min. • **BAKE:** 30 min.
MAKES: 8 servings

- 1½ lbs. ground beef
- 1½ tsp. ground cumin
- 1 Tbsp. chili powder
- ¼ tsp. garlic powder
- ¼ tsp. cayenne pepper
- 1 tsp. salt or to taste
- 1 tsp. pepper or to taste
- 1 can (14½ oz.) diced tomatoes, drained
- 10 to 12 corn tortillas
- 2 cups small curd 4% cottage cheese, drained
- 1 cup shredded pepper jack cheese
- 1 large egg
- ½ cup shredded cheddar cheese
- 2 cups shredded lettuce
- ½ cup chopped tomatoes
- 3 green onions, chopped
- ¼ cup sliced ripe olives

1. In a large skillet, cook beef over medium heat until no longer pink; drain. Add the cumin, chili powder, garlic powder, cayenne, salt, pepper and tomatoes; heat through. Cover the bottom and sides of a greased 13x9-in. baking dish with tortillas.
2. Pour beef mixture over tortillas. Place a layer of tortillas over meat mixture; set aside. Combine cottage cheese, Monterey Jack cheese and egg; pour over tortillas.
3. Bake at 350° for 30 minutes. Remove from oven; sprinkle rows of cheddar cheese, lettuce, tomatoes, green onions and olives diagonally across center of casserole.
1½ CUPS: 381 cal., 19g fat (10g sat. fat), 101mg chol., 785mg sod., 23g carb. (5g sugars, 4g fiber), 30g pro.

UPSIDE-DOWN MEAT PIE

UPSIDE-DOWN MEAT PIE

My sister gave me this recipe more than 30 years ago. It's still perfect whenever friends drop by, a skillet full of beefy goodness that's ready in a jiffy.
—Cora Dowling, Toledo, OH

PREP: 25 min.
BAKE: 20 min.
MAKES: 4 servings

- 1 lb. ground beef
- ½ cup chopped onion
- ½ tsp. salt
- 1 can (15 oz.) tomato sauce
BAKING POWDER BISCUITS
- 1 cup all-purpose flour
- 2 tsp. baking powder
- 1 tsp. celery salt
- 1 tsp. paprika
- ½ tsp. salt
- ¼ tsp. pepper
- 3 Tbsp. butter
- ½ cup milk

1. In a large ovenproof skillet, cook ground beef and onion until the beef is browned and onion is tender; drain. Add salt and tomato sauce; simmer 10-15 minutes.
2. Meanwhile, combine flour, baking powder, celery salt, paprika, salt and pepper in a bowl. Cut in butter until mixture resembles coarse meal. Add milk and stir until a soft dough forms. Drop dough by tablespoonfuls onto the meat mixture.
3. Bake, uncovered, at 475° for about 20 minutes or until biscuits are golden.
1 SERVING: 421 cal., 20g fat (11g sat. fat), 83mg chol., 1827mg sod., 33g carb. (5g sugars, 2g fiber), 26g pro.

THREE-CHEESE JUMBO SHELLS

For me, cooking doesn't mean fancy gourmet foods. It's more challenging to make enticing down-home foods —this irresistible casserole included— with ingredients from the refrigerator and my pantry shelves.

—Marjorie Carey, Alamosa, CO

PREP: 45 min. • **BAKE:** 35 min.
MAKES: 8 servings

- 1 lb. ground beef
- ⅔ cup chopped onion
- 2 cups water
- 2 cans (6 oz. each) tomato paste
- 1 Tbsp. beef bouillon granules
- 1½ tsp. dried oregano
- 1 carton (15 oz.) ricotta cheese
- 2 cups shredded part-skim mozzarella cheese, divided
- ½ cup grated Parmesan cheese
- 1 large egg, lightly beaten
- 24 jumbo pasta shells, cooked and drained

1. In a large skillet, cook beef and onion over medium heat until the meat is no longer pink; drain. Stir in the water, tomato paste, bouillon and oregano. Cover and simmer for 30 minutes.
2. Meanwhile, in a large bowl, combine the ricotta cheese, 1 cup mozzarella, Parmesan cheese and egg. Stuff shells with the cheese mixture.
3. Arrange shells in a greased shallow 3-qt. baking dish. Spoon meat sauce over shells. Cover and bake at 350° for 30 minutes. Uncover; sprinkle with the remaining mozzarella cheese. Bake for 3-5 minutes longer or until the cheese is melted.
FREEZE OPTION: After assembling, sprinkle casserole with the remaining mozzarella cheese. Cover and freeze unbaked casserole. To use, partially thaw in refrigerator overnight. Remove from refrigerator 30 minutes before baking. Preheat oven to 350°. Bake the casserole as directed, increasing time as necessary to heat through and for a thermometer inserted in center to read 165°.
3 STUFFED SHELLS: 442 cal., 20g fat (10g sat. fat), 102mg chol., 706mg sod., 35g carb. (9g sugars, 2g fiber), 32g pro.

FAST PHILLY CHEESESTEAK PIZZA

Cheesesteak meets pizza in this amazing combo. Top a crust with roast beef, cheese, peppers and onions to feast Philly-style.

—Jackie Hannahs, Cedar Springs, MI

TAKES: 30 min. • **MAKES:** 6 slices

- 1 tube (13.8 oz.) refrigerated pizza crust
- 2 cups frozen pepper and onion stir-fry blend
- 2 Tbsp. Dijon-mayonnaise blend
- ½ lb. thinly sliced deli roast beef, cut into wide strips
- 1½ cups shredded cheddar cheese

1. Preheat oven to 425°. Grease a 12-in. pizza pan. Unroll and press dough to fit prepared pan. Pinch edge to form a rim. Bake 8-10 minutes or until edge is lightly browned.
2. Meanwhile, place a large nonstick skillet coated with cooking spray over medium-high heat. Add the stir-fry blend; cook and stir for 3-5 minutes or until heated through.
3. Spread the mayonnaise blend over the crust; top with the roast beef and vegetables. Sprinkle with cheese. Bake 10-15 minutes or until cheese is melted.
1 SLICE: 330 cal., 13g fat (7g sat. fat), 51mg chol., 983mg sod., 34g carb. (6g sugars, 1g fiber), 20g pro.

THREE-CHEESE
JUMBO SHELLS

MINI REUBEN CASSEROLES

NANA'S ITALIAN ROULADE

My great-aunt from Sicily taught my mother how to stuff and bake a steak like a jelly roll. For us, this recipe always means family.
—Roseanne McDonald, Days Creek, OR

PREP: 30 min. • **COOK:** 1½ hours
MAKES: 8 servings

- 6 bacon strips
- 2 garlic cloves, minced
- ¾ tsp. Italian seasoning
- ½ tsp. salt
- ½ tsp. pepper
- 1 beef flank steak (1½ to 2 lbs.)
- ¼ cup grated Parmesan cheese
- 3 hard-boiled large eggs, sliced
- ¼ cup minced fresh parsley
- 2 Tbsp. olive oil
- 3 jars (24 oz. each) meatless pasta sauce
  Hot cooked spaghetti
  Additional minced fresh parsley

1. Preheat oven to 350°. Place bacon on a microwave-safe plate lined with paper towels. Cover with additional paper towels; microwave 3-5 minutes or until partially cooked but not crisp. In a small bowl, mix the garlic, Italian seasoning, salt and pepper.
2. Starting at one long side, cut the steak horizontally in half to within ½ in. of opposite side. Open the steak flat; cover with plastic wrap. Pound with a meat mallet to ¼-in. thickness; remove plastic.
3. Spread garlic mixture over steak; sprinkle with cheese. Layer with eggs and bacon to within 1 in. of edges; sprinkle with the parsley. Starting with a long side of the steak, roll up jelly-roll style (along the grain); tie at 1½-in. intervals with kitchen string.
4. In a Dutch oven, heat the oil over medium-high heat. Brown meat on all sides. Add pasta sauce. Bake, covered, 1½-1¾ hours or until meat is tender.
5. Remove roulade from pot; remove string and cut into slices. Serve with sauce over spaghetti. Sprinkle with additional parsley.
1 SLICE WITH ¾ CUP SAUCE: 331 cal., 15g fat (5g sat. fat), 119mg chol., 1491mg sod., 24g carb. (17g sugars, 4g fiber), 26g pro.

MINI REUBEN CASSEROLES

Topped with toasty bites of rye, these individual roast beef casseroles have the classic flavor of a Reuben sandwich.
—*Taste of Home* Test Kitchen

PREP: 20 min. • **BAKE:** 20 min.
MAKES: 4 servings

- 1 medium onion, chopped
- 1 medium green pepper, chopped
- 2 tsp. olive oil
- 2 cups cubed cooked beef roast
- 1 can (14 oz.) sauerkraut, rinsed and well drained
- 1 can (10¾ oz.) condensed cream of chicken soup, undiluted
- 1¼ cups shredded Swiss cheese, divided
- ⅓ cup 2% milk
- ½ cup Thousand Island salad dressing
- 2 slices rye bread, cubed
- 1 Tbsp. butter, melted
- ½ tsp. onion powder

1. Preheat oven to 350°. In a large skillet, saute onion and pepper in oil until tender. Stir in meat, sauerkraut, soup, 1 cup cheese, milk and salad dressing; heat through. Transfer the mixture to four greased 10-oz. custard cups or ramekins. Place the cups on a baking sheet.
2. In a small bowl, toss the bread cubes with melted butter and onion powder. Arrange over tops. Bake, uncovered, 15 minutes. Sprinkle with remaining cheese. Bake until cheese is melted, 5-10 minutes longer.
1 SERVING: 650 cal., 41g fat (15g sat. fat), 130mg chol., 1782mg sod., 31g carb. (12g sugars, 5g fiber), 37g pro.

"Delicious. I used beef pastrami in place of roast beef. My initial thought was that mixing all the ingredients would blur them together but I was pleased that each ingredient held its flavor. Have made this twice this month alone!"
—TLBOUQUET, TASTEOFHOME.COM

NANA'S
ITALIAN
ROULADE

STANDING RIB ROAST

Treat family and friends to tender standing rib roast for a marvelous main dish. The blend of seasonings builds succulent flavor on other cuts of beef roast, too.

—Lucy Meyring, Walden, CO

PREP: 5 min.
BAKE: 2¼ hours + standing
MAKES: 10 servings

- 3 tsp. lemon-pepper seasoning
- 3 tsp. paprika
- 1½ tsp. garlic salt
- 1 tsp. dried rosemary, crushed
- ½ tsp. cayenne pepper
- 1 bone-in beef rib roast (6 to 7 lbs.)
- 2 cups beef stock

1. Preheat oven to 325°. In a small bowl, mix the first five ingredients. Place roast in a roasting pan, fat side up; rub with seasoning mixture.
2. Roast 2 to 2½ hours or until meat reaches desired doneness (medium-rare, 135°; medium, 140°; medium-well, 145° on a thermometer). Remove the roast from oven; tent with foil. Let stand 15 minutes before carving.
3. Meanwhile, pour drippings and loosened browned bits from roasting pan into a small saucepan. Skim fat. Add beef stock to drippings; bring to a boil. Serve with roast.
4 OZ. COOKED BEEF WITH ABOUT 3 TBSP. JUS: 322 cal., 18g fat (7g sat. fat), 0 chol., 438mg sod., 1g carb. (1g sugars, 0 fiber), 37g pro.

PIZZA MEAT LOAF CUPS

Fix and freeze these moist little meat loaves packed with pizza flavor. They reheat quickly for after-school snacks or dinner on soccer nights. My family likes to drizzle extra pizza sauce on top.

—Susan Wollin, Marshall, WI

TAKES: 30 min. • **MAKES:** 1 dozen

- 1 large egg, lightly beaten
- ½ cup pizza sauce
- ¼ cup seasoned bread crumbs
- ½ tsp. Italian seasoning
- 1½ lbs. ground beef
- 1½ cups shredded part-skim mozzarella cheese
  Additional pizza sauce and basil leaves, optional

1. Preheat oven to 375°. In a large bowl, mix first four ingredients. Add beef; mix lightly but thoroughly. Divide into 12 portions; press each portion onto the bottom and up sides of a greased muffin cup. Add cheese to centers.
2. Bake until meat is cooked through, 15-18 minutes. If desired, top with meat loaves with additional pizza sauce and basil before serving.
FREEZE OPTION: Freeze cooled meat loaves in freezer containers. To use, partially thaw portions in refrigerator overnight. Microwave, covered, on high in a microwave-safe dish until meat loaves are heated through.
2 MEAT LOAF CUPS: 167 cal., 10g fat (4g sat. fat), 63mg chol., 177mg sod., 3g carb. (1g sugars, 0 fiber), 16g pro.

PIZZA MEAT LOAF CUPS

GARLIC SPAGHETTI
SQUASH WITH
MEAT SAUCE

GARLIC SPAGHETTI SQUASH WITH MEAT SAUCE

I have reduced grains and other starches in my diet for health reasons, so I was looking for satisfying meals that don't use pasta or potatoes. While tinkering with this recipe, I discovered just how fun spaghetti squash can be.
—Becky Ruff, McGregor, IA

PREP: 15 min. • **BAKE:** 45 min.
MAKES: 4 servings

- 1 medium spaghetti squash (about 4 lbs.)
- 1 lb. lean ground beef (90% lean)
- 2 cups sliced fresh mushrooms
- 4 garlic cloves, minced, divided
- 4 plum tomatoes, chopped
- 2 cups pasta sauce
- ½ tsp. pepper, divided
- 1 Tbsp. olive oil
- ¼ tsp. salt
  Grated Parmesan cheese, optional

1. Preheat oven to 375°. Cut squash lengthwise in half; remove and discard seeds. Place squash in a 13x9-in. baking pan, cut side down; add ½ in. of hot water. Bake, uncovered, 40 minutes. Drain water from pan; turn squash cut side up. Bake 5-10 minutes longer or until squash is tender.
2. Meanwhile, in a large skillet, cook beef and mushrooms over medium heat 6-8 minutes or until beef is no longer pink, breaking up the beef into crumbles; drain. Add half the garlic; cook and stir 1 minute. Stir in the tomatoes, pasta sauce and ¼ tsp. pepper; bring to a boil. Reduce heat; simmer, uncovered, 15-20 minutes.
3. When the squash is cool enough to handle, use a fork to separate strands. In a large skillet, heat oil over medium heat. Add remaining garlic; cook and stir 1 minute. Stir in squash, salt and the remaining pepper; heat through. Serve with meat sauce and, if desired, Parmesan cheese.

1¼ CUPS SQUASH WITH 1 CUP MEAT SAUCE: 443 cal., 17g fat (5g sat. fat), 71mg chol., 770mg sod., 49g carb. (12g sugars, 11g fiber), 29g pro. **DIABETIC EXCHANGES:** 3 starch, 3 lean meat, 1 vegetable, ½ fat.

MIDWEST MEATBALL CASSEROLE

I've relied on this recipe many times as a soothing finish to a hectic day. All of the ingredients are usually on hand, so there's never a last-minute rush to the store, either.

—Judy Larson, Greendale, WI

PREP: 40 min. • **BAKE:** 20 min.
MAKES: 6 servings

- 2 cans (8 oz. each) tomato sauce, divided
- 1 large egg
- ¼ cup dry bread crumbs
- ¼ cup chopped onion
- 1 tsp. salt
- 1 lb. lean ground beef (90% lean)
- 1 pkg. (10 oz.) frozen mixed vegetables
- ½ tsp. dried thyme
- ⅛ tsp. pepper
- 1 pkg. (16 oz.) frozen shredded hash brown potatoes, thawed
- 1 Tbsp. butter, melted
- 3 slices process American cheese, cut into ½-in. strips

1. In a large bowl, combine 2 Tbsp. tomato sauce with egg, crumbs, onion and salt. Crumble beef over mixture and mix well. Shape the meat mixture into 1-in. balls.
2. Place meatballs on a greased rack in a shallow baking pan and bake at 375° for 15-20 minutes or until meatballs are no longer pink; drain.
3. Meanwhile, in a skillet, combine remaining tomato sauce with mixed vegetables and seasonings. Cover and simmer 10-15 minutes or until heated through; stir in meatballs and set aside.
4. Place potatoes in a greased 11x7-in. baking dish. Brush with butter and bake at 375° for 15-20 minutes or until lightly browned. Remove from the oven; top with the meatball mixture. Arrange the cheese strips in a lattice pattern on top. Bake, uncovered, for 20-25 minutes longer or until heated through and cheese is melted.
1 SERVING: 310 cal., 12g fat (6g sat. fat), 97mg chol., 884mg sod., 27g carb. (4g sugars, 4g fiber), 23g pro.

BUFFALO BLUE CHEESE MEAT LOAF

BUFFALO BLUE CHEESE MEAT LOAF

I made meat loaf with wing sauce for my guy, who prefers food with bold flavors. He went crazy for it, and now likes it even more than traditional Buffalo wings!

—Latesha Harris, Beaverton, OR

PREP: 20 min. • **BAKE:** 40 min.
MAKES: 4 servings

- 1 large egg, lightly beaten
- 1 small onion, finely chopped
- ¼ cup panko (Japanese) bread crumbs
- ¼ cup Buffalo wing sauce
- 1 tsp. dried oregano
- ½ tsp. pepper
- 1 lb. ground beef

TOPPING
- ¼ cup Buffalo wing sauce
- ¼ cup crumbled blue cheese

1. Preheat oven to 350°. In a large bowl, combine the first six ingredients. Add beef; mix lightly but thoroughly. Shape into an 8x4-in. loaf in a greased 11x7-in. baking dish.
2. Bake 20 minutes. Spread wing sauce over top; sprinkle with cheese. Bake for 20-30 minutes longer (a thermometer should read 160°). Let stand 5 minutes before slicing.
1 SLICE: 286 cal., 17g fat (7g sat. fat), 123mg chol., 1093mg sod., 7g carb. (1g sugars, 1g fiber), 24g pro.

"I really liked this as a change of pace from traditional meat loaf. I added in more panko because the meat loaf was initially too wet. The flavor was excellent."
—ENDA MH, TASTEOFHOME.COM

HAMBURGER CORNBREAD CASSEROLE

Welcome friends in from the cold with a comforting dish that all ages will love. A layer of cornbread makes this meal both filling and delicious!

—Kathy Garrison, Fort Worth, TX

PREP: 25 min. • **BAKE:** 15 min.
MAKES: 6 servings

- 1   lb. lean ground beef (90% lean)
- 1   small onion, chopped
- 1   can (15 oz.) Ranch Style beans (pinto beans in seasoned tomato sauce)
- 1   can (14½ oz.) diced tomatoes, undrained
- 1   tsp. chili powder
- 1   tsp. Worcestershire sauce

TOPPING

- ½   cup all-purpose flour
- ½   cup cornmeal
- 2   Tbsp. sugar
- 2   tsp. baking powder
- ¼   tsp. salt
- 1   egg, beaten
- ½   cup fat-free milk
- 1   Tbsp. canola oil

1. Preheat oven to 425°. In a large skillet, cook the beef and onion over medium heat until meat is no longer pink; drain. Add beans, tomatoes, chili powder and Worcestershire sauce; bring to a boil. Reduce heat; simmer, uncovered, 5 minutes.

2. Transfer to an 11x7-in. baking dish coated with cooking spray. For the topping, in a small bowl, combine flour, cornmeal, sugar, baking powder and salt. Combine egg, milk and oil; stir into the dry ingredients just until moistened. Spoon over filling; gently spread to cover the top.

3. Bake, uncovered, 14-18 minutes or until filling is bubbly and a toothpick inserted into topping comes out clean. Let stand 5 minutes before cutting.

1 SERVING: 339 cal., 10g fat (3g sat. fat), 73mg chol., 722mg sod., 38g carb. (9g sugars, 6g fiber), 22g pro. **DIABETIC EXCHANGES:** 3 lean meat, 2 starch, 1 vegetable, ½ fat.

MOM'S TAMALE PIE

I don't believe my mom ever used a recipe for her tamale pie, but I came up with this version that tastes very much like the one she used to make. It's been popular at church gatherings and faculty luncheons—and with my own kids.

—Waldine Guillott, DeQuincy, LA

PREP: 25 min. • **BAKE:** 20 min.
MAKES: 12 servings

- 2   lbs. ground beef
- 1   large onion, chopped
- 1   large green pepper, chopped
- 1   can (15¼ oz.) whole kernel corn, undrained
- 1½   cups chopped fresh tomatoes
- 5   Tbsp. tomato paste
- 1   envelope chili seasoning
- 1½   tsp. sugar
- 1   tsp. garlic powder
- 1   tsp. dried basil
- 1   tsp. dried oregano
- 6   cups cooked grits (prepared with butter and salt)
- 1½   tsp. chili powder, divided
- 1½   cups shredded cheddar cheese

1. Preheat oven to 325°. In a large skillet, cook beef, onion and green pepper over medium heat until the meat is no longer pink; drain. Add the corn, tomatoes, tomato paste, chili seasoning, sugar, garlic powder, basil and oregano. Cook and stir until heated through; keep warm.

2. Spread half of the grits in a greased 3-qt. baking dish. Sprinkle with 1 tsp. chili powder. Top with beef mixture and cheese. Pipe the remaining grits around edge of dish; sprinkle with remaining chili powder.

3. Bake, uncovered, 20-25 minutes or until the cheese is melted. Let stand 5 minutes before serving.

1 SERVING: 296 cal., 12g fat (6g sat. fat), 52mg chol., 725mg sod., 27g carb. (5g sugars, 2g fiber), 20g pro.

MOM'S TAMALE PIE

NO-FUSS LASAGNA

FREEZE OPTION: After assembling, sprinkle lasagna with the remaining cheddar and mozzarella cheeses. Cover and freeze unbaked lasagna. To use, partially thaw in refrigerator overnight. Remove from refrigerator 30 minutes before baking. Preheat oven to 350°. Bake lasagna as directed, increasing time as necessary to heat through and for a thermometer inserted in center to read 165°.

1 PIECE: 632 cal., 23g fat (13g sat. fat), 149mg chol., 1210mg sod., 60g carb. (12g sugars, 5g fiber), 46g pro.

PRIME RIB WITH HORSERADISH SAUCE

To ring in the New Year, we invite friends for dinner. A menu featuring prime rib is festive, yet simple to prepare. A pepper rub and mild horseradish sauce complement the beef's mouth-watering flavor.
—Paula Zsiray, Logan, UT

PREP: 5 min. • **BAKE:** 3 hours
MAKES: 8 servings

- 1 bone-in beef rib roast (4 to 6 lbs.)
- 1 Tbsp. olive oil
- 1 to 2 tsp. coarsely ground pepper

HORSERADISH SAUCE
- 1 cup sour cream
- 3 to 4 Tbsp. prepared horseradish
- 1 tsp. coarsely ground pepper
- ⅛ tsp. Worcestershire sauce

1. Preheat oven to 450°. Brush roast with oil; rub with pepper. Place roast, with fat side up, on a rack in a shallow roasting pan. Bake, uncovered, for 15 minutes.
2. Reduce heat to 325°. Bake roast for 2¼ hours or until meat reaches desired doneness (for medium-rare, a thermometer should read 135°; medium, 140°; medium-well, 145°), basting with pan drippings every 30 minutes.
3. Let stand 10-15 minutes before slicing. Meanwhile, in a small bowl, combine the sauce ingredients. Serve with beef.

4 OZ. COOKED BEEF: 325 cal., 21g fat (9g sat. fat), 7mg chol., 115mg sod., 2g carb. (1g sugars, 0 fiber), 31g pro.

FREEZE IT
NO-FUSS LASAGNA

I like this recipe because it can be prepared a day ahead and baked just before serving, ideal for avoiding that last-minute rush when attending a potluck. Not having to pre-boil the noodles makes lasagna preparation especially quick.
—Denise Goedeken, Platte Center, NE

PREP: 25 min. + chilling
BAKE: 1¼ hours + standing
MAKES: 8 servings

- 1½ lbs. lean ground beef (90% lean)
- 1 can (12 oz.) tomato paste
- 3 cups water
- 2 pkg. (1½ oz. each) spaghetti sauce mix
- 1 Tbsp. sugar
- 4 tsp. dried parsley flakes
- ½ tsp. salt
- ½ tsp. garlic powder
- ¼ tsp. pepper
- 2 large eggs, beaten
- 2 cups cream-style cottage cheese
- 2 cups shredded cheddar cheese, divided
- 2 cups shredded mozzarella cheese, divided
- 1 pkg. (16 oz.) lasagna noodles, uncooked

1. In a Dutch oven, cook the beef over medium heat until no longer pink; drain. Add tomato paste, water, spaghetti sauce mix, sugar, parsley, salt, garlic powder and pepper to the Dutch oven. Simmer, partially covered, for 20 minutes. Stir occasionally.
2. In a bowl, combine eggs, cottage cheese, half of the cheddar cheese and half of the mozzarella. Set aside. Spoon a third of the meat sauce into a 13x9-in. baking dish. Place half of the uncooked noodles over the sauce. Top with a third of meat sauce and press down. Spoon cottage cheese mixture over all. Cover with remaining noodles and meat sauce. Cover and refrigerate lasagna overnight.
3. Bake, covered, at 350° for 1 hour. Uncover; sprinkle with the remaining cheddar and mozzarella cheeses. Bake an additional 15 minutes. Let stand for 10 minutes before cutting.

BEEF & GROUND BEEF | OVEN ENTREES **173**

PROVOLONE BEEF PASTRY POCKETS

POTLUCK TACO CASSEROLE

Bright with color and tempting taco taste, this is the dish I take most often to potluck events.

—Kim Stoller, Smithville, OH

PREP: 25 min. • **BAKE:** 20 min.
MAKES: 8 servings

- 2 lbs. ground beef
- 2 envelopes taco seasoning
- 4 large eggs
- ¾ cup 2% milk
- 1¼ cups biscuit/baking mix
  Dash pepper
- ½ cup sour cream
- 2 to 3 cups chopped lettuce
- ¾ cup chopped tomato
- ¼ cup chopped green pepper
- 2 green onions, chopped
- 2 cups shredded cheddar cheese

1. Preheat oven to 400°. In a large skillet, cook beef over medium heat 10-12 minutes or until no longer pink, breaking into crumbles; drain. Add taco seasoning and prepare according to package directions. Spoon meat into a greased 13x9-in. baking dish.
2. In a large bowl, beat eggs and milk. Stir in biscuit mix and pepper. Pour over meat. Bake casserole, uncovered, 20-25 minutes or until golden brown. Cool 5-10 minutes.
3. Spread sour cream over top; sprinkle with lettuce, tomato, green pepper, onions and cheese.
FREEZE OPTION: Cool baked casserole; cover and freeze. To use, partially thaw in refrigerator overnight. Remove from refrigerator 30 minutes before baking. Preheat oven to 350°. Unwrap dish and reheat on a lower oven rack until a thermometer inserted in center reads 165°. Cool casserole for 5-10 minutes, then top as directed.
1 SERVING: 472 cal., 27g fat (14g sat. fat), 205mg chol., 1360mg sod., 24g carb. (3g sugars, 1g fiber), 32g pro.

PROVOLONE BEEF PASTRY POCKETS

My children always make sure they're home when they find out we're having these pockets for dinner. They're a smart way to use leftover pot roast.

—Karen Burkett, Reseda, CA

PREP: 25 min. • **BAKE:** 20 min.
MAKES: 6 servings

- 1 Tbsp. butter
- 2 cups finely chopped fresh mushrooms
- 1 small onion, finely chopped
- 1 pkg. (15 oz.) refrigerated beef roast au jus
- 1 large egg
- 1 Tbsp. water
- 1 pkg. (17.3 oz.) frozen puff pastry, thawed
- 6 slices provolone cheese

1. Preheat oven to 425°. In a large skillet, heat butter over medium-high heat. Add mushrooms and onion; cook and stir 5-7 minutes or until tender and the liquid is evaporated. Remove from pan; cool completely.
2. Drain beef, discarding sauce or saving for another use. Coarsely chop beef. In a small bowl, whisk the egg and water.
3. Unfold one sheet of puff pastry. On a lightly floured surface, roll the pastry into a 15x9-in. rectangle; cut crosswise into thirds, making three 5-in.-wide rectangles.
4. Place a cheese slice on one half of each rectangle, trimming cheese to fit. Top each with a rounded tablespoon of the mushroom mixture and a scant 3 Tbsp. beef. Lightly brush edges of pastry with egg mixture. Fold pastry over filling; press edges with a fork to seal. Transfer to a parchment paper-lined baking sheet. Repeat with the remaining pastry sheet and filling.
5. Brush tops with egg mixture. Bake 17-20 minutes or until golden brown. Serve warm.
FREEZE OPTION: Freeze the unbaked pastry pockets on a waxed paper-lined baking sheet until firm. Transfer to a resealable plastic freezer bag; return o freezer. To use, bake frozen pastries on a parchment paper-lined baking sheet in a preheated 400° oven for 20-25 minutes or until golden brown and heated through.
1 POCKET: 628 cal., 36g fat (13g sat. fat), 100mg chol., 725mg sod., 49g carb. (3g sugars, 6g fiber), 29g pro.

POTLUCK
TACO CASSEROLE

ULTIMATE POT ROAST

Pot roast really is the ultimate comfort food. When juicy pot roast simmers in garlic, onions and veggies, everyone wants to know when dinner will be ready. The answer? Just wait—it will be worth it.

—Nick Iverson, Denver, CO

PREP: 55 min.
BAKE: 2 hours • **MAKES:** 8 servings

- 1   boneless beef chuck-eye or other chuck roast (3 to 4 lbs.)
- 2   tsp. pepper
- 2   tsp. salt, divided
- 2   Tbsp. canola oil
- 2   medium onions, cut into 1-in. pieces
- 2   celery ribs, chopped
- 3   garlic cloves, minced
- 1   Tbsp. tomato paste
- 1   Tbsp. minced fresh thyme or 1 tsp. dried thyme
- 2   bay leaves
- 1   cup dry red wine or reduced-sodium beef broth
- 2   cups reduced-sodium beef broth
- 1   lb. small red potatoes, quartered
- 4   medium parsnips, peeled and cut into 2-in. pieces
- 6   medium carrots, cut into 2-in. pieces
- 1   Tbsp. red wine vinegar
- 2   Tbsp. minced fresh parsley
  Salt and pepper to taste

1. Preheat oven to 325°. Pat roast dry with a paper towel; tie at 2-in. intervals with kitchen string. Sprinkle roast with the pepper and 1½ tsp. salt. In a Dutch oven, heat oil over medium-high heat. Brown the roast on all sides. Remove from pan.

2. Add onions, celery and ½ tsp. salt to the same pan; cook and stir over medium heat 8-10 minutes or until onions are browned. Add the garlic, tomato paste, thyme and bay leaves; cook and stir 1 minute longer.

3. Add the wine, stirring to loosen the browned bits from pan; stir in broth. Return roast to pan. Arrange potatoes, parsnips and carrots around roast; bring to a boil. Bake, covered, until meat is fork-tender, 2-2½ hours.

4. Remove roast and vegetables from pan; keep warm. Discard bay leaves; skim fat from the cooking juices. On stovetop, bring juices to a boil; cook until liquid is reduced by half (about 1½ cups), 10-12 minutes. Stir in vinegar and parsley; season to taste with salt and pepper.

5. Remove string from roast. Serve with vegetables and sauce.

3 OZ. COOKED BEEF WITH 1 CUP VEGETABLES AND 3 TBSP. SAUCE: 459 cal., 20g fat (7g sat. fat), 112mg chol., 824mg sod., 32g carb. (8g sugars, 6g fiber), 37g pro.

TEST KITCHEN TIP
Chuck is the ideal cut for this type of low-and-slow braising because it has plenty of marbling and collagen. This translates to tenderness and flavor! Brisket is a good choice, too. Very lean cuts, such as rump and round roasts, will work, but they won't be nearly as moist or fall-apart tender.

GREEK PASTA BAKE

My mom taught me to cook, and I love creating new recipes. I developed this casserole on a cold, snowy afternoon many years ago. Or substitute all beef for the beef and lamb mixture.
—Carol Stevens, Basye, VA

PREP: 40 min.
BAKE: 1 hour
MAKES: 6 servings

- ½ lb. ground beef
- ½ lb. ground lamb
- 1 large onion, chopped
- 4 garlic cloves, minced
- 3 tsp. dried oregano
- 1 tsp. dried basil
- ½ tsp. salt
- ¼ tsp. pepper
- ¼ tsp. dried thyme
- 1 can (15 oz.) tomato sauce
- 1 can (14½ oz.) diced tomatoes, undrained
- 1 Tbsp. lemon juice
- 1 tsp. sugar
- ¼ tsp. ground cinnamon
- 2 cups uncooked rigatoni or large tube pasta
- 4 oz. feta cheese, crumbled

1. In a large skillet, cook beef and lamb over medium heat until the meat is no longer pink; drain. Stir in onion, garlic, oregano, basil, salt, pepper and thyme. Add the tomato sauce, tomatoes and lemon juice. Bring to a boil. Reduce the heat; simmer, uncovered, about 20 minutes, stirring occasionally.
2. Stir in sugar and cinnamon. Simmer, uncovered, 15 minutes longer.
3. Meanwhile, cook pasta according to package directions; drain. Stir into meat mixture.
4. Transfer to a greased 2-qt. baking dish. Sprinkle with the feta cheese. Cover and bake at 325° for 45 minutes. Uncover; bake 15 minutes longer or until heated through.
FREEZE OPTION: Cool the unbaked casserole; cover and freeze. To use, partially thaw in refrigerator overnight. Remove from refrigerator 30 minutes before baking. Preheat oven to 325°. Bake casserole as directed, increasing time as necessary to heat through and for a thermometer inserted in center to read 165°.
1 SERVING: 316 cal., 12g fat (6g sat. fat), 54mg chol., 840mg sod., 29g carb. (6g sugars, 4g fiber), 22g pro.

CALIFORNIA CASSEROLE

We might be from Texas, but we sure enjoy eating this colorful casserole named after a West Coast state. It plays well with a variety of side dishes.
—Hope LaShier, Amarillo, TX

PREP: 20 min. • **BAKE:** 1 hour
MAKES: 12-16 servings

- 2 lbs. ground beef
- 1 medium green pepper, chopped
- ¾ cup chopped onion
- 1 can (14¾ oz.) cream-style corn
- 1 can (10¾ oz.) condensed tomato soup, undiluted
- 1 can (10 oz.) tomatoes with green chilies, undrained
- 1 can (8 oz.) tomato sauce
- 1 jar (4½ oz.) whole mushrooms, drained
- 1 jar (4 oz.) chopped pimientos, drained
- 1 can (2¼ oz.) sliced ripe olives, drained
- 1½ tsp. celery salt
- ½ tsp. ground mustard
- ½ tsp. chili powder
- ¼ tsp. pepper
- 8 oz. wide egg noodles, cooked and drained
- 2 cups shredded cheddar cheese

1. Preheat oven to 350°. In a large skillet, cook the beef, green pepper and onion over medium heat until the meat is no longer pink and the vegetables are tender; drain. Stir in the next 11 ingredients. Add noodles.
2. Pour into a greased 13x9-in. baking dish. Cover and bake for 50 minutes. Sprinkle with cheese; bake 10 minutes longer or until cheese is melted.
1 CUP: 248 cal., 11g fat (6g sat. fat), 58mg chol., 658mg sod., 22g carb. (4g sugars, 2g fiber), 17g pro.

GREEK PASTA BAKE

SLOPPY JOE PIE

SLOPPY JOE PIE

To be honest, I don't hear many compliments on this dish...folks are always too busy eating! I developed the recipe by grabbing ingredients from my refrigerator and cupboards one crunch time when I needed an easy dish fast.

—Kathy McCreary, Goddard, KS

PREP: 30 min. • **BAKE:** 20 min.
MAKES: 7 servings

- 1 lb. ground beef
- ½ cup chopped onion
- 1 can (8 oz.) tomato sauce
- 1 can (8¾ oz.) whole kernel corn, drained
- ¼ cup water
- 1 envelope sloppy joe mix
- 2 tubes (6 oz. each) refrigerated buttermilk biscuits
- 2 Tbsp. whole milk
- ⅓ cup cornmeal
- 1 cup shredded cheddar cheese, divided
  Minced fresh parsley, optional

1. Preheat oven to 375°. In a large skillet, cook beef and onion over medium heat until meat is no longer pink; drain. Stir in tomato sauce, corn, water and sloppy joe seasoning; cook until bubbly. Reduce heat and simmer for 5 minutes; remove from heat and set aside.
2. Separate biscuits; flatten each to a 3½-in. circle. Place milk and cornmeal in separate shallow bowls; dip both sides into milk and then into cornmeal. Place seven biscuits around the sides of an ungreased 9-in. pie plate; place three on the bottom.
3. Press biscuits together to form crust, leaving a scalloped edge around rim. Sprinkle with ½ cup cheese. Spoon meat mixture over cheese.
4. Bake until crust is deep golden brown 20-25 minutes. Sprinkle with remaining cheese and, if desired, fresh parsley. Let stand 5 minutes before serving.
1 SERVING: 371 cal., 17g fat (7g sat. fat), 49mg chol., 1174mg sod., 33g carb. (5g sugars, 2g fiber), 19g pro.

DEEP-DISH PIZZA

FREEZE IT
DEEP-DISH PIZZA

My family devours this crusty pan pizza with easy-to-swap toppings. Use a combination of green, red and yellow peppers for extra color.

—Patricia Howson, Carstairs, AB

PREP: 25 min. + standing
BAKE: 20 min. • **MAKES:** 8 servings

- 1 pkg. (¼ oz.) active dry yeast
- 1 cup warm water (110° to 115°)
- 1 tsp. sugar
- 1 tsp. salt
- 2 Tbsp. canola oil
- 2½ cups all-purpose flour
- 1 lb. ground beef, cooked and drained
- 1 can (10¾ oz.) condensed tomato soup, undiluted
- 1 tsp. each dried basil, oregano and thyme
- 1 tsp. dried rosemary, crushed
- ¼ tsp. garlic powder
- 1 small green pepper, julienned
- 1 can (8 oz.) mushroom stems and pieces, drained
- 1 cup shredded part-skim mozzarella cheese

1. In a large bowl, dissolve yeast in warm water. Add the sugar, salt, oil and 2 cups flour. Beat until smooth. Stir in enough remaining flour to form a soft dough. Cover and let rest for 20 minutes.
2. On a floured surface, roll dough into a 13x9-in. rectangle. Transfer to greased 13x9-in. baking pan. Sprinkle with beef.
3. In a small bowl, combine the soup and seasonings; spoon over beef. Top with the green pepper, mushrooms and cheese.
4. Bake at 425° for 20-25 minutes or until the pizza crust and cheese are lightly browned.
FREEZE OPTION: Cover and freeze unbaked pizza. To use, partially thaw in refrigerator overnight. Remove from refrigerator 30 minutes before baking. Preheat oven to 425°. Bake pizza as directed, increasing time as necessary.
1 SLICE: 364 cal., 14g fat (5g sat. fat), 49mg chol., 704mg sod., 39g carb. (5g sugars, 3g fiber), 20g pro.

Poultry

TURKEY MEAT LOAF

TURKEY MEAT LOAF

I first made this when my husband and I had to start watching our diet. Since then, I've been asked to make my turkey meat loaf many times.
—Ruby Rath, New Haven, IN

PREP: 15 min. • **BAKE:** 1 hour + standing
MAKES: 10 servings

- 1 cup quick-cooking oats
- 1 medium onion, chopped
- ½ cup shredded carrot
- ½ cup fat-free milk
- ¼ cup egg substitute
- 2 Tbsp. ketchup
- 1 tsp. garlic powder
- ¼ tsp. pepper
- 2 lbs. lean ground turkey

TOPPING
- ¼ cup ketchup
- ¼ cup quick-cooking oats

1. Preheat oven to 350°. Combine first eight ingredients. Add turkey; mix lightly but thoroughly.
2. Transfer mixture to a 9x5-in. loaf pan coated with cooking spray. Mix the topping ingredients; spread over loaf. Bake until a thermometer reads 165°, 60-65 minutes. Let stand about 10 minutes before slicing.

1 SLICE: 195 cal., 8g fat (2g sat. fat), 63mg chol., 188mg sod., 12g carb. (4g sugars, 1g fiber), 20g pro. **DIABETIC EXCHANGES:** 3 lean meat, 1 starch.

"I loved this meat loaf. It is hard to find a good turkey meat loaf —this is very moist—and I love the topping."
—DCSCAKE_OH, TASTEOFHOME.COM

PASTRY-TOPPED TURKEY CASSEROLE

3. For the crust, whisk together both flours with baking powder and salt; stir in 3 Tbsp. milk and oil. On a lightly floured surface, roll dough to ⅛-in. thickness; cut into short strips. Arrange over filling. Brush strips with remaining milk; sprinkle with paprika.

4. Bake, uncovered, until the filling is bubbly, 20-25 minutes. Let stand for 10 minutes before serving.

1 SERVING: 280 cal., 4g fat (1g sat. fat), 39mg chol., 696mg sod., 38g carb. (9g sugars, 6g fiber), 23g pro. **DIABETIC EXCHANGES:** 2 starch, 2 lean meat, 1 vegetable, ½ fat.

HERB-ROASTED TURKEY BREAST

Whenever we're in the mood for turkey, this is the recipe I use. It bakes up delectably with butter, herbs and other kitchen staples.
—Cheryl King, West Lafayette, IN

PREP: 15 min.
BAKE: 1¼ hours + standing
MAKES: 6 servings

- 6 Tbsp. butter, cubed
- 2 Tbsp. lemon juice
- 1 Tbsp. soy sauce
- 1 Tbsp. chopped green onion
- ½ tsp. dried thyme
- ½ tsp. dried marjoram
- ¼ to ½ tsp. rubbed sage
- ¼ tsp. salt, optional
- ⅛ tsp. pepper
- 1 boneless skinless turkey breast half (2 lbs.)

1. In a small saucepan, combine the first nine ingredients. Bring to a boil; remove from the heat and set aside to cool.

2. Place the turkey breast on a rack in a greased shallow roasting pan. Spoon some of the butter mixture over the top. Cover and bake at 325° for 1¼-1¾ hours (a thermometer inserted in turkey reads 165°); baste occasionally with butter mixture.

3. Let the turkey breast stand for 10-15 minutes before slicing.

4 OUNCES COOKED TURKEY: 104 cal., 11g fat (7g sat. fat), 31mg chol., 368mg sod., 1g carb. (0 sugars, 0 fiber), 1g pro.

EAT SMART
PASTRY-TOPPED TURKEY CASSEROLE

My friends tell me this is the best potpie. Hearty and full-flavored, this reinvented classic never lets on that it's also low in fat and a good source of fiber.
—Agnes Ward, Stratford, ON

PREP: 45 min. • **BAKE:** 20 min. + standing
MAKES: 6 servings

- 2 cups diced red potatoes
- 1 large onion, finely chopped
- 2 celery ribs, chopped
- 2 tsp. chicken bouillon granules
- ½ tsp. dried rosemary, crushed
- ¼ tsp. garlic powder
- ¼ tsp. dried thyme
- ⅛ tsp. pepper
- 1 can (14½ oz.) reduced-sodium chicken broth
- ½ cup water
- 3 Tbsp. all-purpose flour
- ⅔ cup fat-free evaporated milk
- 3 cups frozen mixed vegetables, thawed and drained
- 2 cups cubed cooked turkey breast

CRUST
- ¼ cup all-purpose flour
- ¼ cup whole wheat flour
- ½ tsp. baking powder
- ⅛ tsp. salt
- 4 Tbsp. fat-free milk, divided
- 1 Tbsp. canola oil
  Paprika

1. Preheat oven to 400°. Place first 10 ingredients in a large saucepan; bring to a boil. Reduce heat; simmer, covered, until potatoes are tender, 10-15 minutes.

2. Whisk flour and evaporated milk until smooth; stir into pan. Bring to a boil, stirring constantly; cook and stir until thickened, about 2 minutes. Add frozen vegetables and turkey; heat through, stirring occasionally. Transfer to an ungreased 8-in. square baking dish.

TURKEY LEGS WITH MUSHROOM GRAVY

We farmed 20 acres for 30 years and grew plenty of fruits and vegetables to go with this family favorite. Nestle these tender turkey legs onto a platter of noodles to catch every bit of the mushroomy gravy.
—Wanda Swenson, Lady Lake, FL

PREP: 5 min. • **BAKE:** 1¾ hours
MAKES: 4 servings

- 4 turkey drumsticks (12 oz. each)
- ¼ cup lemon juice
- 2 Tbsp. canola oil
- 1 tsp. garlic powder
- 1 tsp. dried oregano
- 1 tsp. dried basil
- ¼ tsp. pepper

MUSHROOM GRAVY
- 1 Tbsp. cornstarch
- 1 cup cold water
- 1 can (10½ oz.) mushroom gravy
- 1 can (4 oz.) sliced mushrooms, drained
- 1 Tbsp. minced fresh parsley
- 1 tsp. garlic powder
- 1 tsp. finely chopped onion
  Hot cooked noodles, optional

1. Place turkey legs in a roasting pan. In a small bowl, combine the lemon juice, oil and seasonings. Pour over turkey legs.
2. Bake, uncovered, at 375° about 45 minutes or until lightly browned. Turn legs twice and baste occasionally with pan drippings. Remove from the oven.
3. For the gravy, in a small saucepan, combine cornstarch and water until smooth. Bring to a boil over medium heat. Cook and stir for 1-2 minutes or until thickened and bubbly. Stir in the gravy, mushrooms, parsley, garlic powder and onion, heating through. Spoon over turkey legs.
4. Cover loosely with foil. Bake about 1 hour or until a thermometer inserted in turkey reads 180°, basting frequently with pan drippings. If desired, serve with noodles.
1 SERVING: 467 cal., 21g fat (7g sat. fat), 177mg chol., 714mg sod., 10g carb. (2g sugars, 1g fiber), 57g pro.

STUFFED TURKEY ZUCCHINI BOATS

EAT SMART
STUFFED TURKEY ZUCCHINI BOATS

When I worked in the school library, my co-workers were my taste testers. They approved this healthy and happy spin on stuffed zucchini.
—Stephanie Cotterman, West Alexandria, OH

PREP: 30 min. • **BAKE:** 35 min.
MAKES: 6 servings

- 6 medium zucchini
- 1 lb. lean ground turkey
- 1 small onion, chopped
- 1 celery rib, chopped
- 1 garlic clove, minced
- 1½ tsp. Italian seasoning
- ¾ tsp. salt
- ¼ tsp. cayenne pepper
- ¼ tsp. paprika
- 1 cup salad croutons, coarsely crushed
- 1 cup shredded part-skim mozzarella cheese, divided

1. Preheat oven to 350°. Cut each zucchini lengthwise in half. Scoop out pulp, leaving a ¼-in. shell; chop pulp.
2. In a large skillet, cook the turkey, onion, celery, garlic and seasonings over medium heat for 6-8 minutes or until the turkey is no longer pink; break up meat into crumbles. Stir in croutons, ½ cup cheese and zucchini pulp. Spoon into zucchini shells.
3. Transfer to two ungreased 13x9-in. baking dishes; add ¼ in. water. Bake, covered, for 30-35 minutes or until the zucchini is tender. Sprinkle with remaining cheese. Bake for 5 minutes or until cheese is melted.
2 STUFFED ZUCCHINI HALVES: 240 cal., 11g fat (4g sat. fat), 63mg chol., 556mg sod., 13g carb. (5g sugars, 2g fiber), 23g pro. **DIABETIC EXCHANGES:** 3 lean meat, 1 vegetable, ½ starch.

CHEDDAR CHICKEN POTPIE

Cheese soup is one of my favorites but a bit too rich for my husband's taste. By changing the ingredients a little, I came up with a variation of potpie that we both enjoy. (If I'm in a hurry and don't have the time this takes to bake, I'll skip the crust, add extra milk and serve it as a chowder.)
—Sandra Cothran, Ridgeland, SC

PREP: 30 min. • **BAKE:** 40 min.
MAKES: 6 servings

CRUST
- 1 cup all-purpose flour
- ½ tsp. salt
- 5 Tbsp. cold butter, cubed
- 3 Tbsp. cold water

FILLING
- 1½ cups chicken broth
- 2 cups peeled cubed potatoes
- 1 cup sliced carrots
- ½ cup sliced celery
- ½ cup chopped onion
- ¼ cup all-purpose flour
- 1½ cups whole milk
- 2 cups shredded sharp cheddar cheese
- 4 cups cubed cooked chicken
- ¼ tsp. poultry seasoning
  Salt and pepper to taste

1. For crust, in a small bowl, combine flour and salt. Cut butter in flour until the mixture resembles coarse crumbs. Gradually add the water, mixing gently with a fork. Gather into a ball. Cover dough with plastic wrap; chill at least 30 minutes.
2. For filling, place broth in a Dutch oven; bring to a boil over high heat. Add vegetables. Reduce heat; simmer for 10-15 minutes or until vegetables are tender.
3. In a small bowl, combine flour and milk; stir into broth mixture. Cook and stir over medium heat until slightly thickened and bubbly. Stir in cheese, chicken, poultry seasoning, salt and pepper. Heat until cheese melts. Spoon into a 10-in. (2½ to 3-qt.) casserole. Set aside.
4. On a lightly floured surface, roll crust to fit top of casserole, trimming edges as necessary. Place on casserole over filling; seal edges. Make several slits in center of crust for steam to escape.
5. Bake at 425° for 40 minutes or until golden brown.

1 PIECE: 603 cal., 31g fat (18g sat. fat), 161mg chol., 902mg sod., 38g carb. (6g sugars, 3g fiber), 42g pro.

OVEN BARBECUED CHICKEN

Chicken and Sunday dinner always go together in my mind. During 20 years of married life on a dairy farm, I would often brown chicken and mix up sauce while my husband milked, then pop it in the oven when we left for church.
—Esther Shank, Harrisonburg, VA

PREP: 25 min. • **BAKE:** 45 min.
MAKES: 8 servings

- 2 Tbsp. canola oil
- 1 broiler/fryer chicken (3 to 4 lbs.), cut up
- 3 Tbsp. butter
- ⅓ cup chopped onion
- ¾ cup ketchup
- ½ cup water
- ⅓ cup cider vinegar
- 3 Tbsp. brown sugar
- 1 Tbsp. Worcestershire sauce
- 2 tsp. prepared mustard
- ¼ tsp. salt
- ⅛ tsp. pepper

1. Preheat oven to 350°. In a large skillet, heat oil over medium heat. Brown the chicken on both sides. Remove to paper towels to drain.
2. Meanwhile, in a small saucepan, heat butter over medium-high heat. Add onion; cook and stir until tender. Stir in remaining ingredients. Bring sauce to a boil. Reduce heat; simmer, uncovered, 15 minutes.
3. Place chicken in an ungreased 13x9-in. baking dish. Pour the sauce over chicken. Bake, uncovered, for 45-60 minutes or until the chicken juices run clear, basting occasionally.

4 OZ. COOKED CHICKEN: 302 cal., 18g fat (6g sat. fat), 77mg chol., 483mg sod., 12g carb. (12g sugars, 0 fiber), 21g pro.

CHEDDAR CHICKEN POTPIE

TURKEY & BLACK BEAN ENCHILADAS

Ground turkey keeps these slimmed-down enchiladas moist and delicious.
—Sarah Burleson, Spruce Pine, NC

PREP: 30 min. • **BAKE:** 15 min.
MAKES: 8 servings

- 2 cans (15 oz. each) black beans, rinsed and drained, divided
- 1 lb. lean ground turkey
- 1 medium green pepper, chopped
- 1 small onion, chopped
- 1 can (15 oz.) enchilada sauce, divided
- 1 cup shredded reduced-fat Mexican cheese blend, divided
- 8 whole wheat tortillas (8 in.), warmed

1. Preheat oven to 425°. In a small bowl, mash one can black beans; set aside. In a large nonstick skillet, cook the turkey, pepper and onion over medium heat until meat is no longer pink; drain. Add the mashed beans, remaining beans, half the enchilada sauce and ½ cup cheese; heat through.
2. Place ⅔ cupfuls of bean mixture down the center of each tortilla. Roll up filled tortillas and place, seam side down, in two 11x7-in. baking dishes coated with cooking spray.
3. Pour remaining enchilada sauce over the top; sprinkle with remaining cheese. Bake enchiladas, uncovered, 15-20 minutes or until heated through.
FREEZE OPTION: Cover and freeze unbaked casseroles up to 3 months. To use, partially thaw in refrigerator overnight. Remove from refrigerator 30 minutes before baking. Preheat oven to 425°. Bake the enchiladas as directed, increasing time as necessary to heat through and for a thermometer inserted in center to read 165°.
1 SERVING: 363 cal., 11g fat (3g sat. fat), 55mg chol., 808mg sod., 42g carb. (3g sugars, 7g fiber), 24g pro.

CURRIED CHICKEN TURNOVERS

Whenever I have leftover chicken, it's time to put turnovers are on the menu. Curry is the real reason to make these.
—Laverne Kohut, Manning, AB

PREP: 30 min. • **BAKE:** 15 min.
MAKES: 8 servings

- 1 cup finely chopped cooked chicken
- 1 medium apple, peeled and finely chopped
- ½ cup mayonnaise
- ¼ cup chopped cashews or peanuts
- 1 green onion, finely chopped
- 1 to 2 tsp. curry powder
- ¼ tsp. salt
- ¼ tsp. pepper
- Pastry for double-crust pie
- 1 large egg, lightly beaten

1. Preheat oven to 425°. In a small bowl, combine first eight ingredients. Divide the dough into eight portions.
2. On a lightly floured surface, roll each portion into a 5-in. circle. Place about ¼ cup filling on one side. Moisten the edges of pastry with water. Fold the dough over filling; press edges with a fork to seal.
3. Place on greased baking sheets. Brush with egg. Cut ½-in. slits in top of each. Bake 15-20 minutes or until golden brown.
1 TURNOVER: 512 cal., 37g fat (17g sat. fat), 101mg chol., 526mg sod., 34g carb. (2g sugars, 2g fiber), 11g pro.

CURRIED CHICKEN TURNOVERS

BUFFALO
CHICKEN
LASAGNA

BUFFALO CHICKEN LASAGNA

This recipe was inspired by my daughter's favorite food—Buffalo wings! Enjoy all the heat and tang layered in lasagna noodles.
—Melissa Millwood, Lyman, SC

PREP: 1½ hours
BAKE: 40 min. + standing
MAKES: 12 servings

- 1   Tbsp. canola oil
- 1½ lbs. ground chicken
- 1   small onion, chopped
- 1   celery rib, finely chopped
- 1   large carrot, grated
- 2   garlic cloves, minced
- 1   can (14½ oz.) diced tomatoes, drained
- 1   bottle (12 oz.) Buffalo wing sauce
- ½   cup water
- 1½ tsp. Italian seasoning
- ½   tsp. salt
- ¼   tsp. pepper
- 9   lasagna noodles
- 1   carton (15 oz.) ricotta cheese
- 1¾ cups crumbled blue cheese, divided
- ½   cup minced Italian flat-leaf parsley
- 1   large egg, lightly beaten
- 3   cups shredded part-skim mozzarella cheese
- 2   cups shredded white cheddar cheese

1. In a Dutch oven, heat the oil over medium heat. Add chicken, onion, celery and carrot; cook and stir until meat is no longer pink and vegetables are tender. Add garlic; cook 2 minutes longer. Stir in tomatoes, wing sauce, water, Italian seasoning, salt and pepper; bring to a boil. Reduce heat; cover and simmer 1 hour.

2. Meanwhile, cook noodles according to package directions; drain. In a small bowl, mix the ricotta cheese, ¾ cup blue cheese, parsley and egg. Preheat oven to 350°.

3. Spread 1½ cups sauce into a greased 13x9-in. baking dish. Layer with three noodles, 1½ cups sauce, ⅔ cup ricotta mixture, 1 cup mozzarella cheese, ⅔ cup cheddar cheese and ⅓ cup blue cheese. Repeat the layers twice.

4. Bake lasagna, covered, 20 minutes. Uncover; bake until bubbly and cheese is melted, 20-25 minutes. Let stand for 10 minutes before serving.

1 PIECE: 466 cal., 28g fat (15g sat. fat), 124mg chol., 1680mg sod., 22g carb. (6g sugars, 2g fiber), 33g pro.

TEST KITCHEN TIP

For a phenomenal pairing, serve this lasagna with a cool, crisp celery salad or celery sticks on the side. You can tone down the heat by reducing the Buffalo wing sauce to ½ cup and adding an 8-oz. can of tomato sauce.

MEXICAN
TURKEY SKILLET

MEXICAN TURKEY SKILLET

This main dish with turkey, black beans and vegetables has marvelous Mexican flavor that may seem indulgent, but it's really delightfully light.
—*Taste of Home* Test Kitchen

PREP: 20 min. • **BAKE:** 30 min.
MAKES: 8 servings

- 1 lb. lean ground turkey
- 1 cup chopped zucchini
- ½ cup chopped sweet red pepper
- 2 tsp. canola oil
- 2 cups cooked rice
- 1 can (15 oz.) black beans, rinsed and drained
- 1 can (14½ oz.) Mexican stewed tomatoes
- 1 can (8 oz.) tomato sauce
- ½ tsp. ground cumin
- ¼ tsp. salt
- ¼ tsp. pepper
- 1 cup shredded reduced-fat Mexican cheese blend
  Chopped avocado, optional

1. In a large nonstick ovenproof skillet, cook turkey over medium heat until no longer pink; drain. Set turkey aside. In the same skillet, saute the zucchini and red pepper in oil for 2 minutes or until crisp-tender.
2. Stir in turkey, rice, beans, tomatoes, tomato sauce, cumin, salt and pepper. Cover and bake at 350° for 30 minutes. Sprinkle with cheese. Let stand about 5 minutes before serving. Garnish with avocado if desired.
1 CUP: 254 cal., 9g fat (3g sat. fat), 55mg chol., 616mg sod., 25g carb. (4g sugars, 4g fiber), 19g pro. **DIABETIC EXCHANGES:** 2 lean meat, 1 starch, 1 vegetable, ½ fat.

CHEESY CHICKEN & SHELLS

CHEESY CHICKEN & SHELLS

When our friend served this entree, I asked her for the recipe right away. It was so good, I thought that I would share it with others. I make enough for a meal or two, but it doubles or triples easily for larger crowds.
—Jodee Harding, Mount Vernon, OH

PREP: 15 min. • **BAKE:** 30 min.
MAKES: 4 servings

- 1½ cups uncooked medium shell pasta
- 2 Tbsp. all-purpose flour
- ¼ cup water
- 1¼ cups chicken broth
- 1 can (10¾ oz.) condensed cream of chicken soup, undiluted
- ½ cup diced process cheese (Velveeta)
- ¼ tsp. salt
- ¼ tsp. pepper
- ¼ tsp. poultry seasoning
- ⅛ tsp. paprika
- 1½ cups cubed cooked chicken
- 3 Tbsp. dry bread crumbs
- 1 Tbsp. butter, melted

1. Preheat oven to 350°. Cook pasta according to package directions.
2. Meanwhile, in a saucepan, combine flour and water, stirring until smooth. Gradually stir in broth. Bring to a boil; cook and stir about 2 minutes or until thickened. Reduce heat; add the soup, cheese and seasonings. Cook and stir 5 minutes or until cheese is melted.
3. Drain pasta; place in a bowl. Stir in soup mixture and chicken. Transfer to a greased 1½-qt. baking dish. Toss the bread crumbs and butter; sprinkle over top. Bake, uncovered, 30 minutes or until golden brown.
1 CUP: 429 cal., 16g fat (7g sat. fat), 70mg chol., 1304mg sod., 44g carb. (4g sugars, 2g fiber), 27g pro.

BULGUR TURKEY MANICOTTI

Wholesome bulgur brings added nutrition to this zesty and flavorful Italian entree.

—Mary Gunderson, Conrad, IA

PREP: 20 min. + standing
BAKE: 1¼ hours
MAKES: 7 servings

- ¼ cup bulgur
- ⅔ cup boiling water
- ¾ lb. lean ground turkey
- 1 tsp. dried basil
- 1 tsp. dried oregano
- ¼ tsp. pepper
- 1½ cups 2% cottage cheese
- 1 jar (24 oz.) meatless pasta sauce
- 1 can (8 oz.) no-salt-added tomato sauce
- ½ cup water
- 14 uncooked manicotti shells
- 1 cup shredded part-skim mozzarella cheese

1. Combine bulgur and boiling water; let stand, covered, until the liquid is absorbed, about 30 minutes. Drain; squeeze dry.

2. Preheat oven to 350°. In a large nonstick skillet, cook and crumble turkey over medium-high heat until no longer pink, 5-7 minutes. Stir in the seasonings, cottage cheese and bulgur.

3. Mix the pasta sauce, tomato sauce and ½ cup water. Spread 1 cup sauce mixture into a 13x9-in. baking dish coated with cooking spray. Fill the uncooked manicotti shells with the turkey mixture; place in prepared dish. Top with remaining sauce mixture.

4. Bake, covered, until sauce is bubbly and shells are tender, 70-75 minutes. Uncover; sprinkle with the mozzarella cheese. Bake until cheese is melted, about 5 minutes.

2 MANICOTTI: 346 cal., 9g fat (4g sat. fat), 46mg chol., 717mg sod., 42g carb. (12g sugars, 4g fiber), 25g pro. **DIABETIC EXCHANGES:** 3 starch, 3 lean meat, ½ fat.

SANTA FE CHICKEN PITA PIZZAS

Pita breads makes fabulous individual pizzas with a western kick. Tailor the toppings to personal tastes.

—Athena Russell, Greenville, SC

TAKES: 30 min. • **MAKES:** 4 servings

- 4 whole pita breads
- ½ cup refried black beans
- ½ cup salsa
- 1 cup cubed cooked chicken breast
- 2 Tbsp. chopped green chilies
- 2 Tbsp. sliced ripe olives
- ¾ cup shredded Colby-Monterey Jack cheese
- 1 green onion, chopped
- ½ cup reduced-fat sour cream

1. Preheat oven to 350°. Place whole pita breads on an ungreased baking sheet; spread with beans. Top with the salsa, chicken, chilies and olives; sprinkle with cheese.

2. Bake 8-10 minutes or until cheese is melted. Top with green onion; serve with sour cream.

1 PIZZA: 380 cal., 11g fat (6g sat. fat), 56mg chol., 776mg sod., 44g carb. (4g sugars, 3g fiber), 24g pro. **DIABETIC EXCHANGES:** 3 starch, 2 lean meat, 1 fat.

BULGUR TURKEY MANICOTTI

resembles coarse crumbs. In a small bowl, combine buttermilk and oil; stir into dry ingredients just until moistened. Drop mixture by heaping teaspoonfuls over filling.

3. Bake, uncovered, until topping is golden brown and filling is bubbly, 20-25 minutes. Let stand 5 minutes before serving.

1 SERVING: 314 cal., 11g fat (4g sat. fat), 49mg chol., 701mg sod., 34g carb. (8g sugars, 3g fiber), 20g pro. **DIABETIC EXCHANGES:** 2 starch, 2 lean meat, 1½ fat.

TURKEY ASPARAGUS CASSEROLE

This creamy casserole is ready for the oven in just 10 minutes. Crunchy onions lend a decadent touch, or toss cracker crumbs and a little melted butter as a topping substitute.

—Cheryl Schut, Grand Rapids, MI

PREP: 10 min. • **BAKE:** 30 min.
MAKES: 4 servings

- 1 pkg. (10 oz.) frozen cut asparagus
- 2 cups cubed cooked turkey or chicken
- 1 can (10¾ oz.) condensed cream of chicken soup, undiluted
- ¼ cup water
- 1 can (2.8 oz.) french-fried onions

In a small saucepan, cook asparagus in a small amount of water for 2 minutes; drain. Place in a greased 11x7-in. baking dish. Top with turkey. Combine soup and water; spoon over turkey. Bake, uncovered, at 350° for 25-30 minutes. Sprinkle with onions. Bake 5 minutes longer or until golden brown.

1½ CUPS: 328 cal., 18g fat (5g sat. fat), 59mg chol., 800mg sod., 16g carb. (2g sugars, 2g fiber), 24g pro.

TURKEY & MUSHROOM POTPIES

TURKEY & MUSHROOM POTPIES

I always use the leftovers from our big holiday turkey to prepare this recipe. I think my family enjoys the potpies more than the original feast!

—Lily Julow, Lawrenceville, GA

PREP: 40 min. • **BAKE:** 20 min.
MAKES: 8 servings

- 4⅓ cups sliced baby portobello mushrooms
- 1 large onion, chopped
- 1 Tbsp. olive oil
- 2½ cups cubed cooked turkey
- 1 pkg. (16 oz.) frozen peas and carrots
- ¼ tsp. salt
- ¼ tsp. pepper
- ¼ cup cornstarch
- 2½ cups chicken broth
- ¼ cup sour cream

TOPPING
- 1½ cups all-purpose flour
- 2 tsp. sugar
- 1½ tsp. baking powder
- 1 tsp. dried thyme
- ¼ tsp. baking soda
- ¼ tsp. salt
- 2 Tbsp. cold butter
- 1 cup buttermilk
- 1 Tbsp. canola oil

1. Preheat oven to 400°. In a Dutch oven, saute mushrooms and onion in oil until tender. Stir in turkey, peas and carrots, salt and pepper. Combine the cornstarch and broth until smooth; gradually stir into pan. Bring to a boil. Reduce heat; cook and stir 2 minutes or until thickened. Stir in sour cream. Transfer the mixture to eight greased 8-oz. ramekins.

2. In a large bowl, combine flour, sugar, baking powder, thyme, baking soda and salt. Cut in butter until mixture

SAGE CHICKEN
CORDON BLEU

SAGE CHICKEN CORDON BLEU

It's always nice to surprise the family with special meals like this during the week. I usually double the recipe so we can enjoy leftovers the next day.
—Martha Stine, Johnstown, PA

PREP: 20 min. • **BAKE:** 40 min.
MAKES: 6 servings

- 6 boneless skinless chicken breast halves (4 oz. each)
- ½ to ¾ tsp. rubbed sage
- 6 slices thinly sliced deli ham
- 6 slices part-skim mozzarella cheese, halved
- 1 medium tomato, seeded and chopped
- ⅓ cup dry bread crumbs
- 2 Tbsp. grated Parmesan cheese
- 2 Tbsp. minced fresh parsley
- 4 Tbsp. butter, divided

1. Preheat oven to 350°. Pound the chicken breasts with a meat mallet to ⅛-in. thickness; sprinkle with sage. Place ham, mozzarella cheese and tomato down the center of each; roll up chicken from a long side, tucking in ends. Secure with toothpicks.
2. In a shallow bowl, toss the bread crumbs with Parmesan cheese and parsley. In a shallow microwave-safe dish, microwave 3 Tbsp. butter until melted. Dip chicken in butter, then roll in crumb mixture. Place in a greased 11x7-in. baking dish, seam side down. Melt the remaining butter; drizzle over top.
3. Bake, uncovered, for 40-45 minutes or until a thermometer inserted in the chicken reads 165°. Discard toothpicks before serving.
1 SERVING: 328 cal., 17g fat (9g sat. fat), 112mg chol., 575mg sod., 8g carb. (2g sugars, 1g fiber), 35g pro.

PAN-ROASTED CHICKEN & VEGETABLES

Quick prep time pays big dividends when this sheet-pan supper comes out of the oven. The rosemary gives it a rich flavor, and the meat juices cook the veggies to perfection.
—Sherri Melotik, Oak Creek, WI

PREP: 15 min.
BAKE: 45 min.
MAKES: 6 servings

2 lbs. red potatoes (about 6 medium), cut into ¾-in. pieces
1 large onion, coarsely chopped
2 Tbsp. olive oil
3 garlic cloves, minced
1¼ tsp. salt, divided
1 tsp. dried rosemary, crushed, divided
¾ tsp. pepper, divided
½ tsp. paprika
6 bone-in chicken thighs (about 2¼ lbs.), skin removed
6 cups fresh baby spinach (about 6 oz.)

1. Preheat oven to 425°. In a large bowl, combine potatoes, onion, oil, garlic, ¾ tsp. salt, ½ tsp. rosemary and ½ tsp. pepper; toss to coat. Transfer to a 15x10x1-in. baking pan coated with cooking spray.
2. In a small bowl, mix paprika and the remaining salt, rosemary and pepper. Sprinkle chicken with paprika mixture; arrange over vegetables. Roast until a thermometer inserted in the chicken reads 170°-175° and vegetables are just tender, 35-40 minutes.
3. Remove chicken to a serving platter; keep warm. Top the vegetables with spinach. Roast until the vegetables are tender and the spinach is wilted, 8-10 minutes longer. Stir vegetables to combine; serve with chicken.

1 CHICKEN THIGH WITH 1 CUP VEGETABLES: 357 cal., 14g fat (3g sat. fat), 87mg chol., 597mg sod., 28g carb. (3g sugars, 4g fiber), 28g pro. **DIABETIC EXCHANGES:** 4 lean meat, 1½ starch, 1 vegetable, 1 fat.

TURKEY CLUB PIZZA

Here is a cheesy pizza with all the flavor of a turkey club sandwich. The only bit missing is the lettuce, which is an excellent excuse for a side salad.
—Pippa Milburn, Dover, OH

TAKES: 20 min. • **MAKES:** 8 servings

1 prebaked 12-in. pizza crust
½ cup mayonnaise
1½ cups shredded Monterey Jack cheese
1 cup diced cooked turkey
½ cup bacon bits
2 plum tomatoes, sliced

Place the pizza crust on a baking sheet; spread with the mayonnaise. Top with 1 cup cheese, turkey, bacon and tomatoes. Sprinkle with remaining cheese. Bake at 450° for 10-12 minutes or until cheese is melted.
1 SLICE: 367 cal., 22g fat (6g sat. fat), 42mg chol., 688mg sod., 23g carb. (1g sugars, 0 fiber), 18g pro.

> **TEST KITCHEN TIP**
> To add a healthy variation, top each slice of pizza with spinach or watercress that you've tossed with a little Italian dressing or red wine vinaigrette.

PAN-ROASTED CHICKEN & VEGETABLES

**GLAZED
CORNISH HENS**

FAVORITE COMPANY CASSEROLE

Even my friends who don't eat a lot of broccoli or mushrooms admit that this casserole is a winner.
—Suzann Verdun, Lisle, IL

PREP: 15 min. • **BAKE:** 45 min.
MAKES: 8 servings

- 1 pkg. (6 oz.) wild rice, cooked
- 3 cups frozen chopped broccoli, thawed
- 1½ cups cubed cooked chicken
- 1 cup cubed cooked ham
- 1 cup shredded cheddar cheese
- 1 jar (4½ oz.) sliced mushrooms, drained
- 1 cup mayonnaise
- 1 tsp. prepared mustard
- ½ to 1 tsp. curry powder
- 1 can (10¾ oz.) condensed cream of mushroom soup, undiluted
- ¼ cup grated Parmesan cheese

1. Preheat oven to 350°. In a greased 2-qt. baking dish, layer the first six ingredients in order listed. Combine mayonnaise, mustard, curry and soup. Spread over top. Sprinkle Parmesan cheese over the casserole.
2. Bake, uncovered, 45-60 minutes or until top is light golden brown.
1 CUP: 405 cal., 32g fat (8g sat. fat), 61mg chol., 872mg sod., 11g carb. (1g sugars, 2g fiber), 18g pro.

GLAZED CORNISH HENS

If you're looking to add a touch of elegance to your dinner table, we suggest these Cornish game hens topped with a sweet apricot glaze.
—*Taste of Home* Test Kitchen

PREP: 5 min. • **BAKE:** 1 hour
MAKES: 4 servings

- 2 Cornish game hens (20 to 24 oz. each), split lengthwise
- ¼ tsp. salt
- ⅛ tsp. white pepper
- ⅓ cup apricot spreadable fruit
- 1 Tbsp. orange juice

1. Preheat oven to 350°. Place hens, breast side up, on a rack in a shallow roasting pan. Sprinkle with salt and pepper. Bake, uncovered, 30 minutes.
2. In a small bowl, combine spreadable fruit and orange juice. Spoon some of the apricot mixture over the Cornish hens. Bake until golden brown and juices run clear, 30-35 minutes, basting several times with remaining apricot mixture. Let stand about 5 minutes before serving.
½ HEN: 402 cal., 24g fat (7g sat. fat), 175mg chol., 233mg sod., 14g carb. (11g sugars, 0 fiber), 30g pro.

"I fixed this for Sunday dinner. It turned out beautifully! Such an easy recipe—such spectacular results. Served with baked sweet potato and steamed asparagus. Mmmmmm!"
—MYCATATOM, TASTEOFHOME.COM

**FAVORITE COMPANY
CASSEROLE**

MAKEOVER SOUR CREAM CHICKEN ENCHILADAS

My husband knows he's in for a treat when I begin rolling the enchiladas. This is his favorite dish, even in this lightened-up makeover version. We think it's a home run.

—Rynnetta Garner, Dallas, TX

PREP: 30 min. • **BAKE:** 15 min.
MAKES: 12 servings

- 4 cups cubed cooked chicken breast
- 1 Tbsp. chili powder
- 1 tsp. garlic salt
- 1 tsp. ground cumin
- 12 flour tortillas (8 in.), warmed

SAUCE

- 2 Tbsp. all-purpose flour
- 1½ cups reduced-sodium chicken broth
- 1½ cups reduced-fat sour cream
- 1 cup shredded Monterey Jack cheese
- 1 cup shredded Mexican cheese blend
  Chopped tomatoes, optional

1. In a large bowl, combine chicken, chili powder, garlic salt and cumin. Place ⅓ cup chicken mixture down the center of each tortilla. Roll up the enchiladas and place seam side down in two 13x9-in. baking dishes coated with cooking spray.
2. In a large saucepan, whisk flour and broth until smooth. Bring to a boil; cook and stir for 2 minutes. Reduce heat; stir in sour cream and Monterey Jack cheese until melted. Pour sauce over enchiladas; sprinkle with Mexican cheese blend.
3. Bake enchiladas, uncovered, at 350° for 15-20 minutes or until bubbly. Top with tomatoes if desired.

1 ENCHILADA: 338 cal., 13g fat (6g sat. fat), 63mg chol., 645mg sod., 29g carb. (2g sugars, 0 fiber), 25g pro. **DIABETIC EXCHANGES:** 3 lean meat, 2 starch, 1 fat.

CHICKEN & SWISS STUFFING BAKE

CHICKEN & SWISS STUFFING BAKE

I love to cook but just don't have much time. This chicken casserole is both comforting and fast, which makes it my favorite kind of recipe. I often serve it with a fresh salad.

—Jena Coffey, Sunset Hills, MO

PREP: 20 min. • **BAKE:** 25 min.
MAKES: 8 servings

- 1 can (10¾ oz.) condensed cream of mushroom soup, undiluted
- 1 cup whole milk
- 1 pkg. (6 oz.) stuffing mix
- 2 cups cubed cooked chicken breast
- 2 cups fresh broccoli florets, cooked
- 2 celery ribs, finely chopped
- 1½ cups shredded Swiss cheese, divided

1. In a large bowl, combine soup and milk until blended. Add stuffing mix with contents of seasoning packet, chicken, broccoli, celery and 1 cup cheese. Transfer to a greased 13x9-in. baking dish.
2. Bake, uncovered, at 375° for about 20 minutes or until heated through. Sprinkle with the remaining cheese; bake 5 minutes longer or until cheese is melted.

FREEZE OPTION: Sprinkle remaining cheese over unbaked casserole. Cover and freeze. To use, partially thaw in refrigerator overnight. Remove from refrigerator 30 minutes before baking. Preheat oven to 375°. Bake casserole as directed, increasing time as necessary to heat through and for a thermometer inserted in center to read 165°.

1 CUP: 247 cal., 7g fat (4g sat. fat), 42mg chol., 658mg sod., 24g carb. (0 sugars, 3g fiber), 22g pro.

SPINACH & TURKEY TURNOVERS

No one will mind the leftover turkey reappearing as tempting turnovers. The re-do on cranberry sauce is the bonus round. We serve these pastry pockets as a quick meal or snack.

—Anjli Sabharwal, Marlboro, NJ

PREP: 25 min. • **BAKE:** 15 min.
MAKES: 8 servings

- 1½ tsp. olive oil
- 2 green onions, chopped
- 1 garlic clove, minced
- ½ tsp. dried rosemary, crushed
- ¼ tsp. dried thyme
- 1 cup cubed cooked turkey
- 1 pkg. (10 oz.) frozen chopped spinach, thawed and squeezed dry
- ½ cup shredded Monterey Jack cheese
- ¼ cup turkey gravy
- ¼ tsp. salt
- ¼ tsp. pepper
- 1 pkg. (17.3 oz.) frozen puff pastry, thawed
- 1 large egg, lightly beaten
- 1 Tbsp. water

SAUCE
- 1 cup whole-berry cranberry sauce
- ¼ cup orange juice
- 1 Tbsp. grated orange zest

1. Preheat oven to 400°. In a large skillet, heat oil over medium-high heat. Add the green onions, garlic, rosemary and thyme; cook and stir 1 minute. Remove from heat. Stir in turkey, spinach, cheese, gravy, salt and pepper.
2. Unfold puff pastry; cut each sheet into four squares. Transfer to greased baking sheets. Spoon turkey mixture onto center of each square. In a small bowl, whisk egg and water; brush over edges of pastry. Fold one corner of dough diagonally over filling, forming triangles; press the edges with a fork to seal. Brush the tops with the egg mixture. Bake 12-14 minutes or until golden brown.
3. Meanwhile, in a small saucepan, combine cranberry sauce and orange juice. Bring to a boil; cook and stir for 3-4 minutes or until slightly thickened. Stir in the orange zest. Serve dipping sauce with turnovers.

1 TURNOVER WITH 2 TBSP. SAUCE:
435 cal., 21g fat (6g sat. fat), 47mg chol., 397mg sod., 50g carb. (9g sugars, 6g fiber), 13g pro.

TURKEY FLORENTINE

For this main course, I tuck Swiss cheese and spinach into browned turkey slices and bake with store-bought spaghetti sauce. Just a little oven time later, dinner is served.

—Lillian Butler, Stratford, CT

TAKES: 30 min. • **MAKES:** 8 servings

- 1 cup seasoned bread crumbs
- 1 lb. boneless skinless turkey breast, cut into 8 slices
- 2 Tbsp. canola oil
- 4 slices Swiss cheese, halved
- 1 pkg. (10 oz.) frozen chopped spinach, thawed and squeezed dry
- 3 cups meatless spaghetti sauce

1. Preheat oven to 400°. Place bread crumbs in a large resealable plastic bag. Add turkey; toss to coat. In a large skillet, heat oil over medium heat. Add turkey in batches; brown on both sides. Remove from skillet.
2. Place half of a cheese slice and 2 Tbsp. spinach down the center of each turkey slice. Fold turkey slice over filling; secure with toothpicks.
3. Place in a greased 11x7-in. baking dish. Top with spaghetti sauce. Bake, uncovered, for 12-15 minutes or until a thermometer inserted in turkey reads 165°. Discard toothpicks.
1 SERVING: 480 cal., 16g fat (6g sat. fat), 95mg chol., 1409mg sod., 40g carb. (13g sugars, 6g fiber), 43g pro.

SPINACH & TURKEY TURNOVERS

SPECIAL TURKEY SANDWICHES

Every Saturday night, our family's tradition is having lunch for dinner. With a rich cream cheese spread, these turkey sandwiches have become a favorite.

—Maria Bertram, Waltham, MA

TAKES: 25 min. • **MAKES:** 4 servings

- 4 oz. reduced-fat cream cheese
- ½ cup finely chopped fresh spinach
- ½ cup minced fresh basil
- ⅓ cup shredded Parmesan cheese
- 1 garlic clove, minced
- ½ large red onion, sliced
- 2 Tbsp. dry red wine or reduced-sodium beef broth
- 8 slices whole wheat bread, toasted
- ¾ lb. sliced deli turkey
- 8 slices tomato
- 8 lettuce leaves

1. In a small bowl, beat the cream cheese, spinach, basil, cheese and garlic until blended; set aside. In a small skillet, cook onion in wine until tender; set aside.
2. Place four slices of toast on a broiler pan; top with turkey. Place remaining toast on broiler pan; spread with cream cheese mixture.
3. Broil 3-4 in. from the heat for 2-3 minutes or until heated through. Layer the onion, tomato and lettuce over turkey. Place cream cheese toasts over sandwiches.

1 SERVING: 348 cal., 11g fat (6g sat. fat), 63mg chol., 1426mg sod., 36g carb. (6g sugars, 5g fiber), 29g pro.

"This sandwich was amazing. It was like eating a restaurant sandwich. I will probably end up making it for company. And it was super easy."
—ADSIMO, TASTEOFHOME.COM

PARMESAN CHICKEN

Chicken breasts bake up moist and tender when surrounded by savory Parmesan-kissed crumbs. Anyone hoping for leftovers needs to make bigger batches.

—Schelby Thompson, Camden Wyoming, DE

PREP: 10 min. • **BAKE:** 25 min.
MAKES: 6 servings

- ½ cup butter, melted
- 2 tsp. Dijon mustard
- 1 tsp. Worcestershire sauce
- ½ tsp. salt
- 1 cup dry bread crumbs
- ½ cup grated Parmesan cheese
- 6 boneless skinless chicken breast halves (7 oz. each)

1. Preheat oven to 350°. In a shallow bowl, combine the butter, mustard, Worcestershire sauce and salt. Place bread crumbs and cheese in another shallow bowl. Dip chicken in butter mixture, then in bread crumb mixture, patting to help coating adhere.
2. Place in an ungreased 15x10x1-in. baking pan. Drizzle chicken with any remaining butter mixture. Bake pieces, uncovered, for 25-30 minutes or until a thermometer inserted in chicken reads 165°.

1 CHICKEN BREAST HALF : 270 cal., 16g fat (9g sat. fat), 82mg chol., 552mg sod., 10g carb. (1g sugars, 0 fiber), 21g pro.

PARMESAN CHICKEN

CHICKEN TORTILLA BAKE

CHICKEN TORTILLA BAKE

My mother frequently made this heartwarming casserole when I was growing up. Chicken and cheese with zippy green chilies still make for an amazingly scrumptious combo.

—Jerri Moror, Rio Rancho, NM

PREP: 20 min. • **BAKE:** 30 min.
MAKES: 8 servings

3 cups shredded cooked chicken
2 cans (4 oz. each) chopped green chilies
1 cup chicken broth
1 can (10¾ oz.) condensed cream of mushroom soup, undiluted
1 can (10¾ oz.) condensed cream of chicken soup, undiluted
1 small onion, finely chopped
12 corn tortillas, warmed
2 cups shredded cheddar cheese

1. In a large bowl, combine chicken, chilies, broth, soups and onion; set aside. Layer half the warm tortillas in a greased 13x9-in. baking dish, cutting to fit pan if desired. Top with half the chicken mixture and half the cheese. Repeat layers.

2. Bake, uncovered, at 350° for about 30 minutes or until heated through.

FREEZE OPTION: Cover and freeze the unbaked casserole. To use, partially thaw in refrigerator overnight. Remove from refrigerator for 30 minutes before baking. Preheat oven to 350°. Bake as directed, increasing time as necessary for a thermometer inserted in center to read 165°.

1 PIECE: 359 cal., 17g fat (8g sat. fat), 81mg chol., 1007mg sod., 26g carb. (2g sugars, 3g fiber), 25g pro.

Pork

HAM & LEEK PIES

HAM & LEEK PIES

I've been making these pies for years, so lots of friends and family now have the recipe. If you can't find leeks, sweet or mild onions work just as well.
—Bonny Tillman, Acworth, GA

PREP: 40 min. • **BAKE:** 20 min.
MAKES: 4 servings

- ¼ cup butter, cubed
- 4 cups sliced leeks (white portion only)
- ½ lb. sliced fresh mushrooms
- 3 medium carrots, sliced
- ½ cup all-purpose flour
- 1¼ cups 2% milk
- 1¼ cups vegetable broth
- 1¾ cups cubed fully cooked ham
- 2 Tbsp. minced fresh parsley
- ¼ to ½ tsp. ground nutmeg
  Dash pepper
- 1 sheet frozen puff pastry, thawed
- 1 large egg, lightly beaten

1. Preheat oven to 425°. In a large saucepan, heat butter over medium-high heat. Add leeks, mushrooms and carrots; cook and stir until tender.
2. Stir in flour until blended. Gradually stir in milk and broth. Bring to a boil over medium heat, stirring constantly; cook and stir 2 minutes or until thickened. Remove from heat; stir in ham, parsley, nutmeg and pepper.
3. On a lightly floured surface, unfold puff pastry; roll to ¼-in. thickness. Using a 10-oz. ramekin as a template, cut out four tops for pies. Fill four greased 10-oz. ramekins with leek mixture; top with pastry. Cut slits in pastry. Brush tops with egg.
4. Bake 18-22 minutes or until golden brown. Let pies stand 5 minutes before serving.
1 PIE: 713 cal., 37 g fat (15 g sat. fat), 123 mg chol., 1,461 mg sod., 72 g carb., 9 g fiber, 25 g pro.

CREOLE PORK TENDERLOIN WITH VEGETABLES

3 OZ. COOKED PORK WITH 1 CUP VEGETABLES: 247 cal., 10g fat (2g sat. fat), 64mg chol., 575mg sod., 15g carb. (7g sugars, 5g fiber), 25g pro. **DIABETIC EXCHANGES:** 3 lean meat, 2 vegetable, 1 fat.

SAUSAGE BROCCOLI CALZONE

Impress guests with a few easy ingredients, such as French bread dough, sausage and cheeses. This tasty calzone is a real crowd-pleaser.
—Angie Colombo, Oldsmar, FL

PREP: 20 min. • **BAKE:** 20 min.
MAKES: 6 servings

- 12 oz. bulk pork sausage
- 1½ tsp. minced fresh sage
- 1 tube (11 oz.) refrigerated crusty French loaf
- 2 cups frozen chopped broccoli, thawed and drained
- 1 cup shredded part-skim mozzarella cheese
- 1 cup shredded cheddar cheese

1. In a small skillet, cook sausage over medium heat until no longer pink; drain. Stir in sage.
2. On an ungreased baking sheet, unroll dough starting at the seam; pat into a 14x12-in. rectangle. Spoon sausage lengthwise across center of dough. Sprinkle with broccoli and cheeses. Bring long sides of dough to the center over filling; pinch seams to seal. Turn calzone seam side down.
3. Bake at 350° until golden brown, 20-25 minutes. Serve warm.
1 SLICE: 369 cal., 21g fat (11g sat. fat), 51mg chol., 773mg sod., 27g carb. (5g sugars, 2g fiber), 18g pro.

"Before I put it in the oven, I sprayed the dough with butter spray and sprinkled garlic salt and a little sage on the outside. Everyone went back for a second helping."
—KRISTIBEATTY, TASTEOFHOME.COM

EAT SMART

CREOLE PORK TENDERLOIN WITH VEGETABLES

Fresh summer vegetables are paired with lean pork and tasty Greek olives for a healthy and quick dinner that's great for family or friends.
—Judy Armstrong, Prairieville, LA

PREP: 30 min. • **BAKE:** 20 min.
MAKES: 8 servings

- 3½ tsp. reduced-sodium Creole seasoning, divided
- 2 pork tenderloins (1 lb. each)
- 2 Tbsp. canola oil
- 2 medium fennel bulbs, trimmed and cut into 1-in. wedges
- 1 medium eggplant, cut into 1-in. cubes
- 2 medium yellow summer squash, halved and cut into ½-in. slices
- 1 large sweet red pepper, cut into 1-in. pieces
- 2 shallots, thinly sliced
- ½ cup pitted Greek olives, coarsely chopped
- 3 garlic cloves, minced
- ½ cup vegetable broth
- 4 tsp. minced fresh thyme or 1¼ tsp. dried thyme

1. Preheat oven to 350°. Sprinkle 3 tsp. Creole seasoning over tenderloins. In a 6-qt. stockpot, heat oil over medium-high heat. Brown tenderloins on all sides. Transfer to a roasting pan.
2. Add fennel, eggplant, squash, pepper and shallots to stockpot; cook and stir over medium heat 3-4 minutes or until lightly browned. Add olives and garlic; cook and stir 1 minute longer. Stir in broth, thyme and remaining Creole seasoning; bring to a boil. Reduce heat; simmer, covered, 6-8 minutes or until fennel is crisp-tender. Spoon vegetables and liquid around pork.
3. Bake, uncovered, 20-25 minutes or until vegetables are tender and a thermometer inserted in pork reads 145°. Let stand 5 minutes before serving. Cut pork into slices; serve with vegetables.

BROCCOLI MAC & CHEESE

Because the casserole bakes in two pans, you could freeze one for later, depending on your needs.

—Nancy Foust, Stoneboro, PA

PREP: 40 min. • **BAKE:** 25 min.
MAKES: 12 servings

- 1 pkg. (16 oz.) elbow macaroni
- 4 cups fresh broccoli florets
- ½ cup finely chopped onion
- ½ cup butter, cubed
- ½ cup all-purpose flour
- 1 tsp. ground mustard
- 1 tsp. salt
- ¼ tsp. pepper
- 6 cups 2% milk
- 1 jar (15 oz.) process cheese sauce
- 2 cups shredded cheddar cheese, divided
- 4 cups cubed fully cooked ham

1. Preheat oven to 350°. Cook the macaroni according to package directions, adding broccoli during the last 3-4 minutes; drain.
2. In a large Dutch oven, saute onion in butter 2 minutes. Stir in flour, mustard, salt and pepper until blended. Gradually stir in milk. Bring to a boil; cook and stir 2 minutes or until thickened. Stir in cheese sauce and 1 cup cheddar cheese until blended.
3. Remove from heat; stir in ham, macaroni and broccoli. Divide mixture between a greased 13x9-in. baking dish and a greased 8-in. square baking dish. Sprinkle with remaining cheese.
4. Bake, uncovered, 25-35 minutes or until bubbly and heated through.
1¼ CUPS: 532 cal., 28g fat (17g sat. fat), 95mg chol., 1610mg sod., 44g carb. (9g sugars, 2g fiber), 27g pro.

CHICKEN CORDON BLEU PIZZA

This recipe is a combination of my two favorite foods—pizza and chicken Cordon Bleu. I have made this for my family and also the teachers at my school. Now my teachers ask me to make it for them for lunch!!

—Justin Rippel, Colgate, WI

TAKES: 30 min. • **MAKES:** 6 servings

- 1 tube (13.8 oz.) refrigerated pizza crust
- ½ cup Alfredo sauce
- ¼ tsp. garlic salt
- 1 cup shredded Swiss cheese
- 1½ cups cubed fully cooked ham
- 10 breaded chicken nuggets, thawed, cut into ½-in. pieces
- 1 cup shredded part-skim mozzarella cheese

1. Preheat oven to 425°. Unroll and press dough onto bottom of a greased 15x10x1-in. pan, pinching the edges to form a rim if desired. Bake until edges are light brown, 8-10 minutes.
2. Spread crust with Alfredo sauce; sprinkle with garlic salt. Top with remaining ingredients. Bake until crust is golden brown and cheese is melted, 8-10 minutes.
1 SERVING: 438 cal., 20g fat (9g sat. fat), 65mg chol., 1386mg sod., 39g carb. (5g sugars, 2g fiber), 27g pro.

CHICKEN CORDON BLEU PIZZA

**BRAISED PORK
WITH TOMATILLOS**

SPICY PORK TENDERLOIN SALAD

A friend served this flavorful salad at a luncheon, and I adjusted it to fit our tastes. Since it's a meal in one, it's perfect for weeknights. And the pretty presentation makes it ideal for entertaining.
—Pat Sellon, Monticello, WI

PREP: 30 min. • **BAKE:** 25 min.
MAKES: 4 servings

4½ tsp. lime juice
1½ tsp. orange juice
1½ tsp. Dijon mustard
½ tsp. curry powder
¼ tsp. salt
⅛ tsp. pepper
2 Tbsp. olive oil
SPICE RUB
½ tsp. salt
½ tsp. ground cumin
½ tsp. ground cinnamon
½ tsp. chili powder
¼ tsp. pepper
1 pork tenderloin (1 lb.)
2 tsp. olive oil
⅓ cup packed brown sugar
6 garlic cloves, minced
1½ tsp. hot pepper sauce
1 pkg. (6 oz.) fresh baby spinach

1. In a small bowl, whisk the first six ingredients; gradually whisk in oil. Cover and refrigerate vinaigrette. Combine the salt, cumin, cinnamon, chili powder and pepper; rub over the meat.
2. In an ovenproof skillet, brown meat on all sides in oil, about 8 minutes. Combine the brown sugar, garlic and hot pepper sauce; spread over meat.
3. Bake at 350° until a thermometer inserted in pork reads 160°, 25-35 minutes. Let stand for 5 minutes before slicing.
4. Toss spinach with the vinaigrette. Arrange spinach on four salad plates; top with sliced pork. Drizzle with the pan juices.
1 SERVING: 301 cal., 13g fat (3g sat. fat), 63mg chol., 591mg sod., 22g carb. (18g sugars, 2g fiber), 24g pro. **DIABETIC EXCHANGES:** 3 lean meat, 1 starch, 1 vegetable, ½ fat.

BRAISED PORK WITH TOMATILLOS

A pork braise is a sure way to make people's mouths water. The tomatillos in this dish offer a subtle hint of lightness to the meat. For ultimate flavor, make the dish one day ahead and reheat.
—Matthew Lawrence, Vashon, WA

PREP: 25 min. • **BAKE:** 3 hours
MAKES: 6 servings

1 Tbsp. coriander seeds
1 Tbsp. cumin seeds
1 bone-in pork shoulder roast (3 to 4 lbs.)
¼ tsp. salt
¼ tsp. pepper
1 Tbsp. canola oil
15 tomatillos, husks removed, chopped
1 medium onion, chopped
2 garlic cloves, peeled and halved
1 cup white wine
8 cups chicken broth
POLENTA
4 cups chicken broth
1 cup yellow cornmeal

1. In a small dry skillet over medium heat, toast coriander and cumin seeds until aromatic, 1-2 minutes. Remove from skillet. Crush seeds using a spice grinder or mortar and pestle; set aside.
2. Sprinkle pork with salt and pepper. In an ovenproof Dutch oven, brown roast in oil on all sides. Remove and set aside. Add tomatillos and onion to the pan; saute until tomatillos are tender and lightly charred. Add the garlic and crushed spices; cook 1 minute longer.
3. Add wine, stirring to loosen the browned bits from pan. Stir in 8 cups broth and return roast to pan. Bring to a boil. Cover and bake at 350° until pork is tender, 3-3½ hours.
4. Meanwhile, in a large heavy saucepan, bring 4 cups broth to a boil. Reduce heat to a gentle boil; slowly whisk in cornmeal. Cook and stir with a wooden spoon until the polenta is thickened and pulls away cleanly from the sides of the pan, 15-20 minutes. Serve with pork.
1 SERVING: 514 cal., 24g fat (7g sat. fat), 120mg chol., 1160mg sod., 30g carb. (6g sugars, 3g fiber), 41g pro.

HAM & SWISS
STROMBOLI

HAM & SWISS STROMBOLI

This is perfect food to take to someone for dinner. It's also easy to change the recipe with your favorite meats or cheeses.

—Tricia Bibb, Hartselle, AL

TAKES: 30 min. • **MAKES:** 6 servings

1   tube (11 oz.) refrigerated crusty French loaf
6   oz. sliced deli ham
¼   cup finely chopped onion
8   bacon strips, cooked and crumbled
6   oz. sliced Swiss cheese Honey mustard, optional

1. Preheat oven to 375°. Unroll dough on a baking sheet. Place ham down center third of dough to within 1 in. of ends; top with onion, bacon and cheese. Fold long sides of dough over filling, pinching seam and ends to seal; tuck ends under. Cut several slits in top.

2. Bake 20-25 minutes or until golden brown. Cut into slices. If desired, serve with honey mustard.

FREEZE OPTION: Securely wrap and freeze cooled unsliced stromboli in heavy-duty foil. To use, reheat stromboli on an ungreased baking sheet in a preheated 375° oven until heated through and a thermometer inserted in center reads 165°.

1 SLICE: 272 cal., 11g fat (5g sat. fat), 40mg chol., 795mg sod., 26g carb. (3g sugars, 1g fiber), 18g pro.

PORK CHOPS WITH ORANGE RICE

My husband is delighted every time we have this pork and rice bake for dinner. I've also made it for new moms who need meals brought over.

—Karen Hossink, Lansing, MI

PREP: 15 min. • **BAKE:** 30 min.
MAKES: 4 servings

4   bone-in pork loin chops, (½ in. thick and 8 oz. each)
1   Tbsp. canola oil

1⅓ cups uncooked instant rice
1   cup orange juice
    Salt and pepper to taste
1   can (10½ oz.) condensed chicken with rice soup, undiluted

1. Preheat oven to 350°. In a large skillet, brown pork chops in oil on both sides. Sprinkle rice into a greased 9-in. square baking dish. Add juice; arrange chops over rice. Sprinkle with salt and pepper. Pour soup over chops.

2. Cover and bake 25-30 minutes or until a thermometer reads 145° and rice is tender. Let meat stand 5 minutes before serving.

1 SERVING: 549 cal., 23g fat (8g sat. fat), 114mg chol., 559mg sod., 41g carb. (6g sugars, 1g fiber), 40g pro.

"My mom made this dinner often while I was growing up. I am in my 40s and I still love it."
—MOIRAINE1209, TASTEOFHOME.COM

HAM & RICE HOT DISH

One of my best friends shared this recipe with me. My family loves it because it includes one of our favorite vegetables: broccoli. It's a creative way to use up leftover ham.

—Margaret Allen, Abingdon, VA

PREP: 20 min. • **BAKE:** 30 min.
MAKES: 8 servings

- 2 pkg. (10 oz. each) frozen cut broccoli
- 2 cups cooked rice
- 6 Tbsp. butter, cubed
- 2 cups fresh bread crumbs (about 2½ slices)
- 1 medium onion, chopped
- 3 Tbsp. all-purpose flour
- 1 tsp. salt
- ¼ tsp. pepper
- 3 cups milk
- 1½ lbs. fully cooked ham, cubed
  Shredded cheddar or Swiss cheese

1. Preheat oven to 350°. Cook broccoli according to package directions; drain. Spoon rice into a 13x9-in. baking pan. Place broccoli over rice.
2. Melt butter in a large skillet. Sprinkle 2 Tbsp. of the melted butter over the bread crumbs and set aside. In the remaining butter, saute onion until soft. Add the flour, salt and pepper, stirring constantly until blended; stir in milk. Bring to a boil; cook and stir for 2 minutes or until thickened. Add ham.
3. Pour over rice and broccoli. Sprinkle with crumbs. Bake 30 minutes or until heated through. Sprinkle with cheese; let stand 5 minutes before serving.
1 CUP: 379 cal., 19g fat (10g sat. fat), 81mg chol., 1583mg sod., 29g carb. (6g sugars, 2g fiber), 22g pro.

EAT SMART

MOM'S GARLIC PORK ROAST

Mom cooked for 11 children, so her menus usually featured simple foods. But on New Year's Day, she always treated us to this special pork roast. All of us kids agree this was our mom's best meal!

—Ruby Williams, Bogalusa, LA

PREP: 10 min.
BAKE: 1¼ hours + standing
MAKES: 8 servings

- ½ cup chopped celery
- ½ medium green pepper, finely chopped
- ½ cup thinly sliced green onions
- 8 garlic cloves, minced
- 1 bone-in pork loin roast (5 lbs.)
- 1 tsp. salt
- ¼ tsp. cayenne pepper

1. Preheat oven to 350°. In a small bowl, mix celery, green pepper, green onions and garlic.
2. Place roast in a roasting pan, fat side up. With a sharp knife, make deep slits into top of roast, cutting between ribs. Fill slits with vegetable mixture. Sprinkle roast with salt and cayenne.
3. Roast until meat reaches desired doneness (for medium-rare, a thermometer should read 145°; medium, 160°), 1¼ to 1½ hours. Remove roast from oven; tent with foil. Let stand 15 minutes before carving.
1 SERVING: 298 cal., 13g fat (5g sat. fat), 114mg chol., 399mg sod., 2g carb. (1g sugars, 1g fiber), 40g pro. **DIABETIC EXCHANGES:** 5 lean meat.

HAM & RICE HOT DISH

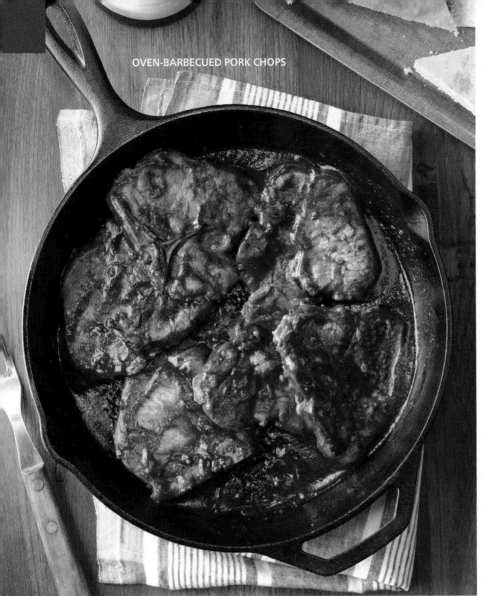

OVEN-BARBECUED PORK CHOPS

SPAGHETTI WITH BACON

As children, we always requested this dish for our birthday dinners. Our mother got the recipe from her grandmother. Now I pass on our tasty tradition.

—Ruth Keogh, North St. Paul, MN

PREP: 20 min. • **BAKE:** 40 min.
MAKES: 4 servings

- 8 oz. uncooked spaghetti
- ½ lb. bacon strips, chopped
- 1 medium onion, chopped
- 1 can (14½ oz.) diced tomatoes, undrained
- 1 can (8 oz.) tomato sauce

1. Preheat oven to 350°. Cook spaghetti according to package directions for al dente.
2. In a large skillet, cook bacon and onion over medium heat until bacon is crisp, stirring occasionally; drain. Stir in tomatoes and tomato sauce; bring to a boil.
3. Drain spaghetti; transfer to a greased 11x7-in. baking dish. Spread the sauce over top. Bake, covered, 40-45 minutes or until bubbly.
1 SERVING: 159 cal., 6g fat (2g sat. fat), 11mg chol., 498mg sod., 18g carb. (4g sugars, 2g fiber), 7g pro.

OVEN-BARBECUED PORK CHOPS

My mother has fixed this recipe for years and now I prepare it for my family. The chops are delicious with scalloped potatoes and home-baked bread.

—Teresa King, Whittier, CA

PREP: 10 min. • **BAKE:** 40 min.
MAKES: 6 servings

- 6 bone-in pork loin chops (¾ in. thick)
- 1 Tbsp. Worcestershire sauce
- 2 Tbsp. vinegar
- 2 tsp. brown sugar
- ½ tsp. pepper
- ½ tsp. chili powder
- ½ tsp. paprika
- ¾ cup ketchup
- ⅓ cup hot water

Place chops, overlapping slightly if necessary, in a large cast-iron or other ovenproof skillet. Combine remaining ingredients; pour over meat. Bake, uncovered, at 375° for 40 minutes, turning chops halfway through cooking.
1 PORK CHOP: 359 cal., 18g fat (7g sat. fat), 111mg chol., 491mg sod., 10g carb. (10g sugars, 0 fiber), 36g pro.

TEST KITCHEN TIP
Sugar, vinegar and ketchup create a classic flavor combination that's both sweet and sour. The sauce would also be tasty with smoked kielbasa or popcorn chicken.

SPAGHETTI
WITH BACON

PORCINI-CRUSTED PORK WITH POLENTA

Hints of rosemary and Parmesan meet earthy mushroom undertones in this restaurant-quality dish you can proudly call your own.
—Casandra Rittenhouse, North Hollywood, CA

PREP: 20 min. • **BAKE:** 20 min.
MAKES: 4 servings

- 1 pkg. (1 oz.) dried porcini mushrooms
- ¼ tsp. salt
- ¼ tsp. pepper
- 4 bone-in pork loin chops (7 oz. each)
- 2 tsp. olive oil
- 1 tube (1 lb.) polenta
- ½ cup grated Parmesan cheese
- ¼ tsp. dried rosemary, crushed

1. Process mushrooms in a food processor until coarsely chopped. Transfer to a shallow bowl; stir in salt and pepper. Press one side of each pork chop into mushroom mixture.
2. In a large ovenproof skillet coated with cooking spray, heat oil over medium-high heat. Place chops, mushroom side down, in skillet; cook for 2 minutes. Turn over; cook 2 minutes longer. Bake, uncovered, at 375° until a thermometer inserted in pork reads 145°, 20-25 minutes. Let stand 5 minutes before serving.
3. Prepare polenta according to package directions for soft polenta. Stir in cheese and rosemary. Serve with pork chops.
1 SERVING: 397 cal., 14g fat (5g sat. fat), 94mg chol., 825mg sod., 26g carb. (2g sugars, 3g fiber), 38g pro.

"This was a hit with my entire family. It was especially good with the polenta. We will for sure keep this on our list!"
—DAY_MAGS, TASTEOFHOME.COM

STUFFED IOWA CHOPS

STUFFED IOWA CHOPS

Here's a hearty dish for big appetites. The corn and apples make a flavorful stuffing for the chops.
—Judith Smith, Des Moines, IA

PREP: 20 min. • **BAKE:** 50 min.
MAKES: 4 servings

- 4 bone-in pork loin chops (1½ in. thick and 8 oz. each)
- 1 Tbsp. canola oil
- 1 Tbsp. finely chopped onion
- 1 Tbsp. minced fresh parsley
- 1 Tbsp. 2% milk
- ¼ tsp. salt
- ¼ tsp. rubbed sage
- ¼ tsp. pepper
- 1 cup chopped peeled apple
- 1 cup whole kernel corn
- 1 cup dry bread crumbs
- SAUCE
- ⅓ cup honey
- 3 to 4 Tbsp. Dijon mustard
- ¾ tsp. minced fresh rosemary or ⅛ tsp. dried rosemary, crushed

1. Preheat oven to 350°. Cut a pocket in each pork chop by slicing almost to the bone. In a large skillet, heat oil over medium heat. Brown chops on each side; cool slightly.
2. In a bowl, mix onion, parsley, milk and seasonings. Add apple, corn and bread crumbs; toss to combine. Spoon into pork chops; place in a greased 13x9-in. baking dish.
3. In a small bowl, mix the sauce ingredients; reserve half for brushing. Pour remaining sauce over pork chops. Bake, uncovered, 50-60 minutes or until a thermometer inserted in the stuffing reads 165°, brushing occasionally with reserved sauce during the last 20 minutes.
1 STUFFED PORK CHOP: 601 cal., 24g fat (8g sat. fat), 112mg chol., 875mg sod., 54g carb. (31g sugars, 3g fiber), 41g pro.

SPINACH & GOUDA-STUFFED PORK CUTLETS

This started as a restaurant copycat dish that I re-created at home. Cheese just oozes out of the center, and mustard lends a lot of flavor.
—Joan Oakland, Troy, MT

TAKES: 30 min. • **MAKES:** 2 servings

- 3 Tbsp. dry bread crumbs
- 2 Tbsp. grated Parmesan cheese
- 2 pork sirloin cutlets (3 oz. each)
- ¼ tsp. salt
- ⅛ tsp. pepper
- 2 slices smoked Gouda cheese (about 2 oz.)
- 2 cups fresh baby spinach
- 2 Tbsp. horseradish mustard

1. Preheat oven to 400°. In a shallow bowl, mix the bread crumbs and Parmesan cheese.
2. Sprinkle cutlets with the salt and pepper. Layer one end of each with Gouda cheese and spinach. Fold the cutlets in half, enclosing filling; secure with toothpicks. Brush mustard over outsides of pork; dip in the bread crumb mixture, patting to help the coating adhere.
3. Place on a greased foil-lined baking sheet. Bake 12-15 minutes or until golden brown and pork is tender. Discard toothpicks before serving.
1 STUFFED CUTLET: 299 cal., 16g fat (7g sat. fat), 91mg chol., 898mg sod., 10g carb. (2g sugars, 2g fiber), 30g pro.

SAVORY PORK LOIN ROAST

My recipe is one of my family's favorites. The pork is always tender and fragrant.
—DeEtta Rasmussen, Fort Madison, IA

PREP: 15 min. • **BAKE:** 70 min. + standing
MAKES: 8 servings (2 cups sauce)

- ¼ cup reduced-sodium soy sauce
- 6 garlic cloves, minced
- 1 Tbsp. each minced fresh basil, rosemary and sage
- 1 Tbsp. ground mustard
- 1 pork loin roast (3½ lbs.), trimmed
- 1 cup water
- 8 green onions, chopped
- 2 Tbsp. butter
- ¼ cup brown gravy mix
- 2½ cups beef broth
- 1¼ cups sour cream
- 2 Tbsp. prepared horseradish

1. Preheat oven to 350°. In a small bowl, combine soy sauce, garlic, herbs and mustard; rub over roast. Place on a rack in a shallow roasting pan. Pour water into the pan.
2. Bake the roast, uncovered, until a thermometer inserted in pork reads 145°, 70-90 minutes. Remove roast from oven; tent with foil. Let stand 15 minutes before slicing.
3. Meanwhile, in a large saucepan, saute onions in butter until tender. Combine gravy mix and broth until smooth; stir into pan. Bring to a boil. Reduce heat; cook and stir until thickened. Stir in sour cream and horseradish; heat through (do not boil). Serve with pork.
1 SERVING: 386 cal., 19g fat (9g sat. fat), 131mg chol., 1127mg sod., 6g carb. (3g sugars, 1g fiber), 43g pro.

SPINACH & GOUDA-STUFFED PORK CUTLETS

HONEY-GLAZED PORK TENDERLOINS

Honey, smoky chipotle pepper and soy sauce help to flavor this no-fuss pork tenderloin. Serve it with veggies or rice for a satisfying meal.
—Diane Cotton, Franklin, NC

PREP: 15 min. • **BAKE:** 20 min.
MAKES: 6 servings

- ½ tsp. garlic powder
- ½ tsp. ground chipotle pepper
- ½ tsp. pepper
- 2 pork tenderloins (1 lb. each)
- 1 Tbsp. canola oil
- ½ cup honey
- 2 Tbsp. reduced-sodium soy sauce
- 1 Tbsp. balsamic vinegar
- 1 tsp. sesame oil

1. Preheat oven to 350°. Combine the first three ingredients; rub over pork. In a large ovenproof skillet, brown pork in canola oil on all sides.
2. In a small bowl, combine honey, soy sauce, vinegar and sesame oil; spoon over pork. Bake, uncovered, 20-25 minutes or until a thermometer reads 145°, basting occasionally with pan juices. Let stand 5 minutes before slicing. Serve with pan juices if desired.
4 OZ. COOKED PORK: 288 cal., 8g fat (2g sat. fat), 84mg chol., 265mg sod., 24g carb. (24g sugars, 0 fiber), 31g pro.

HAM & CHEESE POTATO CASSEROLE

With this recipe you get two cheesy casseroles. Have one tonight and put the other on ice for a future busy weeknight. It's like having money in the bank when things get hectic!
—Kari Adams, Fort Collins, CO

PREP: 15 min. • **BAKE:** 50 min. + standing
MAKES: 2 casseroles (5 servings each)

- 2 cans (10¾ oz. each) condensed cream of celery soup, undiluted
- 2 cups (16 oz.) sour cream
- ½ cup water
- ½ tsp. pepper
- 2 pkg. (28 oz. each) frozen O'Brien potatoes
- 1 pkg. (16 oz.) process cheese (Velveeta), cubed
- 2½ cups cubed fully cooked ham

1. Preheat oven to 375°. In a large bowl, mix the soup, sour cream, water and pepper until blended. Stir in potatoes, cheese and ham.
2. Transfer to two greased 2-qt. baking dishes. Bake, covered, 40 minutes. Uncover; bake 10-15 minutes longer or until bubbly. Let stand 10 minutes before serving.
FREEZE OPTION: Cover and freeze unbaked casseroles. To use, partially thaw in refrigerator overnight. Remove from refrigerator 30 minutes before baking. Preheat oven to 375°. Bake casseroles as directed, increasing time as necessary to heat through and for a thermometer inserted in center to read 165°.
1⅓ CUPS: 474 cal., 26g fat (14g sat. fat), 92mg chol., 1555mg sod., 36g carb. (7g sugars, 4g fiber), 20g pro.

HAM & CHEESE
POTATO CASSEROLE

CUBAN PORK WRAPS

CUBAN PORK WRAPS

Hot and juicy pork in tortillas may remind you of a Cuban sandwich with ham and cheese. We always include the pickles, of course.

—Aimee Bachmann, North Bend, WA

TAKES: 20 min. • **MAKES:** 4 servings

- ¾ lb. thin boneless pork loin chops, cut into strips
- 1 Tbsp. canola oil
- ⅛ tsp. pepper
- 1 Tbsp. Dijon mustard
- 4 multigrain tortillas (10 in.)
- 8 oz. sliced deli ham
- 8 slices Swiss cheese
- 4 thin sandwich pickle slices
- ¼ cup thinly sliced red onion

1. Preheat oven to 350°. In a bowl, toss pork with oil and pepper. Place a large skillet over medium-high heat. Add pork; cook and stir 2-3 minutes or until browned. Remove from heat.

2. To assemble, spread mustard onto center of tortillas; layer with ham, cheese, pickle, onion and pork. Fold bottom and sides of tortillas over filling and roll up. Place wraps on an ungreased baking sheet; bake 4-6 minutes or until heated through.
1 WRAP: 501 cal., 22g fat (8g sat. fat), 86mg chol., 1230mg sod., 37g carb. (5g sugars, 7g fiber), 39g pro.

ITALIAN SHREDDED PORK STEW

Need a warm meal for a blustery night? Throw together this slow-cooked stew loaded with nutritious sweet potatoes and kale. The shredded pork is so tender, you'll want to make the recipe again and again.

—Robin Jungers, Campbellsport, WI

PREP: 20 min. • **COOK:** 8 hours
MAKES: 9 servings (3½ qt.)

- 2 medium sweet potatoes, peeled and cubed
- 2 cups chopped fresh kale
- 1 large onion, chopped
- 3 garlic cloves, minced
- 1 boneless pork shoulder butt roast (2½ to 3½ lbs.)
- 1 can (14 oz.) cannellini beans, rinsed and drained
- 1½ tsp. Italian seasoning
- ½ tsp. salt
- ½ tsp. pepper
- 3 cans (14½ oz. each) chicken broth Sour cream, optional

1. Place the sweet potatoes, kale, onion and garlic in a 5-qt. slow cooker. Place roast on vegetables. Add the beans and seasonings. Pour broth over top. Cook, covered, on low until meat is tender, 8-10 hours.
2. Remove meat; cool slightly. Skim fat from cooking juices. Shred pork with two forks and return to slow cooker; heat through. If desired, garnish with sour cream.
1½ CUPS: 283 cal., 13g fat (5g sat. fat), 78mg chol., 860mg sod., 15g carb. (4g sugars, 3g fiber), 24g pro.

BAKED SAUCY
PORK CHOPS

BAKED SAUCY PORK CHOPS

Baked pork chop recipes are always handy to feed my hungry family. This entree brightens up the usual routine. I reach for this recipe when our appetites are hearty and I feel like baking pork chops.
—Dorothy Toben, Blackwell, OK

TAKES: 30 min. • **MAKES:** 2 servings

- 2 Tbsp. butter
- 2 bone-in pork loin chops (¾ in. thick)
- ¼ cup chopped onion
- ¼ cup maple syrup
- 2 Tbsp. water
- 1 Tbsp. cider vinegar
- 2 tsp. Worcestershire sauce
- 1 tsp. chili powder
- ¼ tsp. salt
- ¼ tsp. pepper
- ⅛ tsp. garlic powder

1. Preheat oven to 350°. In a large skillet, heat butter over medium heat. Brown pork chops on both sides. Transfer chops to a greased 11x7-in. baking dish; sprinkle with onion.
2. In a bowl, mix the remaining ingredients; pour over chops. Bake, covered, until a thermometer inserted in pork reads 145°, 15-20 minutes. Let stand 5 minutes before serving.
1 PORK CHOP: 442 cal., 19g fat (7g sat. fat), 111mg chol., 472mg sod., 31g carb. (26g sugars, 1g fiber), 37g pro.

DID YOU KNOW?

Chili powder is a seasoning blend made primarily from dried chili peppers. Other ingredients commonly include garlic, onion, salt, oregano, cumin, coriander, cloves, cinnamon and even cocoa powder.

FIVE-CHEESE MACARONI WITH PROSCIUTTO BITS

FIVE-CHEESE MACARONI WITH PROSCIUTTO BITS

Macaroni is baked with smoked Gouda, Swiss, white cheddar, goat cheese and Parmesan and topped with crispy prosciutto – so worth it!
—Mya Zeronis, Washington, D.C.

PREP: 25 min. • **BAKE:** 20 min.
MAKES: 12 servings

- 1 pkg. (16 oz.) elbow macaroni
- ⅓ cup unsalted butter, cubed
- 1 medium onion, halved and thinly sliced
- 1 garlic clove, minced
- ⅓ cup all-purpose flour
- ½ cup white wine or reduced-sodium chicken broth
- 4 cups heavy whipping cream
- 1 tsp. white pepper
- ¼ tsp. salt
- 5 oz. fresh goat cheese, crumbled
- 5 oz. white cheddar cheese, shredded
- 5 oz. Swiss cheese, shredded
- 3 oz. smoked Gouda cheese, shredded
- ¾ cup grated Parmesan cheese
- ½ cup panko (Japanese) bread crumbs
- 4 oz. thinly sliced prosciutto, chopped

1. Cook macaroni according to package directions until al dente.
2. Meanwhile, in a Dutch oven, heat butter over medium-high heat. Add onion; cook and stir for 4-6 minutes or until golden brown. Add garlic; cook 1 minute longer. Stir in flour until blended; gradually stir in wine. Add cream, pepper and salt; bring to a boil, stirring constantly. Cook and stir for 2 minutes or until thickened.
3. Reduce heat to medium-low. Add goat cheese; stir gently until melted. Gradually stir in the remaining cheeses; cook until melted. Remove from the heat.
4. Drain macaroni; stir into sauce. Transfer to a greased 13x9-in. baking dish. Sprinkle with bread crumbs. Bake, uncovered, at 375° for 15-20 minutes or until lightly browned.
5. Meanwhile, in a small nonstick skillet, cook prosciutto over medium heat for 5-7 minutes or until crisp, stirring frequently. Sprinkle over macaroni just before serving.
1¼ CUPS: 667 cal., 48g fat (30g sat. fat), 155mg chol., 558mg sod., 37g carb. (4g sugars, 2g fiber), 21g pro.

WHITE CHEDDAR SCALLOPED POTATOES

This recipe has evolved over the past eight years. After I added the thyme, ham and sour cream, my husband declared, "This is it!" I like to serve these rich and saucy potatoes with a salad and homemade French bread.

—Hope Toole, Muscle Shoals, AL

PREP: 40 min. • **BAKE:** 70 min.
MAKES: 10 servings

- ¼ cup butter
- 1   medium onion, finely chopped
- ¼ cup all-purpose flour
- 1   tsp. salt
- 1   tsp. dried parsley flakes
- ½ tsp. dried thyme
- ½ tsp. pepper
- 3   cups 2% milk
- 1   can (10¾ oz.) condensed cream of mushroom soup, undiluted
- 1   cup (8 oz.) sour cream
- 8   cups thinly sliced peeled potatoes
- 3½ cups cubed fully cooked ham
- 2   cups shredded sharp white cheddar cheese

1. Preheat oven to 375°. In a large saucepan, heat butter over medium-high heat. Add onion; cook and stir until tender. Stir in the flour and seasonings until blended; gradually whisk in milk. Bring to a boil, stirring constantly; cook and stir 2 minutes or until thickened. Stir in soup. Remove from heat; stir in sour cream.

2. In a greased 13x9-in. baking dish, layer half of each of the following: potatoes, ham, cheese and sauce. Repeat layer.

3. Bake, covered, 30 minutes. Bake, uncovered, 40-50 minutes longer or until potatoes are tender.

1 SERVING: 417 cal., 20g fat (12g sat. fat), 88mg chol., 1267mg sod., 37g carb. (7g sugars, 3g fiber), 22g pro.

EAT SMART
PEPPER-CRUSTED PORK TENDERLOIN

Guests will be impressed by this elegant entree and its golden crumb coating with peppery pizzazz. The meat slices up so moist and tender, you can serve it without sauce and still have a succulent taste-tempting main dish.

—Ellen Riley, Murfreesboro, TN

PREP: 25 min. • **BAKE:** 30 min.
MAKES: 6 servings

- 3   Tbsp. Dijon mustard
- 1   Tbsp. buttermilk
- 2   tsp. minced fresh thyme
- 1   to 2 tsp. coarsely ground pepper
- ¼ tsp. salt
- 2   pork tenderloins (¾ lb. each)
- ⅔ cup soft bread crumbs

1. Preheat oven to 425°. Mix first five ingredients. To make a double roast, arrange tenderloins side by side, thick end to thin end; tie together with kitchen string at 1½-in. intervals. Place on a rack in a 15x10x1-in. pan. Spread with mustard mixture; cover with bread crumbs, pressing to adhere.

2. Bake until a thermometer inserted in pork reads 145°, 30-40 minutes. (Tent loosely with foil if needed to prevent overbrowning.) Let stand 5 minutes. Cut into slices; remove the string before serving.

NOTE: To make soft bread crumbs, tear bread into pieces and place in a food processor or blender. Cover and pulse until crumbs form. One slice of bread yields ½ to ¾ cup crumbs.

1 SERVING: 155 cal., 4g fat (1g sat. fat), 64mg chol., 353mg sod., 3g carb. (0 sugars, 0 fiber), 23g pro. **DIABETIC EXCHANGES:** 3 lean meat.

PEPPER-CRUSTED
PORK TENDERLOIN

MINI PORK PIES

FREEZE OPTION: Freeze cooled pies in freezer containers. To use, partially thaw pies in refrigerator overnight. Reheat on ungreased baking sheets in a preheated 350° oven 14-17 minutes or until heated through.

2 PIES: 561 cal., 35g fat (14g sat. fat), 94mg chol., 776mg sod., 40g carb. (3g sugars, 0 fiber), 21g pro.

PINEAPPLE HAM LOAVES

Ham and pineapple is such a classic pairing, and this recipe is perfect for two. You can grind up a ham slice and a boneless pork chop in your food processor or a meat grinder, if you have it, for this recipe.

—Aleatha Smith, Billings, MT

PREP: 15 min. • **BAKE:** 35 min.
MAKES: 2 servings

- 1 can (8 oz.) sliced pineapple
- 2 Tbsp. beaten egg
- 2 Tbsp. 2% milk
- ¼ tsp. Worcestershire sauce
- 3 Tbsp. dry bread crumbs
- ¼ tsp. plus ⅛ tsp. ground mustard, divided
  Dash salt
  Dash pepper
- ¼ lb. ground fully cooked ham (about 1 cup)
- ¼ lb. ground pork
- 1 Tbsp. brown sugar

Drain pineapple, reserving 1 Tbsp. juice. Place a pineapple slice each in two 10-oz. ramekins or custard cups coated with cooking spray; set aside. (Refrigerate remaining pineapple and juice for another use.) In a small bowl, combine the egg, milk, Worcestershire sauce, bread crumbs, ¼ tsp. mustard, salt and pepper. Crumble ham and pork over mixture and mix well. Gently press meat mixture into each ramekin. Combine the brown sugar, remaining mustard and reserved juice; spoon over each loaf. Bake, uncovered, at 350° for 35-40 minutes or until lightly browned and a thermometer reads 160°. Invert onto serving plates.

1 SERVING: 392 cal., 21g fat (8g sat. fat), 135mg chol., 948mg sod., 24g carb. (15g sugars, 1g fiber), 25g pro.

FREEZE IT

MINI PORK PIES

I discovered my love of pork pies as a child when I used to help my father deliver oil on Saturdays and we would stop at a local pork pie place for lunch.

—Renee Murby, Johnston, RI

PREP: 1 hour • **BAKE:** 15 min.
MAKES: 10 servings

- 1 Tbsp. cornstarch
- 1¼ cups reduced-sodium chicken broth
- 2 lbs. ground pork
- 3 garlic cloves, minced
- 1½ tsp. salt
- ½ tsp. pepper
- ⅛ to ¼ tsp. ground cloves
- ⅛ to ¼ tsp. ground nutmeg
- ⅛ tsp. cayenne pepper
- 2 pkg. (14.1 oz. each) refrigerated pie pastry
- 1 large egg
- 2 tsp. 2% milk

1. Preheat oven to 425°. In a small saucepan, mix cornstarch and broth until blended; bring to a boil, stirring constantly. Cook and stir 1-2 minutes or until thickened. Remove from heat.
2. In a large skillet, cook pork, garlic and seasonings over medium heat 6-8 minutes or until pork is no longer pink, breaking up pork into crumbles; drain. Add broth mixture; cook and stir for 1-2 minutes or until thickened. Cool slightly.
3. Unroll each pastry sheet. On a work surface, roll each into a 12-in. circle. Using floured round cookie cutters, cut twenty 4-in. circles and twenty 2¾-in. circles, rerolling scraps as needed. Place large circles in ungreased muffin cups, pressing pastry onto bottoms and up sides.
4. Fill each with 3 Tbsp. pork mixture. Place small circles over filling; press edges with a fork to seal. In a small bowl, whisk egg and milk; brush over tops. Cuts slits in pastry.
5. Bake 15-20 minutes or until golden brown. Carefully remove pies to wire racks. Serve warm.

Fish & Seafood

JAMAICAN SALMON WITH COCONUT CREAM SAUCE

JAMAICAN SALMON WITH COCONUT CREAM SAUCE

We try to eat salmon often because it's so healthy. I love thinking of new ways to make it different and delicious. This easy dazzler with jerk seasoning is my go-to meal for company.
—Joni Hilton, Rocklin, CA

TAKES: 30 min. • **MAKES:** 4 servings

- 4 salmon fillets (6 oz. each)
- 3 Tbsp. mayonnaise
- 4 tsp. Caribbean jerk seasoning
- ⅓ cup sour cream
- ¼ cup cream of coconut
- 1 tsp. grated lime zest
- ¼ cup lime juice
- ½ cup sweetened shredded coconut, toasted

1. Preheat oven to 350°. Place fillets in a greased 13x9-in. baking dish. Spread mayonnaise over fillets; sprinkle with jerk seasoning.
2. Bake until fish just begins to flake easily with a fork, about 18-22 minutes. Meanwhile, for the sauce, in a small saucepan, combine sour cream, cream of coconut, lime zest and juice; cook and stir over medium-low heat until ingredients are blended.
3. Drizzle fillets with sauce; sprinkle with coconut.

1 FILLET WITH 3 TBSP. SAUCE AND 2 TBSP. COCONUT: 497 cal., 34g fat (12g sat. fat), 102mg chol., 467mg sod., 16g carb. (14g sugars, 1g fiber), 30g pro.

"Every element of this recipe was great. I had never used cream of coconut and had a bit of trouble locating it in the grocery store: it's with the cocktail mixers. I expected the jerk seasoning to be a dry herb blend, but the one I chose was a spread. I think this recipe would be wonderful even without coconut-lime sauce—but don't skip it! It really takes things to a whole new level."
—SNOWYTREES, TASTEOFHOME.COM

OVEN-BAKED SHRIMP & GRITS

STUFFED SOLE

Seafood was a staple for my large family when we were growing up. Inspired by my mother's delicious meals, I developed this recipe. The fish is moist and flavorful, and the sauce is so good over rice. You'll likely get as many recipe requests and compliments when serving this dish as I do.
—Winnie Higgins, Salisbury, MD

PREP: 20 min. • **BAKE:** 35 min.
MAKES: 8 servings

- 1 cup chopped onion
- 2 cans (6 oz. each) small shrimp, rinsed and drained
- 1 jar (4½ oz.) sliced mushrooms, drained
- 2 Tbsp. butter
- ½ lb. fresh cooked or canned crabmeat, drained and cartilage removed
- 8 sole or flounder fillets (2 to 2½ lbs.)
- ½ tsp. salt
- ¼ tsp. pepper
- ¼ tsp. paprika
- 2 cans (10¾ oz. each) condensed cream of mushroom soup, undiluted
- ⅓ cup chicken broth
- 2 Tbsp. water
- ⅔ cup shredded cheddar cheese
- 2 Tbsp. minced fresh parsley
  Cooked wild, brown, white or mixed rice, optional

1. In a large saucepan, saute the onion, shrimp and mushrooms in butter until onion is tender. Add crabmeat; heat through. Sprinkle the fillets with salt, pepper and paprika. Spoon crabmeat mixture on fillets; roll up and fasten with a toothpick.
2. Place in a greased 13-in. x 9-in. baking dish. Combine the soup, broth and water; blend until smooth. Pour over fillets. Sprinkle with cheese.
3. Cover and bake fish at 400° for 30 minutes. Sprinkle with parsley; bake 5 minutes or until the fish just begins to flake easily with a fork. Serve with rice if desired.
1 SERVING: 297 cal., 10g fat (5g sat. fat), 170mg chol., 1070mg sod., 6g carb. (2g sugars, 1g fiber), 44g pro.

OVEN-BAKED SHRIMP & GRITS

On chilly days, I doctor up grits and top them with shrimp for a comfy meal. If you're not a seafood lover, add chicken, ham or both.
—Jerri Gradert, Lincoln, NE

PREP: 20 min. • **BAKE:** 45 min.
MAKES: 6 servings

- 1 carton (32 oz.) chicken broth
- 1 cup quick-cooking grits
- 1 can (10 oz.) diced tomatoes and green chilies, drained
- 1 cup shredded Monterey Jack cheese
- 1 cup shredded cheddar cheese, divided
  Freshly ground pepper
- 2 Tbsp. butter
- 1 medium green pepper, chopped
- 1 medium onion, chopped
- 1 lb. uncooked shrimp (31-40 per lb.), peeled and deveined
- 2 garlic cloves, minced

1. Preheat oven to 350°. In a 13x9-in. or 2½-qt. baking dish, combine broth and grits. Bake, uncovered, until the liquid is absorbed and grits are tender, 30-35 minutes.
2. Stir in the tomatoes, Monterey Jack cheese and ½ cup cheddar cheese. Bake, uncovered, until heated through, about 10 minutes. Sprinkle with the pepper and remaining cheese; let grits stand 5 minutes.
3. In a large skillet, heat butter over medium-high heat; saute the green pepper and onion until tender, about 6-8 minutes. Add shrimp and garlic; cook and stir until shrimp turn pink, 2-3 minutes. Spoon over grits.
1⅔ CUPS: 360 cal., 18g fat (10g sat. fat), 141mg chol., 1199mg sod., 26g carb. (2g sugars, 2g fiber), 25g pro.

HERB-CRUMBED SALMON

Often we catch enough of our delicious northwest salmon to send some to Michigan for my sister to enjoy. This crisp, lemony recipe is a great way to prepare it.

—Perlene Hoekema, Lynden, WA

TAKES: 30 min. • **MAKES:** 4 servings

- 1½ cups soft bread crumbs
- 2 Tbsp. minced fresh parsley
- 1 Tbsp. minced fresh thyme or 1 tsp. dried thyme
- 2 garlic cloves, minced
- 1 tsp. grated lemon zest
- ½ tsp. salt
- ¼ tsp. lemon-pepper seasoning
- ¼ tsp. paprika
- 1 Tbsp. butter, melted
- 4 salmon fillets (6 oz. each)

1. Preheat oven to 400°. In a bowl, combine first eight ingredients. Toss with melted butter.
2. Place salmon in a 15x10x1-in. pan coated with cooking spray, skin side down. Top with the crumb mixture, patting gently. Bake until golden brown and fish just begins to flake easily with a fork, 12-15 minutes.

NOTE: To make soft bread crumbs, tear bread into pieces and place in a food processor or blender. Cover and pulse until crumbs form. One slice of bread yields ½ to ¾ cup crumbs.

1 FILLET: 339 cal., 19g fat (5g sat. fat), 93mg chol., 507mg sod., 9g carb. (1g sugars, 1g fiber), 31g pro. **DIABETIC EXCHANGES:** 4 lean meat, 1 fat, ½ starch.

CRAB-TOPPED TOMATO SLICES

CRAB-TOPPED TOMATO SLICES

When camping, my wife and I top large beefsteak tomatoes with spicy chunks of crab. Then we warm this summer treat over the fire.

—Thomas Faglon, Somerset, NJ

TAKES: 30 min. • **MAKES:** 4 servings

- 1 carton (8 oz.) mascarpone cheese
- 2 Tbsp. finely chopped sweet red pepper
- 1½ tsp. grated lemon peel
- 2 Tbsp. lemon juice
- 1 tsp. seafood seasoning
- 1 tsp. hot pepper sauce
- ½ tsp. salt
- ¼ tsp. freshly ground pepper
- 2 cans (6 oz. each) lump crabmeat, drained
- 8 slices tomato (½ in. thick) Minced chives

1. Preheat oven to 375°. In a large bowl, combine the first eight ingredients; gently stir in crab.

2. Place tomato slices on a foil-lined baking sheet; top with crab mixture. Bake 12-15 minutes or until heated through. Sprinkle with chives.

1 SERVING: 325 cal., 27g fat (14g sat. fat), 153mg chol., 980mg sod., 3g carb. (1g sugars, 1g fiber), 20g pro.

DID YOU KNOW?

The popular seafood seasoning Old Bay was created in 1940 in Baltimore by Gustav Brunn, a German spice merchant who'd fled the Holocaust. McCormick & Co. bought the Brunn family business in 1990. But the original recipe, which includes paprika, bay leaf, cardamom and 15 other spices, has not changed in more than 75 years.

OYSTER FRICASSEE

I oversee the gardens at Colonial Williamsburg. We've learned that the colonists had a ready source of oysters from Chesapeake Bay. I enjoy this rich, creamy casserole, a special dish from Colonial Williamsburg's holiday recipe collection.

—Susan Dippre, Williamsburg, VA

PREP: 20 min.
BAKE: 25 min. + standing
MAKES: 6 servings

- 1 qt. shucked oysters
- ¾ cup butter, divided
- 2 medium onions, chopped
- 1½ cups chopped celery
- ½ cup all-purpose flour
- 2 cups half-and-half cream
- 2 tsp. minced fresh parsley
- 1 tsp. salt
- 1 tsp. minced fresh thyme or ½ tsp. dried thyme
- ¼ tsp. pepper
- ⅛ tsp. cayenne pepper
- 4 large egg yolks, lightly beaten
- 2 cups crushed Ritz crackers (about 50 crackers)
  Lemon slices
  Fresh thyme sprigs

1. Preheat oven to 400°. Drain oysters, reserving oyster liquor; set aside. In a large saucepan, heat ½ cup butter over medium heat. Add onions and celery; cook and stir until tender, 4-6 minutes. Stir in flour until blended; gradually whisk in cream. Bring to a boil, whisking constantly; cook until thickened, about 2 minutes.
2. Reduce heat; add the next five ingredients and reserved oyster liquor. Cook and stir until smooth, for about 2 minutes. Remove from heat. Stir a small amount of hot liquid into egg yolks; return mixture to pan, stirring sauce constantly.

3. Pour half of sauce into a greased 13x9-in. baking dish. Top with half of the oysters; sprinkle with half of the cracker crumbs. Repeat layers. Melt remaining butter; drizzle over top.
4. Bake, uncovered, until golden brown, 23-28 minutes. Let stand for 10 minutes. Serve with lemon slices and thyme sprigs.
1 SERVING: 639 cal., 44g fat (23g sat. fat), 297mg chol., 1024mg sod., 42g carb. (9g sugars, 2g fiber), 17g pro.

CATFISH PARMESAN

Mississippi is the nation's largest producer of farm-raised catfish. My family loves this dish and asks for it often. One reason I like it is it's so simple to prepare.

—W. D. Baker, Starkville, MS

PREP: 15 min. • **BAKE:** 20 min.
MAKES: 6 servings

- ¾ cup dry bread crumbs
- 3 Tbsp. grated Parmesan cheese
- 2 Tbsp. chopped fresh parsley
- ½ tsp. salt
- ¼ tsp. paprika
- ⅛ tsp. each pepper, dried oregano and basil
- 6 fresh or frozen catfish fillets (3 to 5 oz. each)
- ½ cup butter, melted

1. In a shallow bowl, combine the bread crumbs, Parmesan cheese, parsley and seasonings. Dip catfish in butter, then in crumb mixture. Arrange in a greased 13x9-in. baking dish.
2. Bake catfish, uncovered, at 375° for 20-25 minutes or until fish just begins to flake easily with a fork.
1 SERVING: 219 cal., 18g fat (10g sat. fat), 50mg chol., 522mg sod., 10g carb. (0 sugars, 0 fiber), 5g pro.

OYSTER FRICASSEE

SEAFOOD CASSEROLE

A family favorite, this rice casserole is stuffed with plenty of crab and shrimp to make it a special dish that's also hearty, homey and so easy to make!
—Nancy Billups, Princeton, IA

PREP: 20 min. • **BAKE:** 40 min.
MAKES: 6 servings

- 1 pkg. (6 oz.) long grain and wild rice
- 1 lb. frozen crabmeat, thawed or 2½ cups canned lump crabmeat, drained
- 1 lb. cooked shrimp, peeled, deveined and cut into ½-in. pieces
- 2 celery ribs, chopped
- 1 medium onion, finely chopped
- ½ cup finely chopped green pepper
- 1 can (4 oz.) mushroom stems and pieces, drained
- 1 jar (2 oz.) diced pimientos, drained
- 1 cup mayonnaise
- 1 cup 2% milk
- ½ tsp. pepper
  Dash Worcestershire sauce
- ¼ cup dry bread crumbs

1. Cook rice according to the package directions. Meanwhile, preheat oven to 375°.
2. In a large bowl, combine the crab, shrimp, celery, onion, green pepper, mushrooms and pimientos. In a small bowl, whisk mayonnaise, milk, pepper and Worcestershire sauce; stir into seafood mixture. Stir in rice.
3. Transfer to a greased 13x9-in. baking dish. Sprinkle with bread crumbs. Bake the casserole, uncovered, until bubbly, 40-50 minutes.
1½ CUPS: 585 cal., 34g fat (5g sat. fat), 209mg chol., 1045mg sod., 31g carb. (5g sugars, 2g fiber), 37g pro.

PESTO HALIBUT

The mildness of halibut contrasts perfectly with the robust flavor of pesto in this recipe. It takes only minutes to get the fish ready for the oven, so you can start quickly on your side dishes. Nearly anything goes well with this entree.
—April Showalter, Indianapolis, IN

TAKES: 20 min. • **MAKES:** 6 servings

- 2 Tbsp. olive oil
- 1 envelope pesto sauce mix
- 1 Tbsp. lemon juice
- 6 halibut fillets (4 oz. each)

1. Preheat oven to 450°. In a small bowl, combine oil, sauce mix and lemon juice; brush over both sides of fillets. Place in a greased 13x9-in. baking dish.
2. Bake, uncovered, until the fish just begins to flake easily with a fork, for 12-15 minutes.
1 FILLET: 188 cal., 7g fat (1g sat. fat), 36mg chol., 481mg sod., 5g carb. (2g sugars, 0 fiber), 24g pro. **DIABETIC EXCHANGES:** 3 lean meat, 1 fat.

SEAFOOD CASSEROLE

SPICY SHRIMP

SPICY SHRIMP

Not too hot but full of flavor, these shrimp are one of a kind. They're easy to make and take to parties where they'll impress the other guests.
—Bob Gebhardt, Wausau, WI

TAKES: 30 min. • **MAKES:** 6 servings

- 6 bacon strips, diced
- 1 cup butter, cubed
- 2 Tbsp. seafood seasoning
- 2 Tbsp. Dijon mustard
- 1½ tsp. chili powder
- 1 tsp. pepper
- ½ to 1 tsp. Louisiana-style hot sauce
- ¼ tsp. each dried basil, oregano and thyme
- 2 garlic cloves, minced
- 1½ lbs. uncooked shell-on medium shrimp

1. In a 12-in. oven-proof skillet, cook bacon over medium heat until partially cooked but not crisp; drain. Stir in the butter, seafood seasoning, mustard, chili powder, pepper, hot sauce, basil, oregano and thyme. Cook over low heat for 5 minutes. Add garlic; cook 1 minute longer. Remove from heat and stir in shrimp.
2. Bake, uncovered, at 375° for 20-25 minutes or until the shrimp turn pink, stirring twice.
1 SERVING: 490 cal., 45g fat (24g sat. fat), 265mg chol., 1464mg sod., 2g carb. (0 sugars, 0 fiber), 21g pro.

CRAB-STUFFED PORTOBELLOS

Fans of portobello mushrooms will love these delectable treats. I filled them with tasty crabmeat.
—Pat Ford, Southampton, PA

TAKES: 25 min. • **MAKES:** 2 servings

- 2 large portobello mushrooms
- 2 Tbsp. olive oil
- 1 garlic clove, minced
- 1 can (6 oz.) crabmeat, drained, flaked and cartilage removed
- 5 tsp. mayonnaise
- 2 roasted sweet red pepper halves, drained
- 2 slices provolone cheese

1. Remove and discard stems from the mushrooms. Place caps on a greased baking sheet. Combine the oil and garlic; brush over mushrooms. Broil 4-6 in. from the heat for 4-5 minutes or until tender.
2. In a small bowl, combine crab and mayonnaise. Place a red pepper half on each mushroom; top with crab mixture. Broil for 2-3 minutes or until heated through. Top with cheese; broil 1-2 minutes longer or until the cheese is melted.
1 SERVING: 414 cal., 30g fat (8g sat. fat), 103mg chol., 1014mg sod., 7g carb. (4g sugars, 1g fiber), 25g pro.

TUNA NOODLE CUPS

TUNA NOODLE CUPS

Older kids can get a jump on preparing dinner by stirring up these miniature tuna casseroles. Or serve them for brunch with fresh fruit, a tossed salad and rolls.
—Marlene Pugh, Fort McMurray, AB

PREP: 25 min. • **BAKE:** 30 min.
MAKES: 9 servings

- 8   oz. uncooked medium egg noodles (about 4 cups)
- 2   cans (5 oz. each) light tuna in water, drained
- 2   cups frozen peas and carrots (about 10 oz.), thawed
- 1   small onion, finely chopped
- 2   cups shredded cheddar cheese, divided
- 3   large eggs
- 1   can (12 oz.) evaporated milk
- ½   cup water
- 1   tsp. garlic salt
- ¼   tsp. pepper

1. Preheat oven to 350°. In a 6-qt. stockpot, cook noodles according to package directions; drain and return to pot. Add tuna, peas and carrots, onion and 1 cup cheese.
2. Whisk together eggs, milk, water and seasonings; toss with noodle mixture. Divide among 18 well-greased muffin cups. Sprinkle with remaining cheese.
3. Bake until heated through, about 30-35 minutes. Cool 5 minutes. Loosen edges with a knife before removing from pans.
2 NOODLE CUPS: 316 cal., 14g fat (7g sat. fat), 131mg chol., 549mg sod., 27g carb. (5g sugars, 2g fiber), 21g pro.

CITRUS COD

EAT SMART
CITRUS COD

We enjoy fish frequently, and this baked version has a tempting mild orange flavor. It comes out of the oven flaky and moist, and it's just the thing to make for a delightful light meal.
—Jacquelyn Dixon, La Porte City, IA

TAKES: 25 min. • **MAKES:** 4 servings

- 4   cod fillets (4 oz. each)
- 2   Tbsp. butter
- ½   cup chopped onion
- 1   garlic clove, minced
- 1   tsp. grated orange zest
- ⅓   cup orange juice
- 1   Tbsp. lemon juice
- ⅛   tsp. pepper
- 1   Tbsp. minced fresh parsley

1. Preheat oven to 375°. Place fillets in an 11x7-in. baking dish coated with cooking spray.
2. In a skillet, heat butter over medium-high heat; saute onion and garlic until tender. Spoon over fish. Mix orange zest and citrus juices; drizzle over fish.
3. Bake, uncovered, until the fish just begins to flake easily with a fork, about 15-20 minutes. Sprinkle with pepper and parsley.
1 COD FILLET: 153 cal., 6g fat (4g sat. fat), 58mg chol., 108mg sod., 5g carb. (3g sugars, 0 fiber), 18g pro. **DIABETIC EXCHANGES:** 3 lean meat, 1½ fat.

LEMON-PARSLEY TILAPIA

I like to include seafood in our weekly dinner rotation but don't want to bother with anything complicated (and it had better taste good or the family will riot). This herbed fish does the trick.
—Trisha Kruse, Eagle, ID

TAKES: 20 min. • **MAKES:** 4 servings

- 4 tilapia fillets (about 4 oz. each)
- 2 Tbsp. lemon juice
- 1 Tbsp. butter, melted
- 2 Tbsp. minced fresh parsley
- 2 garlic cloves, minced
- 2 tsp. grated lemon zest
- ½ tsp. salt
- ¼ tsp. pepper

1. Preheat oven to 375°. Place tilapia in a parchment paper-lined 15x10x1-in. pan. Drizzle with lemon juice, then melted butter.
2. Bake until fish just begins to flake easily with a fork, about 11-13 minutes. Meanwhile, mix the remaining ingredients. Remove fish from oven; sprinkle with parsley mixture.
1 FILLET: 124 cal., 4g fat (2g sat. fat), 63mg chol., 359mg sod., 1g carb. (0 sugars, 0 fiber), 21g pro. **DIABETIC EXCHANGES:** 3 lean meat, 1 fat.

SALMON VEGGIE PACKETS

I feel the spirit of Julia Child when I make lemon-pepper salmon *en papillote* (in parchment). It was the first French recipe I learned, and it makes a healthy, family-friendly meal.
—Renee Murphy, Smithtown, NY

TAKES: 30 min. • **MAKES:** 4 servings

- 2 Tbsp. white wine
- 1 Tbsp. olive oil
- ¼ tsp. salt
- ¼ tsp. pepper
- 2 medium sweet yellow peppers, julienned
- 2 cups fresh sugar snap peas, trimmed

SALMON

- 2 Tbsp. white wine
- 1 Tbsp. olive oil
- 1 Tbsp. grated lemon zest
- ½ tsp. salt
- ¼ tsp. pepper
- 4 salmon fillets (6 oz. each)
- 1 medium lemon, halved

1. Preheat oven to 400°. Cut four 18x15-in. pieces of parchment paper or heavy-duty foil; fold each crosswise in half, forming a crease. In a large bowl, mix wine, oil, salt and pepper. Add the vegetables and toss to coat.
2. In a small bowl, mix the first five salmon ingredients. To assemble, lay open one piece of parchment paper; place a salmon fillet on one side. Drizzle with 2 tsp. wine mixture; top with one-fourth of the vegetables.
3. Fold paper over fish and vegetables; fold the open ends two times to seal. Repeat with remaining packets. Place on baking sheets.
4. Bake until fish just begins to flake easily with a fork, about 12-16 minutes, opening packets carefully to allow steam to escape.
5. To serve, squeeze lemon juice over vegetables.
1 SERVING: 400 cal., 23g fat (4g sat. fat), 85mg chol., 535mg sod., 13g carb. (3g sugars, 3g fiber), 32g pro. **DIABETIC EXCHANGES:** 5 lean meat, 1½ fat, 1 vegetable.

SALMON VEGGIE PACKETS

SHRIMP &
CRAB PIZZA

BROILED SCALLOPS

These quick scallops, perfect for two, look and taste like they were prepared in a fine restaurant.
—Susan Coryell, Huddleston, VA

TAKES: 25 min. • **MAKES:** 2 servings

- 2 green onions, sliced
- 1 garlic clove, minced
- 2 tsp. olive oil
- 12 oz. sea scallops
- 2 tsp. minced fresh parsley
- 1 tsp. finely chopped fresh basil
- ¼ cup vermouth or chicken broth
- ⅛ tsp. salt
- ⅛ tsp. white pepper
- ⅓ cup soft bread crumbs
- 2 tsp. butter

1. In a nonstick skillet, saute onions and garlic in oil until tender. Add the scallops, parsley and basil; cook and stir over medium heat until scallops are firm and opaque. Add the vermouth, salt and pepper; cook, uncovered, over medium-low heat for 1 minute.
2. Divide mixture evenly between two ovenproof 1½-cup dishes. Sprinkle with bread crumbs; dot with butter. Broil 4-6 in. from heat until scallops are firm and opaque and bread crumbs are golden brown.
1 SERVING: 296 cal., 10g fat (3g sat. fat), 66mg chol., 506mg sod., 13g carb. (4g sugars, 1g fiber), 30g pro. **DIABETIC EXCHANGES:** 4 very lean meat, 2 fat, 1 starch.

DID YOU KNOW?
White pepper comes from fully ripened peppercorns that have had their skins removed. It has a milder flavor than black pepper and is helpful in dishes like mashed potatoes where you might not want black flecks to show. You can substitute black pepper (perhaps using a bit less than called for).

SHRIMP & CRAB PIZZA

When we were growing up, my mother made an amazing pizza with shrimp and crab. Now my kids ask for it, and the tradition continues.
—Danielle Woodward,
COLORADO SPRINGS, CO

TAKES: 30 min. • **MAKES:** 6 servings

- ½ lb. uncooked shrimp (61-70 per lb.), peeled and deveined
- 1 cup water
- 2 Tbsp. lemon juice
- 1 Tbsp. butter
- 1¾ cups sliced fresh mushrooms
- 1 small onion, chopped
- 1 small sweet red pepper, cut into strips
- 1 garlic clove, minced
- ¼ tsp. salt
- 1¼ cups coarsely chopped imitation crabmeat (about ½ lb.)
- 1 prebaked 12-in. pizza crust
- ⅓ cup Alfredo sauce
- 2 cups shredded part-skim mozzarella cheese

1. Preheat oven to 450°. In a small bowl, combine shrimp, water and lemon juice. Let stand 10 minutes.
2. Meanwhile, in a large skillet, heat butter over medium-high heat. Add mushrooms, onion and pepper; cook and stir 4-5 minutes or until tender. Add garlic and salt; cook 1 minute longer.
3. Drain shrimp, discarding liquid. Add shrimp and crab to pan; cook and stir 1-2 minutes longer or until the shrimp turn pink.
4. Place crust on an ungreased 12-in. pizza pan or baking sheet; spread with Alfredo sauce. Spoon shrimp mixture over sauce; sprinkle with cheese. Bake 8-10 minutes or until crust is golden and cheese is melted.
1 SLICE: 403 cal., 15g fat (7g sat. fat), 84mg chol., 1014mg sod., 40g carb. (4g sugars, 2g fiber), 27g pro.

CAJUN BAKED CATFISH

CAJUN BAKED CATFISH

This slightly spicy catfish dish gets compliments from family and friends whenever I serve it. It's moist and flaky, and the coating is crispy, crunchy and flecked with paprika.

—Jim Gales, Milwaukee, WI

TAKES: 25 min. • **MAKES:** 2 servings

- 2 Tbsp. yellow cornmeal
- 2 tsp. Cajun or blackened seasoning
- ½ tsp. dried thyme
- ½ tsp. dried basil
- ¼ tsp. garlic powder
- ¼ tsp. lemon-pepper seasoning
- 2 catfish or tilapia fillets (6 oz. each)
- ¼ tsp. paprika

1. Preheat oven to 400°. In a shallow bowl, mix the first six ingredients.

2. Dip fillets in cornmeal mixture to coat both sides. Place on a baking sheet coated with cooking spray. Sprinkle with paprika.

3. Bake until fish begins to flake easily with fork, 20-25 minutes.

1 FILLET: 242 cal., 10g fat (2g sat. fat), 94mg chol., 748mg sod., 8g carb. (0 sugars, 1g fiber), 27g pro. **DIABETIC EXCHANGES:** 4 lean meat, ½ starch.

BAKED PARMESAN FLOUNDER

If you haven't tried it, flounder is delicate and sweet tasting. Bread it with a cornflake-Parmesan mix and put it on the table in 25 minutes.

—Patti Bailey, Chanute, KS

TAKES: 25 min. • **MAKES:** 6 servings

- ¾ cup crushed cornflakes
- ½ cup grated Parmesan cheese
- ½ tsp. salt
- 2 large eggs, lightly beaten
- 2 Tbsp. 2% milk
- 2 lbs. flounder fillets

1. Preheat oven to 450°. In a large resealable plastic bag, combine cornflakes, cheese and salt. In a shallow bowl, combine eggs and milk. Dip fish fillets in egg mixture, then shake in cornflake mixture.

2. Transfer to a greased 15x10x1-in. baking pan. Bake until the fish just begins to flake easily with a fork, 15-20 minutes.

1 SERVING: 211 cal., 5g fat (2g sat. fat), 168mg chol., 513mg sod., 10g carb. (1g sugars, 0 fiber), 30g pro. **DIABETIC EXCHANGES:** 4 lean meat, ½ starch, ½ fat.

FETTUCCINE SHRIMP CASSEROLE

Perfect pasta—a creamy shrimp fettuccine with sour cream, cheddar, green chilies, salsa and cilantro. Then garnish it with lovely slices of avocado.

—Judy Armstrong, Prairieville, LA

PREP: 25 min. • **BAKE:** 40 min.
MAKES: 8 servings

- 6   oz. uncooked fettuccine
- 1   large egg
- ¾   cup half-and-half cream
- ½   cup sour cream
- ½   tsp. salt
- 2   cups shredded cheddar cheese
- ¼   cup canned chopped green chilies
- 3   green onions, thinly sliced
- 1   Tbsp. each minced fresh cilantro, basil and marjoram
- 1   lb. uncooked shrimp (31-40 per lb.), peeled and deveined or frozen cooked crawfish tail meat, thawed
- 1   cup salsa
- ½   cup shredded pepper jack cheese
- 2   cups tortilla chips, crushed
- 2   plum tomatoes, chopped
- 1   medium ripe avocado, peeled and sliced

1. Preheat the oven to 350°. Cook fettuccine according to package directions. In a large bowl, whisk egg, cream, sour cream and salt. Stir in the cheddar cheese, chilies, green onions and herbs. Drain fettuccine.
2. In a greased 13x9-in. baking dish, layer half of the fettuccine, shrimp, cream mixture and salsa. Repeat the layers.
3. Bake, covered, 35 minutes. Sprinkle with pepper jack cheese, chips and tomatoes. Bake, uncovered, for about 5-10 minutes or until bubbly and the cheese is melted. Serve fettuccine with avocado slices.
1 SERVING: 399 cal., 21g fat (12g sat. fat), 163mg chol., 603mg sod., 26g carb. (4g sugars, 3g fiber), 24g pro.

EAT SMART
PECAN-ORANGE SALMON
This healthy baked salmon is a favorite to prepare and share because you can adjust it to suit anyone by dialing up or down the mustard and honey.

—Kari Kelley, Plains, MT

TAKES: 25 min. • **MAKES:** 4 servings

- 1   Tbsp. grated orange zest
- ⅓   cup orange juice
- 1   Tbsp. Dijon mustard
- 1   Tbsp. honey
- 2   tsp. olive oil
- ½   tsp. salt
- ¼   tsp. pepper
- 4   salmon fillets (5 oz. each)
- 2   Tbsp. finely chopped pecans

1. Preheat oven to 425°. In a small bowl, whisk the first seven ingredients until blended.
2. Place salmon in a greased 11x7-in. baking dish. Pour sauce over salmon; sprinkle with pecans. Bake, uncovered, until fish just begins to flake easily with a fork, 15-18 minutes.
1 FILLET: 297 cal., 18g fat (3g sat. fat), 71mg chol., 456mg sod., 8g carb. (6g sugars, 1g fiber), 24g pro. **DIABETIC EXCHANGES:** 4 lean meat, 1½ fat, ½ starch.

FETTUCCINE SHRIMP CASSEROLE

EAT SMART
COD & ASPARAGUS BAKE

In this bright and lively one-pan dish, green and red veggies back up tender fish. Lemon pulls everything together. You can sub Parmesan for Romano.
—Thomas Faglon, Somerset, NJ

TAKES: 30 min. • **MAKES:** 4 servings

    4   cod fillets (4 oz. each)
    1   lb. fresh thin asparagus, trimmed
    1   pint cherry tomatoes, halved
    2   Tbsp. lemon juice
 1½   tsp. grated lemon zest
   ¼   cup grated Romano cheese

1. Preheat oven to 375°. Place cod and asparagus on a 15x10x1-in. baking sheet brushed with oil. Add tomatoes, cut side down. Brush fish with lemon juice; sprinkle with the lemon zest. Sprinkle fish and vegetables with Romano cheese. Bake until the fish just begins to flake easily with a fork, about 12 minutes.
2. Remove pan from oven; preheat broiler. Broil cod mixture 3-4 in. from heat until the vegetables are lightly browned, 2-3 minutes.
1 SERVING: 141 cal., 3g fat (2g sat. fat), 45mg chol., 184mg sod., 6g carb. (3g sugars, 2g fiber), 23g pro. **DIABETIC EXCHANGES:** 3 lean meat, 1 vegetable.

TEST KITCHEN TIP
If asparagus isn't in season, fresh green beans make a great substitute and will cook in about the same amount of time. We tested the recipe with cod fillets that were about ¾ in. thick. You'll need to adjust the bake time up or down if your fillets are thicker or thinner.

SEASONED TILAPIA FILLETS

EAT SMART
SEASONED TILAPIA FILLETS

If you need a healthy, keep-it-simple solution to dinner tonight, you just found it. This restaurant-quality dish relies on spices you're likely to have on hand to deliver big flavor.
—Dana Alexander, Lebanon, MO

TAKES: 25 min. • **MAKES:** 2 servings

    2   tilapia fillets (6 oz. each)
    1   Tbsp. butter, melted
    1   tsp. Montreal steak seasoning
   ½   tsp. dried parsley flakes
   ¼   tsp. paprika
   ¼   tsp. dried thyme
   ⅛   tsp. onion powder
   ⅛   tsp. salt
   ⅛   tsp. pepper
        Dash garlic powder

1. Preheat oven to 425°. Place tilapia in a greased 11x7-in. baking dish; drizzle with butter. In a small bowl, mix remaining ingredients; sprinkle over fillets.
2. Bake, covered, 10 minutes. Uncover; bake until fish just begins to flake easily with a fork, 5-8 minutes.
1 FILLET: 193 cal., 7g fat (4g sat. fat), 98mg chol., 589mg sod., 1g carb. (0 sugars, 0 fiber), 32g pro. **DIABETIC EXCHANGES:** 5 lean meat, 1½ fat.

COD &
ASPARAGUS
BAKE

Bonus: Easy Desserts

COCONUT-LAYERED POUND CAKE

COCONUT-LAYERED POUND CAKE

If you love chocolate, almonds and coconut, this cake is for you. It comes together in a flash and tastes just like an Almond Joy candy bar!
—Linda Nichols, Steubenville, OH

TAKES: 10 min. • **MAKES:** 8 servings

- 1 pkg. (7 oz.) sweetened shredded coconut
- 1 can (14 oz.) sweetened condensed milk
- ½ cup chopped almonds, toasted
- 1 loaf (16 oz.) frozen pound cake, thawed
- 1 cup chocolate fudge frosting

Mix the coconut, milk and almonds. Cut cake horizontally into four layers. Place the bottom layer on a serving plate; top with half of the coconut mixture, one cake layer and ½ cup frosting. Repeat layers. Refrigerate, covered, until serving.

NOTE: To toast nuts, bake in a shallow pan in a 350° oven for 5-10 minutes or cook in a skillet over low heat until lightly browned, stirring occasionally.
1 SLICE: 715 cal., 35g fat (19g sat. fat), 98mg chol., 426mg sod., 93g carb. (72g sugars, 3g fiber), 10g pro.

DID YOU KNOW?
Pound cake gets its name from the traditional formula used to prepare the sweet: a pound each of butter, eggs, sugar and flour.

LIGHT
STRAWBERRY PIE

set, about 3 hours. Garnish each piece with about 1 Tbsp. whipped topping. Refrigerate leftovers.

1 PIECE: 159 cal., 4g fat (2g sat. fat), 0 chol., 172mg sod., 29g carb. (14g sugars, 2g fiber), 2g pro. **DIABETIC EXCHANGES:** 1 starch, 1 fruit, ½ fat.

BANANA SPLIT PUDDING

Our kids love banana splits, so I came up with this simple dessert, which is so fast to fix.
—Sherry Lee, Shelby, AL

TAKES: 10 min. • **MAKES:** 8 servings

- 3   cups cold 2% milk
- 1   pkg. (5.1 oz.) instant vanilla pudding mix
- 1   medium firm banana, sliced
- 1   cup sliced fresh strawberries
- 1   can (8 oz.) crushed pineapple, drained
- 1   carton (8 oz.) frozen whipped topping, thawed
- ¼   cup chocolate syrup
- ¼   cup chopped pecans
      Additional sliced strawberries and bananas, optional

1. In a large bowl, whisk milk and pudding mix for 2 minutes. Let set for 2 minutes or until soft-set. Add banana, strawberries and pineapple.
2. Transfer to a large serving bowl. Dollop with whipped topping. Drizzle with chocolate syrup; sprinkle with pecans. If desired, top with additional strawberries and bananas.

½ CUP: 291 cal., 11g fat (7g sat. fat), 12mg chol., 305mg sod., 43g carb. (34g sugars, 2g fiber), 4g pro.

LIGHT STRAWBERRY PIE

It's no exaggeration to say people rave about this luscious strawberry pie. Best of all, it's a low-sugar and no-guilt treat.
—Lou Wright, Rockford, IL

PREP: 25 min. + chilling
MAKES: 8 servings

- 1   can (8 oz.) unsweetened crushed pineapple
- 1   pkg. (8 oz.) sugar-free cook-and-serve vanilla pudding mix
- 1   pkg. (3 oz.) sugar-free strawberry gelatin
- 3   cups sliced fresh strawberries
- 1   reduced-fat graham cracker crust (8 in.)
- ½   cup reduced-fat whipped topping

1. Drain pineapple, reserving juice in a 2-cup measuring cup. Set pineapple aside. Add enough water to juice to measure 1½ cups liquid; transfer to a saucepan. Whisk in pudding mix and gelatin until combined. Bring to a boil; cook and stir for 1-2 minutes or until thickened. Stir in pineapple. Remove from heat; cool 10 minutes.
2. Add the strawberries; toss gently to coat. Pour into crust. Refrigerate until

S'MOREOS

S'MOREOS

My son introduced us to this twist on the classic s'more when we were camping. Or try spreading Nutella instead of peanut butter for a twist on the twist.
—Christina Smith, Santa Rosa, CA

TAKES: 15 min. • **MAKES:** 4 servings

- 4 Oreo cookies
- 3 Tbsp. creamy peanut butter
- 4 whole graham crackers, halved
- 1 milk chocolate candy bar (1.55 oz.), quartered
- 4 large marshmallows

1. Spread both sides of each Oreo cookie with peanut butter; place each on a graham cracker half. Top with chocolate.
2. Using a long-handled fork or long metal skewer toast marshmallows 6 in. from medium-hot heat until golden brown, turning occasionally. Place on chocolate; cover with the remaining graham crackers. Serve s'mores immediately.
1 SERVING: 271 cal., 13g fat (4g sat. fat), 3mg chol., 223mg sod., 35g carb. (19g sugars, 2g fiber), 5g pro.

"Why didn't we think of this before! This combines my family's favorites all in one s'more. Oreos add great flavor."
—RANDCBRUNS, TASTEOFHOME.COM

CHOCOLATE CINNAMON TOAST

CHOCOLATE CINNAMON TOAST

Looking for a fun dessert or snack? Toast cinnamon bread in a skillet and top with chocolate and fresh fruit. Add a small dollop of whipped cream to each slice to make it extra indulgent.
—Jeanne Ambrose, Milwaukee, WI

TAKES: 10 min. • **MAKES:** 1 serving

- 1 slice cinnamon bread
- 1 tsp. butter, softened
- 2 Tbsp. 60% cacao bittersweet chocolate baking chips
   Sliced banana and strawberries, optional

Spread both sides of bread with the butter. In a small skillet, toast bread over medium-high heat 2-3 minutes on each side, topping with chocolate chips after turning. Remove from heat; spread melted chocolate evenly over toast. If desired, top with fruit.
1 SERVING: 235 cal., 13g fat (8g sat. fat), 10mg chol., 131mg sod., 29g carb. (19g sugars, 3g fiber), 4g pro.

LEMON ICE

Pucker up for this sweet-tart treat. The delicious lemon dessert is a perfectly refreshing way to end a summer meal... or any meal, for that matter.
—Concetta Maranto Skenfield Bakersfield, CA

PREP: 15 min. + freezing
MAKES: 6 servings

- 2 cups sugar
- 1 cup water
- 2 cups lemon juice
   Lemon slices
   Fresh mint leaves, optional

1. In a large saucepan over low heat, cook and stir sugar and water until sugar is dissolved. Remove from the heat; stir in lemon juice.
2. Pour into a freezer container. Freeze for 4 hours, stirring every 30 minutes, or until the mixture becomes slushy. Garnish servings with lemon slices and mint if desired.
½ CUP: 279 cal., 0 fat (0 sat. fat), 0 chol., 2mg sod., 74g carb. (67g sugars, 0 fiber), 0 pro.

CONTEST-WINNING EASY TIRAMISU

Sweet little servings of tiramisu, dusted with a whisper of cocoa, end any meal on a high note. What a fun use for pudding snack cups!
—Betty Claycomb, Alverton, PA

TAKES: 10 min.
MAKES: 2 servings

- 14 vanilla wafers, divided
- 1 tsp. instant coffee granules
- 2 Tbsp. hot water
- 2 snack-size cups (3½ oz. each) vanilla pudding
- ¼ cup whipped topping
- 1 tsp. baking cocoa

1. Set aside four vanilla wafers; coarsely crush remaining wafers. Divide wafer crumbs between two dessert dishes.
2. In a small bowl, dissolve coffee granules in hot water. Drizzle over wafer crumbs. Spoon pudding into dessert dishes. Top with whipped topping; sprinkle with cocoa. Garnish with reserved vanilla wafers.
1 SERVING: 267 cal., 9g fat (4g sat. fat), 4mg chol., 219mg sod., 41g carb. (28g sugars, 1g fiber), 3g pro.

FROZEN BANANA TREATS

I love to make these treats with my 9-year-old son, Sam. He's in charge of cutting the bananas with a butter knife, pushing in the pop sticks and rolling the chocolate-covered bananas in the granola. It's such fun!
—Aimee Lawrence, Wimberley, TX

PREP: 15 min. + freezing
MAKES: 8 servings

- 1½ cups granola without raisins, crushed
- 1 cup (6 oz.) semisweet chocolate chips
- ⅓ cup creamy peanut butter
- 8 wooden pop sticks
- 4 large firm bananas, halved widthwise

1. Sprinkle the granola onto a large piece of waxed paper; set aside. In a microwave, melt chocolate chips; stir until smooth. Stir in peanut butter until blended.
2. Insert a pop stick into each banana half. Spread with chocolate mixture; roll in granola. Wrap in foil and freeze for 24 hours.
1 SERVING: 307 cal., 15g fat (5g sat. fat), 0 chol., 60mg sod., 44g carb. (23g sugars, 7g fiber), 8g pro.

CONTEST-WINNING EASY TIRAMISU

FROZEN HAWAIIAN PIE

FROZEN HAWAIIAN PIE

Cool summer pies are one of Mom's specialties. In this version, pineapple, maraschino cherries and walnuts are folded into a fluffy filling. It's an easy yet tempting no-bake dessert.
—Jennifer Mcquillan, Jacksonville, FL

PREP: 10 min. + freezing
MAKES: 2 pies (8 servings each)

1 can (14 oz.) sweetened condensed milk
1 carton (12 oz.) frozen whipped topping, thawed
1 can (20 oz.) crushed pineapple, drained
½ cup chopped walnuts
½ cup chopped maraschino cherries
2 Tbsp. lemon juice
2 graham cracker crusts (9 in.)
   Fresh mint and additional walnuts and maraschino cherries

1. In a large bowl, combine milk and whipped topping. Fold in pineapple, nuts, cherries and lemon juice. Pour half into each crust. Freeze until firm, about 4 hours.

2. Remove from freezer 20 minutes before serving. Garnish with mint, additional nuts and cherries.

1 SLICE: 328 cal., 14g fat (7g sat. fat), 11mg chol., 168mg sod., 46g carb. (40g sugars, 1g fiber), 4g pro.

QUICK ICEBOX SANDWICHES

EAT SMART
BLACK & BLUE BERRY GRUNT

For something different from the usual cakes and fruit pies, try this old-fashioned dessert. It features a jammy combination of blackberries and blueberries with homemade dumplings on top.

—Kelly Akin, Johnsonville, NY

TAKES: 30 min. • **MAKES:** 8 servings

- 2½ cups fresh or frozen blackberries, thawed
- 2½ cups fresh or frozen blueberries, thawed
- ¾ cup sugar
- ¼ cup water
- 1 Tbsp. lemon juice
- ⅛ tsp. ground cinnamon
- ⅛ tsp. pepper

DUMPLINGS
- 1 cup all-purpose flour
- 2 Tbsp. sugar
- 1 tsp. baking powder
- ½ tsp. baking soda
- ⅛ tsp. salt
- 2 Tbsp. butter, melted
- ½ cup buttermilk
- 1 Tbsp. cinnamon-sugar
  Sweetened whipped cream, optional

1. In a large skillet, combine first seven ingredients. Bring mixture to a boil. Reduce heat; simmer, uncovered, for 5 minutes.
2. Meanwhile, in a large bowl, mix first five dumpling ingredients. Add butter and buttermilk; stir just until moistened. Drop by tablespoonfuls onto berry mixture. Sprinkle with the cinnamon-sugar.
3. Cover skillet tightly; simmer until a toothpick inserted in a dumpling comes out clean, 10-15 minutes. Serve warm; if desired, top with sweetened whipped cream.

1 SERVING: 226 cal., 4g fat (2g sat. fat), 8mg chol., 229mg sod., 47g carb. (31g sugars, 4g fiber), 3g pro.

QUICK ICEBOX SANDWICHES

My mother liked making these cool, creamy treats when I was growing up in the States because they're so quick to fix. Now my three kids enjoy them.

—Sandy Armijo, Naples, Italy

PREP: 20 min. + freezing
MAKES: 2 dozen

- 1 pkg. (3.4 oz.) instant vanilla pudding mix
- 2 cups cold milk
- 2 cups whipped topping
- 1 cup miniature semisweet chocolate chips
- 24 whole graham crackers, halved

1. Mix pudding and milk according to package directions; refrigerate until set. Fold in whipped topping and chocolate chips.
2. Place 24 graham cracker halves on a baking sheet; top each with about 3 Tbsp. filling. Place another graham cracker half on top. Wrap individually in plastic; freeze for 1 hour or until firm. Serve sandwiches frozen.

1 SERVING: 144 cal., 5g fat (3g sat. fat), 3mg chol., 162mg sod., 23g carb. (13g sugars, 1g fiber), 2g pro.

BLACK & BLUE
BERRY GRUNT

SKILLET CHERRY COBBLER

Once a week, my husband and I enjoy a candlelight dinner after our two children are fed and in bed. This is a perfectly sized "date night" dessert. Depending what your date likes, try the stovetop cobbler with apple or blueberry pie filling.
—Kari Damon, Rushford, NY

TAKES: 30 min. • **MAKES:** 2 servings

- ½ cup biscuit/baking mix
- 1½ tsp. sugar
- ½ to 1 tsp. grated orange zest
- 2 Tbsp. 2% milk
- 1 cup cherry pie filling
- ¼ cup orange juice

1. In a small bowl, combine the biscuit mix, sugar and orange zest. Stir in milk just until moistened; set aside.
2. In a small nonstick skillet, combine the pie filling and orange juice; bring to a boil, stirring occasionally. Drop biscuit mixture in two mounds onto boiling cherry mixture. Reduce heat; cover and simmer for 10 minutes. Uncover; simmer for 5-7 minutes longer or until a toothpick inserted into a dumpling comes out clean.
1 SERVING: 262 cal., 6g fat (2g sat. fat), 1mg chol., 397mg sod., 51g carb. (28g sugars, 1g fiber), 4g pro.

DID YOU KNOW?

Carl Smith, a salesman for General Mills, was inspired to create Bisquick on a 1930 train ride to San Francisco. Though the dining car was closed, the train's chef quickly produced fresh biscuits for the hungry Mr. Smith. The chef's secret? A pre-mixed blend of lard, flour, leavening and salt that he kept in the icebox. General Mills cooks soon went to work preparing a shelf-stable mix, and Bisquick debuted in 1931.

CHOCOLATE-COVERED PEANUT BUTTER & PRETZEL TRUFFLES

CHOCOLATE-COVERED PEANUT BUTTER & PRETZEL TRUFFLES

Sweet chocolate, creamy peanut butter and salty pretzels create a to-die-for truffle. It's a little bite of decadence any time.
—Ashley Wisniewski, Champaign, IL

PREP: 40 min. + chilling
MAKES: 3 dozen

- 1¾ cups creamy peanut butter, divided
- ⅓ cup confectioners' sugar
- ¼ cup packed brown sugar
- 2 Tbsp. butter, softened
- ⅛ tsp. salt
- 3¼ cups crushed pretzels, divided
- 3 cups (18 oz.) semisweet chocolate chips
- 3 Tbsp. shortening

1. In a large bowl, beat 1½ cups peanut butter, confectioners' sugar, brown sugar, butter and salt until blended. Stir in 3 cups pretzels.
2. Shape pretzel mixture into 1-in. balls; transfer to waxed paper-lined baking sheets. Refrigerate at least 30 minutes or until firm.
3. In a microwave, melt chocolate chips and shortening; stir until smooth. Dip truffles in chocolate; allow excess to drip off. Return to baking sheets.
4. Microwave the remaining peanut butter on high for 30-45 seconds or until melted. Drizzle over truffles; sprinkle with the remaining pretzels. Refrigerate until set. Store between layers of waxed paper in an airtight container in the refrigerator.
1 TRUFFLE: 176 cal., 11g fat (4g sat. fat), 2mg chol., 186mg sod., 18g carb. (10g sugars, 2g fiber), 4g pro.

ORANGE GELATIN PRETZEL SALAD

Salty pretzels pair nicely with sweet fruit in this refreshing layered salad. It's a family favorite that also makes a pretty potluck dish.

—Peggy Boyd, Northport, AL

PREP: 20 min. + chilling
BAKE: 10 min. + cooling
MAKES: 12 servings

¾ cup butter, melted
1 Tbsp. plus ¾ cup sugar, divided
2 cups finely crushed pretzels
2 cups boiling water
2 pkg. (3 oz. each) orange gelatin
2 cans (8 oz. each) crushed pineapple, drained
1 can (11 oz.) mandarin oranges, drained
1 pkg. (8 oz.) cream cheese, softened
2 cups whipped topping
   Additional whipped topping and mandarin oranges, optional

1. Preheat oven to 350°. Mix melted butter and 1 Tbsp. sugar; stir in pretzels. Press onto bottom of an ungreased 13x9-in. baking dish. Bake 10 minutes. Cool completely on a wire rack.

2. In a large bowl, add boiling water to gelatin; stir for 2 minutes to completely dissolve. Stir in fruit. Refrigerate until partially set, about 30 minutes.

3. Meanwhile, in a bowl, beat cream cheese and remaining sugar until smooth. Fold in whipped topping. Spread over crust.

4. Gently spoon gelatin mixture over top. Refrigerate, covered, until firm, 2-4 hours. To serve, cut into squares. If desired, top with whipped topping and oranges.

1 SERVING: 400 cal., 21g fat (13g sat. fat), 50mg chol., 402mg sod., 51g carb. (38g sugars, 1g fiber), 4g pro.

STRAWBERRY KIWI DESSERT

In the heat of summer, folks will look foreword to this kind of light dessert. The season's finest fruits are slightly sweetened with caramel, orange juice and honey. Serve this fruity finale alone or on top of pound cake, angel food cake or ice cream.

—*Taste of Home* Test Kitchen

TAKES: 10 min. • **MAKES:** 4 servings

3 cups halved fresh strawberries
2 kiwifruit, peeled and sliced
2 Tbsp. caramel ice cream topping
1 Tbsp. orange juice
2 to 3 Tbsp. honey-roasted almonds or toasted almonds

Place fruit in a serving bowl. Combine caramel topping and orange juice; drizzle over fruit. Sprinkle with nuts. May also be served over angel food cake, pound cake or ice cream.

½ CUP: 112 cal., 3g fat (0 sat. fat), 0 chol., 45mg sod., 22g carb. (17g sugars, 5g fiber), 2g pro.

ORANGE GELATIN PRETZEL SALAD

CINNAMON APPLE
PAN BETTY

CINNAMON APPLE PAN BETTY

I found this recipe soon after I was married 47 years ago. It requires just a few ingredients, which you probably have on hand. It's still a favorite of ours during fall and winter, when apples are at their best.
—Shirley Leister, West Chester, PA

TAKES: 15 min. • **MAKES:** 6 servings

3	medium apples, peeled and cubed
½	cup butter
3	cups cubed bread
½	cup sugar
¾	tsp. ground cinnamon

In a large skillet, saute apple in butter for 4-5 minutes or until tender. Add bread cubes. Stir together sugar and cinnamon; sprinkle over apple mixture and toss to coat. Saute mixture until bread is warmed.

⅔ CUP: 279 cal., 16g fat (10g sat. fat), 41mg chol., 208mg sod., 34g carb. (25g sugars, 2g fiber), 2g pro.

GRANDMA'S DIVINITY

Every Christmas my grandmother and I made divinity, just the two of us. I still make it every year.
—Anne Clayborne, Walland, TN

PREP: 5 min. • **COOK:** 40 min. + standing
MAKES: 1½ lbs. (60 pieces)

2	large egg whites
3	cups sugar
⅔	cup water
½	cup light corn syrup
1	tsp. vanilla extract
1	cup chopped pecans

1. Place the egg whites in the bowl of a stand mixer; let egg whites stand at room temperature for 30 minutes. Meanwhile, line three 15x10x1-in. pans with waxed paper.
2. In a large heavy saucepan, combine sugar, water and corn syrup; bring to a boil, stirring constantly to dissolve sugar. Cook mixture, without stirring, over medium heat until a candy thermometer reads 252° (hard-ball stage). Just before the temperature is reached, beat egg whites on medium speed until stiff peaks form.
3. Slowly add hot sugar mixture in a thin stream over egg whites, beating constantly and scraping sides of bowl occasionally. Add vanilla. Beat until the candy holds its shape, 5-6 minutes. (Do not overmix or candy will get stiff and crumbly.) Immediately fold in pecans.
4. Quickly drop mixture by heaping teaspoonfuls onto prepared pans. Let stand at room temperature until dry to the touch. Store between pieces of waxed paper in an airtight container at room temperature.

NOTE: We recommend that you test your candy thermometer before each use by bringing water to a boil; the thermometer should read 212°. Adjust your recipe temperature up or down based on your test.

1 PIECE: 61 cal., 1g fat (0 sat. fat), 0 chol., 4mg sod., 13g carb. (12g sugars, 0 fiber), 0 pro.

GRANDMA'S DIVINITY

BUCKEYES

BUCKEYES

This recipe is always popular at my church's annual Christmas fundraiser. They resemble chestnuts, or buckeyes, hence the name.

—Merry Kay Opitz, Elkhorn, WI

PREP: 30 min. + chilling
MAKES: about 5½ dozen

5½ cups confectioners' sugar
1⅔ cups peanut butter
1 cup butter, melted
4 cups (24 oz.) semisweet chocolate chips
1 tsp. shortening

1. In a large bowl, beat sugar, peanut butter and butter until smooth. Shape mixture into 1-in. balls; set aside.
2. Microwave the chocolate chips and shortening on high until melted; stir until smooth. Dip balls in chocolate, allowing excess to drip off. Place on a wire rack over waxed paper; chill for 15 minutes or until firm. Cover and store in the refrigerator.
2 PIECES: 302 cal., 18g fat (8g sat. fat), 15mg chol., 119mg sod., 35g carb. (31g sugars, 2g fiber), 4g pro.

NO-BAKE PEANUT BUTTER PIE

"Wow!" That's what I hear whenever I serve this creamy peanut butter pie with chocolate cookie crust. Chocolate and peanut butter do have that wow factor. And I love that I can whip this up in just 20 minutes.

—Elaine Sabacky, Litchfield, MN

PREP: 20 min. + chilling
MAKES: 8 servings

3 oz. cream cheese, softened
⅓ cup peanut butter
1 cup confectioners' sugar
¼ cup whole milk
1 carton (8 oz.) frozen whipped topping, thawed
1 chocolate crumb crust (9 in.)
¼ cup chopped peanuts

In a large bowl, beat cream cheese until fluffy. Beat in peanut butter and sugar until smooth. Gradually add the milk; mix well. Fold in the whipped topping. Spoon into crust. Refrigerate pie overnight. Garnish with peanuts.
1 SLICE: 410 cal., 26g fat (11g sat. fat), 13mg chol., 292mg sod., 38g carb. (0 sugars, 1g fiber), 6g pro.

BANANAS FOSTER SUNDAES FOR TWO

I have wonderful memories of eating bananas Foster in New Orleans, and as a dietitian, I wanted a healthier version. This one combines the best of two recipes with my own tweaks to recreate a southern treat. Here it's a lovely dessert for two!
—Lisa Varner, El Paso, TX

TAKES: 15 min. • **MAKES:** 2 servings

- 1 tsp. butter
- 1 Tbsp. brown sugar
- 1 tsp. orange juice
- ⅛ tsp. ground cinnamon
- ⅛ tsp. ground nutmeg
- 1 large banana, sliced
- 2 tsp. chopped pecans, toasted
- ⅛ tsp. rum extract
- 1 cup reduced-fat vanilla ice cream

In a large nonstick skillet, melt butter over medium-low heat. Stir in the brown sugar, orange juice, cinnamon and nutmeg until blended. Add the banana and pecans; cook 2-3 minutes or until banana is glazed and slightly softened, stirring lightly. Remove from the heat; stir in extract. Serve with ice cream.
1 SERVING: 259 cal., 8g fat (4g sat. fat), 26mg chol., 74mg sod., 45g carb. (32g sugars, 2g fiber), 5g pro.

TOFFEE CRUNCH GRAHAMS

My sister gave me the recipe years ago. Only four ingredients are needed to make up these toffee bars loaded with crunchy almonds.
—Carol Ann Horne, Perth, ON

PREP: 15 min. • **BAKE:** 10 min. + cooling
MAKES: 4 dozen

- 12 whole graham crackers
- 1½ cups butter, cubed
- 1 cup packed brown sugar
- 2 cups sliced almonds

1. Line a 15x10x1-in. baking pan with heavy-duty foil. Place the graham crackers in pan. In a saucepan, bring the butter and brown sugar to a boil, stirring constantly. Carefully pour mixture over the graham crackers. Sprinkle with almonds.
2. Bake toffee grahams at 400° for 6-8 minutes or until bubbly. Cool in pan about 4 minutes. Cut each graham cracker into four sections; transfer to wire racks to cool completely.
1 PIECE: 107 cal., 8g fat (4g sat. fat), 15mg chol., 71mg sod., 8g carb. (6g sugars, 1g fiber), 1g pro.

"This is a quick and easy treat. I took it camping this weekend and got rave reviews! I added a mixture of almonds and sunflower seeds. I will make this again for sure."
—MRSMAGOO1996, TASTEOFHOME.COM

BANANAS FOSTER SUNDAES FOR TWO

ICEBOX CAKE

MARMALADE CHEWS

I live in the heart of citrus country and think this cookie really captures the flavor of Florida. Orange marmalade, juice and zest give the cookie and frosting a delightful taste.
—Shirleene Wilkins, Lake Placid, FL

PREP: 20 min.
BAKE: 10 min/batch + cooling
MAKES: about 4½ dozen

¼ cup shortening
½ cup sugar
1 large egg
1½ cups all-purpose flour
¼ tsp. baking soda
¼ tsp. salt
½ cup orange marmalade
½ cup chopped pecans, optional
FROSTING
2 cups confectioners' sugar
2 Tbsp. butter, melted
1 tsp. grated orange zest
2 to 3 Tbsp. orange juice

1. In a large bowl, cream shortening and sugar until light and fluffy. Beat in egg. Combine flour, baking soda and salt; gradually add to creamed mixture and mix well. Stir in the marmalade and, if desired, pecans.
2. Drop by heaping teaspoonfuls 2 in. apart onto greased baking sheets. Bake at 350° for 10-15 minutes or until golden brown. Remove to wire racks to cool.
3. In a small bowl, combine the sugar, butter and orange zest until blended. Add enough orange juice to achieve spreading consistency. Frost cookies.
2 COOKIES: 116 cal., 3g fat (1g sat. fat), 10mg chol., 48mg sod., 22g carb. (16g sugars, 0 fiber), 1g pro.

ICEBOX CAKE

You don't have to bake to serve a showstopping dessert. This "cake" is made from chocolate wafers and whipping cream. The line starts here.
—Cindy Hawkins, New York, NY

PREP: 15 min. + chilling
MAKES: 12 servings

2 cups heavy whipping cream
2 Tbsp. confectioners' sugar
1 tsp. vanilla extract
1 pkg. (9 oz.) chocolate wafers
Chocolate curls, optional

1. In a large bowl, beat cream until soft peaks form. Add the sugar and vanilla; beat until stiff. Spread cream mixture in heaping teaspoonfuls on cookies. Make six stacks of cookies; turn stacks on edge and place on a serving platter, forming a 14-in.-long cake.
2. Frost top and sides with remaining whipped cream. If desired, garnish with chocolate curls. Refrigerate for 4-6 hours before serving.
1 SLICE: 235 cal., 18g fat (10g sat. fat), 55mg chol., 138mg sod., 18g carb. (2g sugars, 1g fiber), 2g pro.

MARMALADE CHEWS

QUICK COCONUT MACAROONS

Coconut lovers will gravitate to these chewy bite-sized cookies, a quick sell at bake sales. Be sure to save some for the family, too!

—Sabrina Shafer, Minooka, IL

TAKES: 25 min. • **MAKES:** 1½ dozen

- 2½ cups sweetened shredded coconut
- ⅓ cup all-purpose flour
- ⅛ tsp. salt
- ⅔ cup sweetened condensed milk
- 1 tsp. vanilla extract

1. Preheat oven to 350°. In a small bowl, combine the coconut, flour and salt. Add milk and vanilla; mix well (batter will be stiff).
2. Drop by tablespoonfuls 1 in. apart onto a greased baking sheet. Bake 15-20 minutes or until golden brown. Remove to wire racks.
1 MACAROON: 110 cal., 6g fat (5g sat. fat), 4mg chol., 65mg sod., 14g carb. (11g sugars, 1g fiber), 2g pro.

LIMONCELLO FRUIT CUPS

This is a refreshing dish to serve for brunch or dessert. The berries offer a powerhouse of nutrition, and the limoncello, an Italian lemon liqueur, adds a burst of citrus flavor.

—Sarah Vasques, Milford, NH

TAKES: 15 min. • **MAKES:** 4 servings

- 2 cups sliced fresh strawberries
- 1 medium banana, sliced
- 1 cup fresh blueberries
- ¼ cup limoncello
- 1 Tbsp. sugar
- ¾ cup plain yogurt
- 3 Tbsp. lemon curd

In a small bowl, combine the first five ingredients; spoon into four dessert dishes. Whisk together yogurt and lemon curd; spoon over fruit.
1 CUP BERRY MIXTURE WITH 3 TBSP. SAUCE: 218 cal., 3g fat (1g sat. fat), 17mg chol., 34mg sod., 40g carb. (32g sugars, 3g fiber), 3g pro.

DESSERT BRUSCHETTA WITH NECTARINE SALSA

This is an easy no-cook dessert for hot summer days. The bright colors and fresh flavors work beautifully together.

—Sally Sibthorpe, Shelby Township, MI

TAKES: 15 min. • **MAKES:** 2 servings

- 1 medium nectarine, chopped
- ¼ cup fresh or frozen raspberries, thawed
- 1 Tbsp. thinly sliced fresh mint leaves
- 2 slices pound cake
- 3 Tbsp. mascarpone cheese
- 2 tsp. honey
  Whipped cream, optional

1. In a small bowl, combine nectarine, raspberries and mint. Let stand about 5 minutes.
2. Spread cake slices with cheese; top with nectarine mixture. Drizzle with honey. If desired, top desserts with whipped cream.
1 SERVING: 358 cal., 26g fat (14g sat. fat), 119mg chol., 143mg sod., 30g carb. (12g sugars, 3g fiber), 6g pro.

QUICK COCONUT MACAROONS

MARSHMALLOW PUFFS

aside. In a bowl, combine cake mix, butter and remaining milk; set half aside and press the other half into a greased 13x9-in. baking pan. Bake at 350° for 6 minutes. Remove from the oven and sprinkle with chocolate chips. Pour caramel mixture over; spoon reserved cake mixture on top. Return to oven for 20 minutes.

1 SERVING: 120 cal., 6g fat (3g sat. fat), 9mg chol., 117mg sod., 17g carb. (12g sugars, 0 fiber), 1g pro.

RASPBERRY CHEESECAKE PARFAITS

This impressive dessert can be as near as the fridge. I also recommend it as an excellent late-night snack.

—Joyce Mart, Wichita, KS

TAKES: 10 min. • **MAKES:** 4 servings

- 1 pkg. (8 oz.) cream cheese, softened
- 2 to 4 Tbsp. sugar
- ½ cup vanilla yogurt
- 2 cups fresh raspberries or berries of your choice
- ½ cup graham cracker crumbs (8 squares)

1. In a large bowl, beat cream cheese and sugar until smooth. Stir in yogurt.
2. In four dessert glasses or bowls, alternate layers of berries, cream cheese mixture and cracker crumbs. Serve immediately or refrigerate for up to 8 hours.

1 SERVING: 328 cal., 22g fat (13g sat. fat), 65mg chol., 251mg sod., 27g carb. (16g sugars, 4g fiber), 7g pro

TEST KITCHEN TIP
You can prepare the cream cheese mixture ahead and refrigerate for up to a week. That way, it's easy to make a parfait or two whenever you like.

MARSHMALLOW PUFFS

With peanut butter, chocolate and marshmallows, these treats were popular with our three kids as they were growing up—and now I make them for our two grandchildren. They're perfect for the holidays when time is so precious.

—Dody Cagenello, Simsbury, CT

PREP: 10 min. + chilling
MAKES: 3 dozen

- 36 large marshmallows
- 1½ cups semisweet chocolate chips
- ½ cup chunky peanut butter
- 2 Tbsp. butter

Line a 9-in. square pan with foil; butter the foil. Arrange marshmallows in pan. In a microwave, melt the chocolate chips, peanut butter and butter; stir until smooth. Pour and spread over the marshmallows. Chill completely. Cut into 1½-in. squares.

1 PIECE: 83 cal., 5g fat (2g sat. fat), 2mg chol., 28mg sod., 11g carb. (8g sugars, 1g fiber), 1g pro.

FIVE-INGREDIENT CHOCOLATE CARAMEL BARS

Even after tasting many wonderful European chocolates, this is still my favorite chocolate recipe. It would be selfish not to share it.

—Carol Lang, Bitburg, Germany

PREP: 15 min. • **BAKE:** 30 min.
MAKES: 3-4 dozen

- 1 pkg. (14 oz.) caramels
- ⅔ cup evaporated milk, divided
- 1 pkg. German chocolate cake mix (regular size)
- ⅔ cup butter, melted
- 1 cup (6 oz.) chocolate chips

Melt caramels in a double boiler or microwave. Stir in ⅓ cup milk and set

MIXED BERRY
SUNDAES FOR TWO

MIXED BERRY SUNDAES FOR TWO

These pretty sundaes are an easy way to add fruit and calcium to your diet. Berries star in the dish, which I like as a simple breakfast or healthy dessert for two.
—Edie DeSpain, Logan, UT

TAKES: 10 min. • **MAKES:** 2 servings

¼ cup halved fresh strawberries
¼ cup each fresh raspberries, blueberries and blackberries
3 tsp. honey, divided
½ cup fat-free plain Greek yogurt
2 Tbsp. pomegranate juice
2 Tbsp. chopped walnuts, toasted

1. In a small bowl, combine berries and 1 tsp. honey; spoon berries into two dessert dishes.
2. Combine the yogurt, pomegranate juice and remaining honey; spoon over berries. Sprinkle with walnuts.
1 SUNDAE: 160 cal., 5g fat (0 sat. fat), 0 chol., 33mg sod., 22g carb. (18g sugars, 3g fiber), 10g pro. **DIABETIC EXCHANGES:** 1 starch, 1 fat, ½ fruit.

TEST KITCHEN TIP
Greek yogurt boasts more protein and fewer sugars and carbs than traditional yogurt. Its creamy, rich texture can't be beat.

DESSERT WAFFLES

DESSERT WAFFLES

Crunchy waffles take center stage for dessert when topped with toasty coconut and creamy ice cream.
—Sheila Watson, Stettler, AB

TAKES: 15 min. • **MAKES:** 6 servings

½ cup sweetened shredded coconut
½ cup packed brown sugar
¼ cup butter, softened
6 frozen waffles, lightly toasted
6 scoops butter pecan ice cream or flavor of your choice

In a small bowl, combine the first three ingredients. Spread over waffles. Broil for 3-4 minutes or until bubbly. Top with ice cream.
1 SERVING: 433 cal., 25g fat (13g sat. fat), 57mg chol., 476mg sod., 49g carb. (34g sugars, 1g fiber), 5g pro.

FLOURLESS PEANUT BUTTER COOKIES

When my mother (who's now a great-grandmother) gave me this recipe for no-flour peanut butter cookies about 15 years ago, I was skeptical. It calls for only three ingredients—and no flour. Mom was right. I've never had a failure, and I make these all the time.
—Maggie Schimmel, Wauwatosa, WI

PREP: 15 min. • **BAKE:** 20 min.
MAKES: 2 dozen

1 large egg, beaten
1 cup sugar
1 cup creamy peanut butter

1. In a large bowl, mix all ingredients. Roll level tablespoons of dough into balls. Place on an ungreased baking sheet; flatten with a fork.
2. Bake at 350° for 18 minutes. Remove to a wire rack to cool.
2 COOKIES: 197 cal., 11g fat (2g sat. fat), 18mg chol., 105mg sod., 21g carb. (18g sugars, 1g fiber), 6g pro.

GINGER-POACHED
PEARS

GINGER-POACHED PEARS

Here's a simply elegant choice for dessert. The fresh pear halves are roasted in a sweet sauce of ginger ale and honey.
—Harriet Millstone, Toronto, ON

PREP: 15 min. • **BAKE:** 25 min.
MAKES: 4 servings

- 4 medium pears
- ½ cup ginger ale
- ½ cup honey
- ½ cup chopped crystallized ginger
- ½ cup chopped pecans, toasted

1. Preheat oven to 375°. Core pears from bottom, leaving stems intact. Peel pears; cut in half vertically. If necessary, cut ¼ in. from bottoms to level. Place in an ungreased 13x9-in. baking dish.
2. Place the ginger ale and honey in a small saucepan. Cook and stir until combined; spoon over pears. Bake, uncovered, 25-30 minutes or until tender, basting occasionally.

3. With a slotted spoon, remove pears to individual serving dishes. Transfer pan juices to a small saucepan; stir in ginger. Cook and stir over medium heat 5-8 minutes or until heated through. Spoon over pears; sprinkle with pecans.

2 PEAR HALVES: 429 cal., 10g fat (1g sat. fat), 0 chol., 23mg sod., 91g carb. (65g sugars, 7g fiber), 2g pro.

TOFFEE PEANUT CLUSTERS

Treat family and friends to peanut clusters with an extra layer of nutty chocolate. The secret is toffee bits.
—Joy Dulaney, Highland Village, TX

TAKES: 30 min. • **MAKES:** 5 dozen

- 1½ lbs. milk chocolate candy coating, coarsely chopped
- 1 jar (16 oz.) dry roasted peanuts
- 1 pkg. (8 oz.) milk chocolate English toffee bits

In a microwave, melt candy coating; stir until smooth. Stir in the peanuts and toffee bits. Drop by rounded tablespoonfuls onto waxed paper-lined baking sheets. Let stand until set. Store in an airtight container.
1 PIECE: 123 cal., 8g fat (4g sat. fat), 3mg chol., 78mg sod., 11g carb. (9g sugars, 1g fiber), 2g pro. **DIABETIC EXCHANGES:** 1½ fat, 1 starch.

SYRUPY APPLES

This fresh, fruity syrup adds delicious flavor to everything from pancakes and waffles to cinnamon ice cream.
—Cindy Walstedt, Maidstone, ON

TAKES: 20 min. • **MAKES:** 1⅓ cups

- 2 Tbsp. butter
- 2 medium tart apples, peeled and thinly sliced
- ⅓ cup packed brown sugar

Melt the butter in a saucepan over medium-low heat. Add apple slices; cook and stir for 5 minutes. Stir in sugar; cook and stir over low heat for 5 minutes.
¼ CUP: 120 cal., 5g fat (3g sat. fat), 12mg chol., 52mg sod., 21g carb. (20g sugars, 1g fiber), 0 pro.

FAST FUDGE SUNDAES

Homemade fudge sauce that's ready in 10 minutes? It's true. I think this thick, warm, chocolaty topping blows the store-bought kind out of the water.
—Sue Gronholz, Beaver Dam, WI

TAKES: 10 min. • **MAKES:** 1¼ cups

- ½ cup semisweet chocolate chips
- 1 oz. unsweetened chocolate
- 3 Tbsp. butter
- 1 cup confectioners' sugar
- 1 can (5 oz.) evaporated milk
- ½ tsp. vanilla extract
  Ice cream
  Maraschino cherries, optional

Place the chocolate and butter in a microwave-safe dish. Microwave, uncovered, on medium-high 30-60 seconds. Stir in the sugar, milk and vanilla; beat until smooth. Microwave, uncovered, on medium for 3-4 minutes or until bubbly. Serve over ice cream; top with a cherry if desired.
2 TBSP.: 150 cal., 8g fat (5g sat. fat), 14mg chol., 50mg sod., 19g carb. (17g sugars, 1g fiber), 2g pro.

TOFFEE PEANUT CLUSTERS

**M&M &
PRETZEL
COOKIES**

CHOCOLATE CARAMEL HAZELNUT PIE

Because I love chocolate, caramel and hazelnuts, I came up with a recipe that has all three. If you don't have a food processor, place crust ingredients in a zip-top freezer bag and smash with a rolling pin.

—Debbie Anderson, Mount Angel, OR

PREP: 25 min. + chilling
MAKES: 8 servings

- 1½ cups salted caramel pretzel pieces
- 12 Lorna Doone shortbread cookies
- ¼ cup sugar
- 6 Tbsp. butter, melted
- 5 Tbsp. caramel topping, divided

FILLING

- 1 pkg. (8 oz.) cream cheese, softened
- ½ cup Nutella
- 1 jar (7 oz.) marshmallow creme
- 1 carton (8 oz.) frozen whipped topping, thawed
- 1 cup miniature marshmallows
- 1 Snickers candy bar (1.86 oz.), chopped

1. Place the pretzel pieces and cookies in a food processor; pulse until fine crumbs form. Add sugar and melted butter; pulse just until blended. Press onto bottom and sides of a 9-in. pie plate. Drizzle with 3 Tbsp. caramel topping. Freeze while preparing filling.
2. For filling, beat cream cheese and Nutella until smooth. Gradually beat in marshmallow creme. Gently fold in whipped topping and marshmallows. Spoon into crust.
3. Refrigerate until set, 3-4 hours. Top with chopped candy and remaining caramel topping before serving.
1 PIECE: 663 cal., 35g fat (19g sat. fat), 60mg chol., 327mg sod., 74g carb. (57g sugars, 1g fiber), 6g pro.

TEST KITCHEN TIP
Short on time? Quick-chill this pie in the freezer in just one hour.

M&M & PRETZEL COOKIES

Kids and grown-ups adore these sweet, chewy and crunchy cookies. M&M's lovers can go crazy with the candy, or add more pretzels for that extra salty bite.

—Madison Allen, Destrehan, LA

PREP: 20 min. + chilling
MAKES: 6 dozen

- ½ cup butter, cubed
- 2 cups sugar
- ½ cup 2% milk
- 2 Tbsp. baking cocoa
- 1 cup creamy peanut butter
- 2 tsp. vanilla extract
- 3 cups quick-cooking oats
- 1 cup coarsely crushed pretzels
- 1 cup milk chocolate M&M's

1. In a large saucepan, combine the butter, sugar, milk and cocoa. Bring to a boil over medium heat, stirring constantly. Cook and stir 1 minute.
2. Remove from heat; stir in peanut butter and vanilla until blended. Stir in oats; let stand 5 minutes to cool. Fold in pretzels and M&M's. Drop the mixture by tablespoonfuls onto waxed paper-lined baking sheets. Refrigerate until set.
1 COOKIE: 87 cal., 4g fat (2g sat. fat), 4mg chol., 46mg sod., 12g carb. (8g sugars, 1g fiber), 2g pro.

**CHOCOLATE CARAMEL
HAZELNUT PIE**

CRANBERRY
PINEAPPLE SALAD

CRANBERRY PINEAPPLE SALAD

This ruby red salad of cranberry and other fruity flavors is a welcome not-too-sweet addition to the fall table. Dollop with whipped cream for a rich accent.

—Dorothy Angley, Carver, MA

PREP: 15 min. + chilling
MAKES: 12 servings

- 2 pkg. (3 oz. each) raspberry gelatin
- 1¾ cups boiling water
- 1 can (14 oz.) jellied cranberry sauce
- 1 can (8 oz.) crushed pineapple, undrained
- ¾ cup orange juice
- 1 Tbsp. lemon juice
- ½ cup chopped walnuts

Add boiling water to gelatin; stir until dissolved, about 2 minutes. Stir in cranberry sauce. Add the pineapple, orange juice and lemon juice. Refrigerate until thickened, about 30 minutes. Stir in the nuts. Pour into an 11x7-in. dish. Refrigerate salad until set.

1 SERVING: 149 cal., 3g fat (0 sat. fat), 0 chol., 49mg sod., 30g carb. (25g sugars, 1g fiber), 2g pro.

"I've been making this cranberry recipe for many years. I lost the TOH cookbook that had this recipe, so I was so glad to find the recipe again. A holiday isn't a holiday without this delicious family favorite! Even the kids gobble this one down."
—KIMBERKANE, TASTEOFHOME.COM

MACADAMIA TOFFEE SNACK CAKE

MACADAMIA TOFFEE SNACK CAKE

Ever since I worked in a restaurant preparing desserts, I've been collecting recipes that make people happy. This mouthwatering cake is loaded with white chocolate chips, macadamia nuts and coconut.

—Marie Zajdowicz, Riva, MD

PREP: 15 min. • **BAKE:** 30 min. + cooling
MAKES: 20 servings

- 2 cups all-purpose flour
- 1½ cups packed brown sugar
- ½ cup cold butter, cubed
- 1 tsp. baking powder
- ½ tsp. salt
- 1 large egg
- 1 cup milk
- 1 tsp. vanilla extract
- 1 cup white baking chips
- ½ cup chopped macadamia nuts
- ¼ cup sweetened shredded coconut

1. In a large bowl, combine the flour and brown sugar. Cut in butter until the mixture resembles coarse crumbs. Set aside 1 cup for topping. Add the baking powder and salt to remaining crumb mixture. In another bowl, whisk egg, milk and vanilla. Stir into crumb mixture just until moistened.
2. Transfer to a greased 13x9-in. dish pan; sprinkle with reserved topping mixture, white baking chips, nuts and coconut. Bake cake at 350° for 30-35 minutes or until golden brown and the edges pull away from sides of pan. Cool cake completely on a wire rack before cutting.
1 PIECE: 235 cal., 11g fat (6g sat. fat), 25mg chol., 146mg sod., 32g carb. (22g sugars, 1g fiber), 3g pro.

Recipe Index